THE
NO-BS
SELF-HELP BOOK

The No-Fluff Guide to Self-Mastery

HONEROD

Paperback ISBN: 978-82-693158-5-1
Hardcover ISBN: 978-82-693158-4-4
e-ISBN: 978-82-693158-6-8

For permissions contact:

🏠 https://www.honerod.com

✉ phonerodb@gmail.com

"Twenty years from now you will be more disappointed by the things you didn't do than by the ones you did do. So, throw off the bowlines. Sail away from the safe harbor. Catch the trade winds in your sails. Explore. Dream. Discover."

— Mark Twain

Contents

CHAPTER 1

INTRODUCTION

"Stay away from those people who try to disparage your ambitions. Small minds will always do that, but great minds will give you a feeling that you can become great too."

— Mark Twain

"Reading is the gateway skill that makes all other learning possible."

— Barack Obama

"Every man has two lives, and the second starts when he realizes he has just one."

— Confucius

Learning Beyond the Classroom

"The swiftest way to triple your success is to double your investment in personal development."

— *Robin Sharma*

HAVE you ever stopped to consider just how much time you spend in a classroom, trying to absorb information that has been taught for years before you even arrived? Let's assume you completed the traditional education journey, from elementary school to obtaining a bachelor's degree. Congratulations on your achievement! But, a degree can only take you so far in life, and to truly succeed, you need to develop a set of life skills.

Earning a degree with good grades indicates your ability to learn new subjects and demonstrate proficiency in them. It does not make you unique, as many others have achieved the same level of knowledge before you. To truly set yourself apart, you must acquire unique life skills that will help you thrive in any situation.

This book is not intended to discourage you from pursuing higher education. Rather, it is meant to demonstrate that you can learn much more outside of a classroom setting. Learning is a lifelong process, and if you've picked up this book, it's likely because you're looking to gain a greater understanding of personal development.

It can be challenging to navigate the vast sea of books and information present on personal development. There are countless books out there, each offering unique insights and approaches to achieving success and happiness in life. With so many choices, it can be difficult to know where to begin.

That's where this book comes in. I've taken the time to filter through the vast array of available literature and compiled the best ideas from the most influential books in four key areas essential to personal growth and development. These areas include:

➤ **Money**

➤ **Productivity**

➤ **Communication**

➤ **Health**

By combining the best ideas and practices from the most influential books in these four key areas, this book provides you with a comprehensive roadmap for personal growth and development. Whether you're looking to build wealth, improve your time management and productivity, enhance your communication skills, or overcome unhealthy habits, the insights and strategies presented in this book will help you achieve your goals.

Fear of the Unknown

People often don't take steps to become the best version of themselves because they are afraid, have problems, or don't know how. We fear change because it means that outcomes are unknown. Our brains are designed to find peace in knowing. When we don't know what will happen, we make up scenarios that create worry. Emotional feelings attached to the fear of change include:

➤ **Loss.**
People are afraid of change because they might lose something. They worry that they will have to give up something in exchange for the loss.

➤ **Confusion.**
People fear change if they don't know why it's happening, so they fight it. Change makes people nervous and forces them out of their comfort zones.

➤ **Lack of competence.**
People worry about change when they think they won't be able to do what needs to be done.

➤ **Extensive work.**
People are afraid of change because they think it will mean more work. Change takes time, and people will always have to come up with and try out new ideas while still doing business as usual. The stress that comes from too much work and insufficient time can make the change seem like a failure.

➤ **Lack of control.**

People fear change because it makes them lose control of their roles. The bigger the change, the more they'll feel like it's being forced on them. No one likes feeling powerless.

When something people know ends, it's hard for them to move on. Fear of failure also plays a role in making people afraid of change. If we don't know how something will turn out, we might not want to try it because it could go wrong. When you try something new, you take a chance. Here are some problems you might have had when trying to change a habit that is related to the main ideas of this book:

➤ **Insufficient knowledge or understanding of financial concepts and principles.**

➤ **Limited time to get things done.**

➤ **Communication is overwhelming and listening is hard.**

➤ **Unrealistic goals, lack of patience, or too high expectations.**

Whether you're struggling to make a career change, start a new business, or take any other major step in your life, this book will provide the guidance and support you need to push through your fears and move forward confidently.

So if you're ready to take that first step toward a life free from the fear of the unknown, then this book is your opening shot. It's the starting point for a journey of self-discovery and growth, and it will provide you with the tools and knowledge you need to overcome your fears and embrace the unknown. I hope you find it helpful and inspire you to take action toward achieving your dreams. So, dive into this book like a harpoon and become the captain of your destiny.

How the Rat Race is Killing Your Dreams

"Stay afraid, but do it anyway. What's important is the action. You don't have to wait to be confident. Just do it and eventually the confidence will follow."

— Carrie Fisher

M ANY people die at 25 but aren't buried until they're 75. Read that again and give yourself a moment to reflect on that sentence. What does it mean?

We've all heard the phrase *rat race* before. It means a pursuit that seems endless, pointless, or even self-defeating, and it's often used to describe a 9-to-5 job or career. People who are stuck in the rat race are unhappy and just going through the motions of life. They go through the daily grind of their jobs feeling unfulfilled, unchallenged, and uninspired until they go home at the end of the day, only to start all over again the next day.

In general, there are two ways to define the rat race. One is:

"It's a way of life in which people are caught up in a fiercely competitive struggle for money or power. It's a routine that is usually exhausting and competitive."

In this situation, it's good to want to get rich and powerful with passion but not desperation. When you want to do something passionately, not desperately, in an intense competition struggle or exhausting routine, you will reach your goal because your beliefs will work together to make it happen sooner or later. Then, getting what you want is fun and satisfying, not a struggle in the rat race.

But if you are in a highly competitive race for money or power, trying to *"Keep up with the Joneses,"* or trying to live a life that is way beyond what you can afford, then you are stuck in the rat race and can't get out.

And then you have the other way to describe it:

"A term used to describe a frustrating and hard-to-break financial lifestyle."

It is a way of life that many people live without recognizing what it is, to the point where they will deny it strongly when asked.

This kind of rat race involves taking on a job that takes up a lot of time and saddling oneself with heavy mortgages/rents, bills, children, and other responsibilities that force the person to keep working hard at the same job. People in this rat race think that getting more money will solve their problems with money. But those who choose to be in this race spend more and more, digging themselves deeper and deeper into the same hole. They will say, *"I'm not interested in money."* Why do they spend their lives working for nothing and always complaining about insufficient money if they aren't?

This kind of rat race is caused by a self-created fear of being poor, a lack of options, bad spending habits, doing the same thing over and over, or an inability to adapt to the changes in the workforce that were happening at the time this definition was made. I'll describe what a typical day in the rat race looks like.

Get Off the Wheel

Okay, so your alarm goes off at 6:30 a.m. You hit snooze. It rings again. You begin to get angry about it. But still, you hit snooze. And you keep doing this until you can't stay in bed any longer because you have to be at your 9-to-5 job today. You go to work tired and have to spend the next eight hours of the day making everyone else richer but yourself. Your boss bought his fourth home in Florida and you probably shouldn't have spent $9.12 on that Starbucks breakfast combo. Your demanding boss told you at 11 a.m. that you're not good enough and should consider a new career path. And at lunch, you realize that people talk about a different person every day, and today it's you. By 3 p.m., you've been in meetings for hours that haven't gotten anywhere. And the only real difference is that you now have more work on your desk. You decide at 4 p.m. to check the time every five minutes to see if it's already 5 p.m. You'd rather be somewhere else. But don't forget that it's only Monday. This is something you have to do four more times this week. And you have to do this for another 50 weeks, assuming you have two weeks off for a holiday. Everyone wants to get out of the rat race because of this.

It's hard to say when you became part of the rat race. It just sort of went that way.

When you were in college, you probably had roommates and shared the rent for a bad apartment. You probably didn't have a fancy car, and you probably ate ramen noodles for food. You could buy some beer or go out to dinner with friends with the money you had left over. Most people like to think back and remember those moments.

After that, you got a job and started making real money. You needed a nice car to drive and a big house to show how successful you had become. But none of the things you got did anything to improve your life. The more money you had, the more stuff you needed. Even when you got a raise or a promotion, you couldn't get ahead because your cost of living stayed the same.

The problem with the rat race is that there is no endpoint. No one is waiting for you at the end with a medal and a cooler of Gatorade to dump on your head. The wheel just keeps spinning. And the longer you stay in this cycle of using, the more normal it feels. You don't remember that it wasn't always this way.

The first step you need to take to get out of the rat race is to be able to see it. When you're just trying to keep up, it's easy to take on a big mortgage and a pricey car payment and tell yourself that's what will make you happy. Because it won't, you will over time have hedonically adapted to the new fancy car or house you bought. Hedonic adaptation is an important concept to understand because it helps explain why we often struggle to find lasting happiness or satisfaction in life. It is a psychological phenomenon that refers to the human tendency to adjust to positive or negative changes in our lives and return to our baseline levels of happiness or well-being, despite the intensity or duration of the change. In other words, it is the process of becoming accustomed to new positive or negative experiences and eventually taking them for granted, thereby diminishing their initial impact on our emotions.

The good news is that you got on the wheel, which means you can get off of it. Here are the most important things you need to do to get off it:

➤ **Recognize where you are right now.**
  You can't move forward in life if you don't know where you are now and how far away you are from where you want to be. You can learn how to get out of the rat race once you realize you don't have to stay where you are now.

➤ **Know your income and expenses.**
  Next, you need to track spending for more than one reason. Keeping track

of your spending lets you know exactly how much you spend each month and how much money you need to make to get out of the rat race.

➤ **Get rid of things that no longer support you.**

Getting out of the rat race means letting go of people, things, and situations that no longer serve you. This can be hard. To grow, you must get rid of the things holding you back. You should have ties to the people and things that help you move in your desired direction. You'll never figure out how to get out of the rat race if you keep one foot in the things that made you comfortable in the past. To take bold steps toward the life you want, you have to let go.

➤ **Use your knowledge, the internet, and social networks to make yourself more valuable.**

With the internet, social media, software, and access to information, you have many great options, whether you want to develop a professional career or start your own business. Regardless of your income model, improving your leadership and content skills can help you make yourself more valuable to a company or customers. The idea is to use what you know about topics you're interested in and feel confident talking about to make videos, written posts, or audio content. You teach, show your expertise, and get people's attention.

➤ **Be consistent, pay attention, and work.**

You already have everything you need to work hard and live the life you want. At the end of the day, how successful you are will depend on how hard you work at it. People don't get out of the rat race because they don't put in the focused work every day. You'll get out of the rat race when you want to. The life you want to live requires it.

➤ **Take one step at a time.**

You probably won't get out of the rat race in a day, a month, or a year unless you win the lottery or get a big inheritance, which you shouldn't count on. Getting out of the rat race takes time and doing small things repeatedly. But small steps can add up to real financial freedom over time.

The Pitfall of the Traditional Education System

We don't want to waste our lives being slaves to money, but we weren't taught how to make money work for us. We are taught to go to college, get a steady job, and work from 9 to 5 until we retire as part of our education. Although many people find this unappealing, our brains start thinking this is the only way to make money. We feel stuck in this rat race and can't think of other ways to make money, so we keep working harder and harder to make ends meet. Even if we get a high-paying job, we still tend to live from paycheck to paycheck because when our pay goes up, so do our bills.

The traditional education system often falls short of equipping individuals with the necessary tools and skills to navigate the challenges of adult life. While schools focus on academic learning, they tend to overlook essential life skills such as effective communication, time management, critical thinking, problem solving, financial management, and personal development. As a result, graduates are often ill-equipped to handle the demands of the workplace and daily life.

Moreover, the rapidly changing nature of the global economy means that skills that were once in demand may no longer be relevant. This makes it even more critical for individuals to continually upskill themselves and seek personal development opportunities. Learning and adapting to new situations is becoming increasingly essential in today's rapidly changing work environment.

As the world evolves and technology advances, individuals must continuously develop new skills and learn how to adapt to new situations. It's not just about achieving a degree or qualification, but about embracing a mindset of a lifelong learning mindset. Personal development should be taken seriously, as it helps individuals to improve their skill sets and to develop the right mindset to tackle the challenges they may encounter in life.

Schools must adapt to the changing world and emphasize equipping individuals with the necessary life skills that they will need in the future. It is equally important for individuals to take their personal development seriously and continually upskill themselves to remain relevant in the workforce. Learning and adapting to new situations is a vital tool that will serve individuals well in their personal and professional lives. But you can't get better if you don't take actions.

Take Actions Now

Knowledge is undoubtedly a powerful tool that can help individuals achieve great things. However, knowledge alone is not enough to bring about change and success. Action is like a gun, and what you know is like bullets. If you don't have a gun (action), the bullets won't do much (knowledge). But if you don't have any bullets (knowledge), you can still hit your target by throwing the gun (action) and get a little ahead. But again, having knowledge without action is useless.

You don't need to know everything before you start. Sometimes, the best way to learn is by doing. Action brings with it new experiences, and these experiences can teach you valuable lessons that no amount of knowledge can.

On the other hand, having too much knowledge can often lead to indecision. We spend so much time acquiring knowledge, thinking it will give us the answers we need, only to find that we are still unsure what to do. The more we know, the more we can get lost in the details, and the more indecisive we become. In contrast, taking action forces us to make decisions and learn from our mistakes.

Sometimes we spend so much time, money, and energy acquiring knowledge that we will not use, and that will leave us paralyzed from taking any action. We become afraid of making mistakes or failing, so we hesitate to take any steps. This fear of failure is one of the biggest obstacles that prevent people from taking action. But the truth is that failure is a part of the learning process. Every failure is an opportunity to learn, grow, and improve. *Albert Einstein* said the same,

> *"Failure is success in progress."*

Growth Mindset vs Fixed Mindset

"If you can manipulate your mindset and begin viewing obstacles as opportunities, you'll have better confidence when entering the situation."

— Lora Jets

HAVE you ever wondered why some people succeed while others don't? Our worldview, cognitive processes, and interpretations of information shape our identities. Ultimately, it all comes down to our thinking patterns and how we apply them to navigate life's challenges. How we perceive our intellect, abilities, and personality affects our emotions and actions, determining whether we can adopt new habits or acquire new skills. Here are some beliefs that distinguish one mindset from another:

Growth Mindset vs **Fixed Mindset**
Accepting challenges with open arms vs **Attempting to avoid challenges**
Persevere despite failure vs **Giving up early**
Ability & talent can be developed vs **Talents and abilities are innate**
Keep the focus on the process vs **Concentrating on the end result**
Take inspiration from others' successes vs **Afraid of others' success**
Embrace criticism vs **Avoid negative feedback**
Find people who challenge you vs **Reinforce their self-esteem**
Deeply involved in the learning process vs **Run from mistakes**

Individuals' perspectives on the world typically fall into two categories: a growth mindset and a fixed mindset. The growth mindset is critical to success and can ultimately help us achieve happiness. This outlook is grounded in the belief that our personalities, intellects, and creative abilities can change over time. Living with a growth mindset involves embracing challenges and welcoming problems, while regarding failure not as a setback but as an opportunity for growth and improvement.

In contrast, the fixed mindset strives to evade failure at any cost, equating success with intelligence. With a fixed mindset, individuals believe their personalities, intellects, and skills are predetermined and unchangeable. These attitudes, which are formed early in life, significantly impact our actions and our views on success and failure in both personal and professional arenas.

In her book, *Mindset: The New Psychology of Success,* Carol Dweck delves more deeply into these two ways of thinking. Dweck's work emphasizes the following: [1]

> *"My work bridges developmental psychology, social psychology, and personality psychology, and examines the self-conceptions (or mindsets) people use to structure the self and guide their behavior. My research looks at the origins of these mindsets, their role in motivation and self-regulation, and their impact on achievement and interpersonal processes."*

The concept of motivation and its influence on human behavior has been a topic of extensive exploration in the book. The author has devoted considerable effort to examining the factors that lead to success or failure and identifying strategies to enhance achievement. Over two decades, the author has conducted research to determine whether personality and intelligence are malleable qualities that can be nurtured and developed from an early age. Based on her findings, she has formulated a theory, which is presented below:

> *"For twenty years, my research has shown that the view you adopt for yourself profoundly affects how you lead your life. It can determine whether you become the person you want to be and whether you accomplish the things you value. How does this happen? How can a simple belief have the power to transform your psychology and, as a result, your life?*
>
> *Believing that your qualities are carved in stone — the fixed mindset — creates an urgency to repeatedly prove yourself. If you have only a certain amount of intelligence, a certain personality, and a certain moral character you'd better prove that you have a healthy dose of them. It simply wouldn't do to look or feel deficient in these basic characteristics.*
>
> [...]
>
> *There's another mindset in which these traits are not simply a hand you're dealt and have to live with, always trying to convince yourself and others that you have a royal flush when you're secretly worried it's a pair*

of tens. In this mindset, the hand you're dealt is the starting point for development. This growth mindset is based on the belief that your basic qualities are things you can cultivate through your efforts. Although people may differ in every which way — in their initial talents and aptitudes, interests, or temperaments — everyone can change and grow through application and experience."

The importance of the mindset we adopt daily cannot be overstated. Our mindset shapes our attitudes, behaviors, and ultimately, our destiny. Choosing the right mindset is a critical step toward achieving success and fulfillment in life. This is why it is crucial to be intentional about the ideas we expose ourselves to and the knowledge we acquire.

One way to cultivate a growth mindset is to commit to learning something new daily. Whether reading a book, listening to a podcast, or attending a seminar, continuous learning helps us expand our knowledge, develop new skills, and broaden our perspectives. Exposing ourselves to new ideas and experiences keeps our minds active and open to possibilities.

In this context, my book is a valuable resource for anyone looking to cultivate a growth mindset. While it may not be feasible to read the entire book in one day, it provides a wealth of information and insights that can be incorporated into daily life. Readers can gradually absorb and apply the ideas presented, without feeling overwhelmed by reading the book in bite-sized chunks.

The book is designed to help readers develop a way of thinking that promotes personal growth and greater fulfillment. The book's concepts and ideas are supported by subject matter experts and real-world instances, making them useful and relevant to a diverse array of situations. By using the book as a tool for personal development, readers can gain a deeper understanding of themselves, their goals, and the world around them.

Adapting to Change

"Everyday of your life is a another lesson. If you learn the lesson well and apply it; whether positive or negative, you determine what happens in your tomorrow."

— David Awusi

I N a world that is always changing, having life skills is an essential part of handling the challenges of everyday life. In the past ten years alone, the world's economies and technology have changed dramatically, significantly impacting education, the workplace, and our home life. To deal with the pace and change of modern life, people need new life skills that will help them adapt and thrive in a constantly evolving world.

Technological changes and the global economy require us to be flexible and adaptable. We must be willing to learn new skills and embrace new ways of doing things if we want to succeed in this rapidly changing world. As a result, traditional skills such as reading, writing, and arithmetic are no longer enough. We must develop new skills such as digital literacy, critical thinking, problem-solving, creativity, and emotional intelligence.

How we develop life skills as children significantly impact our ability to thrive as adults. Children who are taught important life skills such as communication, time management, financial management, and emotional intelligence have a better chance of succeeding in life. They are better equipped to handle the challenges of everyday life, build strong relationships, and navigate difficult situations.[2]

Why Life Skills are Essential

Life skills are important because they enable us to navigate the challenges of everyday life, improve our relationships with others, and achieve personal and professional success. These skills encompass a broad range of abilities and qualities essential for personal growth.

By developing and refining these life skills, we become more resilient and self-reliant, which in turn helps us to manage stress and adapt to change. Strong interpersonal skills such as effective communication and conflict resolution help us build positive and lasting relationships with others. This is essential for our mental health and overall well-being, as studies have shown that strong social connections are critical for our happiness and life satisfaction.[3]

Moreover, life skills are also vital for success in the workplace. Employers are increasingly looking for candidates who possess a broad range of life skills in addition to academic qualifications. These skills help employees work more effectively with colleagues, manage their time and workload, and adapt to the ever-changing demands of the modern workplace.[4]

Beyond personal and professional success, life skills are also important for our communities and wider society. When we develop empathy, teamwork, and leadership skills, we become better equipped to work collaboratively with others and positively contribute to our communities.

Life Skills for a Better Future

The importance of life skills depends on various factors such as age, culture, beliefs, location, and personal circumstances. However, some essential life skills are universally necessary to thrive in life. The World Health Organization (WHO) has identified ten critical life skills: problem solving, critical thinking, effective communication, decision-making, creative thinking, interpersonal relationship skills, self-awareness building skills, empathy, and dealing with stress and emotions.[5]

While all of these skills are valuable, focusing on a more specific set of life skills can be helpful depending on one's personal goals and circumstances. From my perspective, the four critical life skills are *Money, Communication, Productivity,* and *Health.*

Money management is a critical life skill that can help people achieve financial stability and security. It involves budgeting, saving, investing, and managing debt. By learning these skills, individuals can avoid financial stress and make informed decisions about their financial futures.

Effective communication is another vital life skill that can help people build stronger relationships and improve their professional prospects. It involves articulating ideas clearly, listening actively, and responding appropriately to feedback. Good communication skills can help people navigate conflicts, express themselves effectively, and build stronger personal and professional relationships.

Productivity skills are also critical for success in today's fast-paced world. They involve managing one's time, prioritizing tasks, and setting goals effectively. By developing these skills, individuals can optimize their productivity, achieve their goals more efficiently, and reduce stress and anxiety.

Finally, health is a fundamental aspect of our lives, and caring for our bodies and minds is a crucial life skill. This includes proper nutrition, exercise, stress management, and self-care. By prioritizing health, individuals can improve their quality of life, reduce the risk of chronic illnesses, and boost their mental and emotional well-being.

The next sections will discuss the importance of gaining these crucial life skills and how they help advance to the next stage.

The Role of Productivity

"Productivity is never an accident. It is always the result of a commitment to excellence, intelligent planning, and focused effort."

— *Paul Meyer*

TIME is a finite resource, and being productive is the key to achieving the most in our time. Productivity refers to the ability of an individual, a team, or an organization to accomplish its goals efficiently in a given amount of time. Various factors contribute to high productivity, such as motivation, natural talent, training, environment, and time management. Physical factors also boost productivity, including regular exercise, healthy eating habits, and adequate sleep. While some people seem naturally adept at getting things done, others struggle and may need to adopt daily exercises and better habits to improve their productivity.

Mental energy and motivation are crucial for individuals to get things done. Motivation often stems from work that is personally meaningful or valuable. While not all tasks may be intrinsically rewarding, focusing on long-term goals can provide the drive and energy to accomplish mundane daily tasks. Distractions can hinder productivity, as multitasking and constant technological interruptions can slow it down. Avoiding such distractions can help individuals achieve more in a shorter time frame.

Productivity is essential because it allows individuals to work toward their full potential. Being productive enables individuals to balance their work, home lives, hobbies, and family obligations with less stress and worry. While productivity depends on various factors, it is critical to identify the ones that work best for each individual. By prioritizing productivity, individuals can achieve their goals and lead fulfilling lives.

Family, College & Personal Growth

Time is the most precious and finite resource we possess, yet in today's fast-paced, information-rich world, it can be challenging to use it effectively. Many factors consume our time, including the internet, social media, friends, and family obligations.

Consider this real-life example: you strive to learn and grow but must also balance caring for your family while staying competitive at work:

Your mornings begin early with preparing breakfast and clothing for your children, driving your spouse to work, and dropping off your kids at school. The workday demands your best efforts to please both your clients and boss. After an eight-hour day, you return home to pick up your children, make dinner, and transport them to football practice, where they spend a couple of hours. Your evening remains on alert in case an unexpected event arises. Finally, you collect your kids from football practice, prepare them an evening meal, and put them to bed. After such a busy day, you will unlikely find the motivation to pick up a 500-page brick of a book by your bedside.

Alternatively, imagine being a college student repeatedly told that obtaining an A+ is critical to competing with other graduates. As a college student, you are expected to complete assignments, deliver presentations, and perform at the highest level in various subjects while maintaining a healthy lifestyle to make it through each day. Having recently completed college, I understand the limited time to add extra activities to a demanding schedule. Your day is generally divided into two lectures and self-study, leaving little additional time for reading the same brick of 500 pages.

It's evident that our daily lives have become so consumed with mundane tasks that we have limited time for self-development and growth. By continually performing routine duties, you may master them and become efficient.

Picking up your children from school or studying for exams becomes second nature. However, these activities rarely contribute to personal growth. It's vital to remember that you should take some time to learn something new to continue developing and expanding your knowledge base.

How to Learn More Efficiently in a Busy World

Learning a new skill requires time, effort, and commitment, but in today's fast-paced world, finding the time to read and learn can be challenging. If you struggle to fit learning into your busy schedule, book summaries can be invaluable. Rather than reading a 500-page brick, you can extract the key insights in just 5-10 pages, saving you precious time and helping you maintain a healthy, balanced lifestyle.

Book summaries offer a quick and easy way to learn without sacrificing hours of your day. They can enhance the reading experience by providing additional analysis and insights, especially for complex and lengthy works. By using book summaries, you can learn more efficiently and effectively, allowing you to maximize your productivity and achieve your goals.

As time is a finite resource, mastering time management is crucial for your personal and professional success. By prioritizing your tasks and learning how to manage your time effectively, you can make progress and achieve results faster, leading to a more fulfilling and enjoyable life overall. In short, investing in book summaries and time management strategies is a small but powerful step towards a more productive and rewarding life.

That's why this book is the solution. This book summarizes the most impactful and game-changing books in four key categories, presenting the most important concepts in one easily digestible package. Say goodbye to the fluff and hello to enhanced financial literacy, productivity, communication, and health, and achieve your full potential.

Productivity Comes with Emotional Rewards

The sense of accomplishment that comes with doing something meaningful is a profound and powerful feeling. Intrinsic rewards, such as personal satisfaction or a sense of purpose, are often more effective than external rewards, such as pay raises or promotions, because they are not tangible but emotional and deeply personal.

While wealth and success may bring financial security, they cannot replace the sense of purpose and fulfillment that comes from doing meaningful work. Investing our time and energy in work that matters contributes to our personal growth and development and has a positive impact on other areas of our lives. When we give our work meaning and purpose, we experience a sense of satisfaction and personal fulfillment that cannot be obtained through external rewards or recognition.

The key to unlocking this sense of purpose and fulfillment is to engage in deep work that allows us to be truly productive. By focusing our attention on high-value tasks and minimizing distractions, we can achieve greater productivity and unleash our creativity and positive attitude. The result is a sense of satisfaction and accomplishment that is its reward and can help us find balance and meaning in all aspects of our lives.

In short, by investing in personally meaningful work and engaging in deep, focused work, we can experience a profound sense of satisfaction and accomplishment that enriches our lives in countless ways.

The Importance of Financial Responsibility

"Beware of little expenses. A small leak will sink a great ship."

— Benjamin Franklin

T HE ability of an individual to effectively manage their personal finances is often seen as a matter of personal responsibility. However, the impact of one's financial decisions can extend beyond the individual and their immediate family, and have consequences for the larger community and even the economy as a whole.[6,7]

For instance, an individual who has not managed their finances well and is, therefore, unable to qualify for a loan to purchase a home. This can limit their housing options to renting, living with family, or even homelessness. On the other hand, those who can effectively manage their finances have the opportunity to purchase a home and, in doing so, contribute to the stability of the housing market and the broader economy.

For everyone to have access to economic opportunities such as owning a home or starting a business, financial literacy and responsibility are crucial. Individuals with limited means or past credit issues can benefit greatly from financial education that teaches them how to save and re-establish a strong financial foundation. By improving their personal finances, they can improve their own quality of life and contribute to their communities' economic vitality.

Personal financial responsibility is not just a matter of individual choice; it has important implications for the larger community and the economy. Ensuring that everyone has the skills and knowledge to manage their finances effectively is essential to promoting economic growth and stability.

Understand the Value of Money

The concept of money as a tool to pursue more without a clear goal or proven principles is a common pitfall in personal finance. Money, in and of itself, is not enough to guarantee wealth. Rather, it requires careful management and a clear plan to grow and protect it.

People who have substantial financial resources often report that the source of their happiness is not just the acquisition of more wealth, but rather the ability to maintain a steady income that meets their needs and allows them to achieve their life goals while leaving a meaningful legacy for those they care about. [8]

Effective money management involves acquiring key financial skills to build, protect, and sustain wealth per one's individual needs, values, goals, and risk tolerance. It also involves a deeper look at how one's behavior can impact long-term financial decisions and how to mitigate those negative effects.

Moreover, those seeking to accumulate wealth must recognize and combat powerful forces such as taxes, inflation, market volatility, risks, and debt, which can easily erode gains if not proactively managed. Failure to take decisive action in this regard can often result in significant losses.

How Money Spending Habits Affect Us

Over the past two decades, our money habits have changed significantly due to the increasing number of financial products available, making it challenging for many people to determine the best way to handle their money. Previously, people used cash for daily transactions, but credit cards have become the norm in recent years. In 2019, 23% of all payments were made using credit cards, up from 21% in 2017.[9] With the majority of payments now being made electronically, it is easy to take out more credit than we need and accumulate large debts. Poor money management can lead to adverse consequences such as divorce, health issues, depression, and even bankruptcy.[10]

When we don't know how to handle our finances effectively, we become beholden to them, living paycheck to paycheck and always worrying about money. This problem is compounded by the fact that we often unintentionally pick up spending habits from our parents, observing how they manage their finances. If you grew up with parents who were financially responsible, you are fortunate. But for those who grew up watching their parents living from paycheck to paycheck, we may have unconsciously developed similar spending habits.[11] This cycle continues indefinitely, and future generations may continue to be *"slaves"* to money unless we teach them how to handle it appropriately.

Unfortunately, most schools worldwide do not offer *Personal Finance 101* or *Personal Finance 1-2-3* as part of their curriculum. A study conducted by *CreditKarma* revealed that many Americans believed personal finance education should be part of the school curriculum. Despite this, there is a political debate regarding the appropriate age to begin personal finance education and where it should occur. While 63% of respondents to the study stated that personal finance education should be included in the school curriculum, they did not agree on the ideal grade level to introduce the subject.[12] From the study, this is how the participants responded to which grade level was ideal to start learning about proper money management:

➤ 30% selected Elementary School.

➤ 33% selected Middle School.

➤ 32% selected High School.

➤ 5% selected College / University.

Whether you're just starting to learn about personal finance or seeking to deepen your understanding, you have arrived at the right place. In the realm of finance, the vast array of technical terminology can be overwhelming and difficult to comprehend. It can all seem confusing, from the *compound effect* to *emergency funds, index funds*, and *assets vs liabilities*.

However, it's crucial to remember that the ultimate goal is to gain the necessary knowledge to manage your finances. By the time you finish this chapter on *Money*, you'll be able to understand these basic terms and acquire a greater understanding of how to handle your own money. Armed with this knowledge, you'll be equipped to find answers to your questions and ask better ones. Consequently, you'll gain a more profound appreciation for managing your finances, which will help you live a fulfilling and joyful life while securing your financial future.

Many aspire to attain financial freedom, but few know how to achieve it. Some believe that having multiple sources of income is the solution to saving more money. But, even the highest-paid individuals may have a considerable amount of debt if they fail to manage their finances appropriately.

One of the significant benefits of learning how to manage your finances is gaining a clear view of your spending habits. This increased awareness will help you stay within your budget and even facilitate saving more money. Moreover, mastering the art of personal finance will enable you to achieve your financial goals by using your money wisely. With these skills, you'll better understand money and its potential for generating income.

Never Underestimate Communication

"Take advantage of every opportunity to practice your communication skills so that when important occasions arise, you will have the gift, the style, the sharpness, the clarity, and the emotions to affect other people."

— Jim Rohn

COMMUNICATION is the backbone of society, enabling us to share ideas, work together, and achieve common goals. At its core, communication is the act of conveying information from one person to another to ensure that the message is understood.

In its simplest form, communication is universal — babies communicate their needs through sounds and gestures, and humans have used nonverbal cues since the time of ancient. As societies developed, so did the means of communication, with language emerging as a powerful tool for conveying ideas.

Today, communication takes many forms — verbal, nonverbal, and written. Verbal communication relies on spoken language, while nonverbal communication uses gestures, facial expressions, and other nonverbal cues. Written communication allows us to convey complex ideas over long distances and time frames, creating a record that can be revisited and refined.

The importance of effective communication cannot be overstated. Our ability to communicate with one another has become essential as we live in an increasingly interconnected world. It enables us to share knowledge, build relationships, and work towards a common vision.

Technology advances have revolutionized how we communicate, with new tools emerging all the time. From social media to instant messaging to video conferencing — the pace, accuracy, and clarity of communication have never been greater. As we continue to push the boundaries of what is possible, it's clear that communication will remain a vital part of our lives, enabling us to connect with one another in ever more powerful ways.

How Powerful Are You?

The power of communication and speech is often overlooked, yet it is one of the most important tools we have for transferring information between individuals. As *Jordan Peterson*, a renowned psychologist and speaker, noted in his recent conference speech, how we convey information is critical.

In recent years, *Jordan Peterson* has gained recognition for his perspectives on life and recommended approaches to living. His ideas on communication, which emphasize the significance of honest and truthful interactions, have resonated with many individuals.

In reality, we often lie to others, even about trivial things. It's not because we want to be malicious but because we're accustomed to lying to ourselves. We might convince ourselves that we're not lying, but when faced with a situation where the truth may hurt someone, we often resort to dishonesty.

Jordan's advice is simple: we should always strive to tell the truth, regardless of the situation. During his presentation, he emphasized the value of your speech: [13]

> *"One way of conceptualizing yourself is that you are one speck of dust among 7 billion. When you conceptualize yourself that way, what difference does it make for what you say or do? Thinking like this is quite convenient for you because when it doesn't matter what you say or do, you don't have any responsibility and can do whatever you want. The price you pay for that is a bit of nihilism, but if you don't have to shoulder any responsibility, that's a small price to pay. The correct and accurate way of looking at it is that you are a node in a social network and the center of that network. And the way networks work is that information propagates in a networked manner. To understand how powerful you are in this network, let's say you know a thousand people, and they know a thousand people. Using a little bit of arithmetic means you are one person away from a million people and two persons away from a billion people — so don't underestimate the power of your speech."*

Communication is Key

Effective communication is an essential component of sharing and exchanging ideas between individuals. Everyone has a unique set of ideas and wants to communicate them to others. However, people cannot comprehend what a person is thinking or understand their perspective until they share their thoughts.

Additionally, communication is vital for social interaction since humans are social animals. Talking to people and engaging in conversation is critical for getting to know our environment and the people around us. When we communicate, we respond to their questions, actions, or comments, whether consciously or not. Therefore, effective communication is necessary for a healthy and thriving society.

Explaining ideas and concepts to students clearly and concisely is crucial in education. A teacher's communication ability helps students learn and understand more effectively. When information is communicated poorly, students may be unable to comprehend the message, resulting in confusion and misunderstandings.

There is no denying that communication is a crucial aspect of society and life in general. It not only makes it possible for individuals to exchange information and knowledge, but it also allows them to develop stronger relationships. To improve our lives, we talk to people in various contexts, such as family, friends, coworkers, and even strangers. Thus, it is imperative to recognize the importance of communication and continue to communicate effectively.

Health Equals Wealth

"Health is like money, we never have a true idea of its value until we lose it."

— *Josh Billings*

WHEN we hear the word *health,* many of us tend to only think of doctors, hospitals, and medical care. However, the concept of good health is much broader than simply the absence of illness. The World Health Organization defines health as *"a state of complete physical, mental, and social well-being and not merely the absence of disease or infirmity."*

Good health is paramount to living a fulfilling life. It is a foundation for everything else we do, and reaching our potential or achieving our goals is impossible without it. We need energy, vitality, and resilience to thrive in every aspect of our lives. Good health is essential to our success, whether we want to excel at work, play with our children, or pursue our hobbies.

Physical health is an important aspect of overall health. It is the ability to carry out daily activities without experiencing undue fatigue, maintain a healthy weight, and reduce the risk of chronic diseases such as diabetes, heart disease, and cancer. Maintaining good physical health requires regular exercise, proper nutrition, and sufficient sleep.

Mental health is another critical component of overall health. It is the ability to manage our emotions, thoughts, and behaviors in a way that allows us to function in daily life. Good mental health helps us cope with the normal stresses of life, work productively, and build positive relationships with others. Mental health can be promoted through various means, including therapy, self-care practices, and social support.

Social health is a less well-known but equally important aspect of over-all health. It is the ability to form and maintain meaningful relationships with others, to feel a sense of belonging and connection, and to contribute to the well-being of others. Social support and a sense of community are essential for mental and physical well-being. Studies have linked social isolation to var-ious negative health outcomes, including depression, anxiety, and chronic dis-eases.[14]

A healthy society is one in which all people have the opportunity to live healthy, happy lives. This requires access to good medical care, education, housing, employment, and social policies supporting health and well-being. A healthy society is one in which people are free from illness and have the re-sources and support they need to thrive.

Good health is critical to living a fulfilling life. It encompasses not only physical health but also mental and social well-being. To achieve and maintain good health, we need to focus on regular exercise, proper nutrition, sufficient sleep, social support, and mental health care.

How Can You Measure Health?

Measuring health is a complex and multi-dimensional task. One of the most widely used indicators of health is life expectancy. This measure is used to de-termine the average number of years a person can expect to live, and it is influ-enced by factors such as genetics, environment, lifestyle, and access to health care. In addition to life expectancy, other measures such as morbidity rates, disability-adjusted life years, and quality of life indicators are used to measure health. Morbidity rates measure the incidence and prevalence of illnesses and diseases in a population. Disability-adjusted life years measure the impact of a particular disease or condition on an individual's quality of life by combining the number of years lost to premature death with the years lived with a disability.

Quality of life indicators measure a person's physical, social, and emotional well-being and include measures of happiness, satisfaction, and self-perceived health status. These measures are often used to evaluate health interventions and policies and are important tools for health professionals, policymakers, and researchers.

In the end, assessing one's health necessitates a thorough and diverse methodology that considers the bodily and biological components of health and the social and environmental factors that influence health results.

Why is Health Important?

A healthy society prioritizes health promotion and disease prevention rather than simply reacting to illness when it occurs. This involves recognizing the many complex factors that impact individual and community health, including social, cultural, political, economic, commercial, and environmental influences. A healthy society can help to create conditions that support the health and well-being of all its members by addressing these underlying determinants of health, both now and in the future.

Not only does good health benefit individuals, but it also has positive impacts on society as a whole. Healthy people are more productive, better able to learn, and more likely to contribute to their communities. Governments can help to create prosperous and growing societies by investing in programs and policies that promote health and prevent illness.

However, achieving good health is not solely the responsibility of governments or public health agencies. Each of us can take steps to improve our health and well-being, and in doing so, we can contribute to the health of our communities. Developing a personal health and wellness plan that includes regular exercise, healthy eating habits, stress management, and good sleep hygiene can help to improve overall health and well-being.

Good health is a complex and multifaceted concept that extends far beyond just the absence of illness. A healthy society recognizes the importance of addressing the underlying determinants of health and creating conditions that promote health and well-being for all. By prioritizing health promotion and disease prevention, we can all contribute to creating a healthier, happier, and more productive society. So, you see — your health is about so much more than what you eat, how much you exercise, and how much sleep you get.

The Antidote to Our Busy World

"The secret of change is to focus all of your energy, not on fighting the old, but on building the new."

— Socrates

THE *80/20 Principle* is a powerful tool that can help us streamline our lives and focus on what matters most. The 80/20 Principle, also known as the Pareto Principle, is a concept that suggests that roughly 80% of the effects or outcomes come from 20% of the causes or inputs. This principle was introduced by Italian economist *Vilfredo Pareto*, who observed that 80% of Italy's wealth was owned by 20% of the population. [15] While it's easy to get bogged down by the many demands of modern life, the 80/20 Principle reminds us that most of our results come from a relatively small number of activities. Focusing on the critical few and ignoring the trivial many can free up time and energy to devote to what matters.

One of the most significant benefits of the 80/20 Principle is that it helps us avoid burnout. When we try to do everything, we often end up doing nothing well. We become spread too thin, and our productivity suffers. By contrast, when we focus on the 20% of activities that will give us the most significant results, we can achieve more with less effort. We can work more efficiently, reduce our stress levels, and achieve our goals more easily.

Another key benefit of the 80/20 Principle is that it helps us avoid multitasking. Multitasking is a common productivity myth, but it reduces our efficiency and increases our stress levels. When we try to do too many things at once, we end up juggling too many balls, and some inevitably get dropped. In contrast, when we focus on one task at a time and use the 80/20 Principle to identify the most critical tasks, we can work more efficiently and reduce our stress levels.

The 80/20 Principle also helps us live more intentionally. When we identify our key goals and priorities and allocate our time and resources to the activities that will help us achieve them, we are living in alignment with our values. We are making deliberate choices about how we spend our time, rather than simply reacting to the demands of others. Focusing on what matters can create a sense of purpose and meaning in our lives.

Uncovering the Value of Time

We live in a world where time seems to be in endless supply, yet we fail to recognize its value. We often spend only 20% of our time on activities that make a significant impact, while the remaining 80% is wasted on trivial and unimportant tasks. Even a small amount of time can make a big difference for those with a lot of talent. The 80/20 rule comes in here. By focusing on the 20% of activities that generate 80% of results, we can double our productivity and achieve more in less time.

The 80/20 Principle is a counter-intuitive approach to time management that is often overlooked in favor of the *"do more things faster"* philosophy. This approach fails to help us distinguish between the truly important tasks and those that can be deprioritized. The 80/20 Principle encourages us to do fewer things but to do them well. By minimizing distractions and unnecessary tasks, we can devote more time and attention to the projects that matter most.

The concept of the 80/20 Principle can be applied to all areas of our lives, including work, personal relationships, and hobbies. We can make more progress by identifying the 20% of activities that generate the most results and devoting twice as much time and effort to them. This can help us accomplish our goals and achieve greater success in our personal and professional lives.

Here's a glimpse into how you can integrate the 80/20 Principle into your daily life:

➤ **80/20 Happiness.**
Adopting an 80/20 approach to happiness can have a powerful impact on our lives. Rather than passively hoping for happiness to come our way, we can take an active role in cultivating it. By identifying and prioritizing the actions that bring us the most joy, we can create a lasting and cumulative sense of happiness.

➤ **80/20 Success.**
Achieving success is not a one-size-fits-all proposition. It requires that you take the time to discover what works best for you. You will find that you are more productive in some areas than others, and it is crucial to identify those areas to focus your efforts on them. In doing so, you can avoid wasting valuable time and energy on tasks that don't come naturally

to you.

➤ **80/20 Investing.**
To maximize the benefits of the 80/20 Principle in investing, it's critical to adopt a deliberate and well-informed approach to portfolio management. By identifying the investments that will impact your long-term financial success, you can make the most of your resources and achieve your financial objectives more efficiently.

➤ **80/20 Relationships.**
It's the quality of these relationships that matter. In building relationships, it's important to consider where you are in life and what you are doing at the moment. It's important to cultivate a network of relationships that will help you move forward instead of simply having a large network. Remember that the right relationships significantly impact your growth and success.

➤ **80/20 Work.**
In work, the principle states that roughly 80% of the value of an organization or profession comes from the top 20% of its professionals. These high performers tend to be more skilled, experienced, and effective than the rest, often earning more money and prestige as a result. By understanding this principle, you can leverage it to your advantage and focus your attention on the most critical aspects of your work or career.

Accelerate Your Learning with Book Summaries

Book summaries are a great way to save time and quickly understand a book's content without having to read the entire text. They provide a concise and well-written overview of a book's main points, highlighting the most important outcomes of the book's research. It presents a condensed version of the book, encompassing approximately 20% of its content while still imparting 80% of its key outcomes.

Aside from saving time, book summaries often objectively present the content, showcasing both the positive and negative aspects of the book. This helps the reader get a well-rounded understanding of the author and the subject matter. By reading a book summary, you can quickly understand the book and determine whether it's worth reading in full.

Most book summaries are around a quarter of the length of the original text. They provide a quick and easy-to-understand summary of the book's content and can be a valuable tool for acquiring new skills and knowledge.

As you read more summaries, you'll start to develop a deeper understanding of the topics and be able to determine how you can apply these principles to your life. This is why summaries can be a great addition to your lifelong learning journey.

The focus on eliminating extraneous information, such as personal stories and details, and presenting the ideas and concepts in a straightforward and easy-to-understand manner makes this book a valuable resource for those seeking to acquire new skills and knowledge. By reading this book, you can quickly understand its key takeaways and determine whether the full book is worth reading.

Writing this book was an educational experience, and I aimed to share the lessons I've learned with others. By incorporating some of the principles outlined in this book into your daily life, you can set yourself on a path of lifelong learning and personal growth.

This Book is Not a Marathon

"Remember that guy that gave up? Neither does anyone else."

— *Gregg Plitt*

TECHNOLOGICAL advancements have transformed the way we function, from communication to entertainment. However, one significant impact of technology on humans is the decrease in attention span. It is interesting to note that a goldfish, which is typically known for having a short attention span, has an average attention span of 9 seconds. In the year 2000, the average human attention span was 12 seconds. However, according to a recent study conducted by Microsoft, the average attention span of a human has now decreased to 8 seconds. [16]

With the ability to multitask, individuals may be able to handle several tasks simultaneously, but it has become increasingly challenging to focus on a single task for an extended period. Given the current state of attention spans, it is reasonable to wonder how people can absorb large volumes of information from text, particularly regarding to reading.

Despite these challenges, reading remains one of the most effective ways for individuals to learn new things. A reading state can aid in one's personal growth and development, with learning being one of its primary benefits. However, people often cite a lack of time as a reason for not reading, even though the same people may have time to binge-watch all seasons of *The Office* in just a few days. Reading, like any other skill, requires consistent practice and improvement.

As an avid reader myself, I have spent the last few years reading over a hundred books on self-improvement and personal growth. The learning curve has been exponential, leading to my growth and development on a personal level. Fortunately, you don't have to spend years reading to achieve the same results. I have summarized the most significant concepts from the books I have read in one easily digestible package. This book is not a marathon and doesn't have to be read in a day. It's my pleasure to share this work of art with you.

Less is More

"Strive for excellence in few things, rather than good performance in many."

— Richard Koch

L EARNING everything there is to know about any subject is impossible for humans to achieve. Instead, it's crucial to focus on excelling in the areas that are most important to us. When searching for information on a topic like personal finance, the sheer volume of search results can be overwhelming, making it difficult to determine where to start. However, out of the many books available on any given topic, only a few provide the majority of the essential information. This is the premise of the 80/20 principle, which is explored in detail in this book.

In my quest for self-improvement over the years, I have absorbed myself in countless books, articles, and blog posts on topics related to personal growth.

Along the way, I have been fortunate to connect with many inspiring individuals, attend conventions, receive expert mentorship, and experience significant personal growth. By cultivating a growth mindset and living by the foundational principles that I have learned from these sources, I have been able to navigate life's challenges with greater ease. I am eager to share this knowledge with you through the pages of this book.

One of the most powerful realizations that self-help books have taught me is that many of my problems can be solved by applying core principles. A review of the scientific literature conducted by Cambridge University found that self-help books are highly effective at teaching new life skills, including assertiveness, problem-solving, and personal hygiene.[17] According to the same article, self-help books have been proven to:

1. Change how you see and understand the world to be more positive.

2. Encourage and motivate people to do good things more often.

3. Learn new skills by expanding your knowledge base.

4. Encourage you to break out of your chains and go beyond what you think you can do.

5. Set goals for yourself that will lead to rapid growth.

To avoid getting lost in the sea of information, I have compiled a collection of lessons from the most important books in four key areas: *Money*, *Productivity*, *Communication*, and *Health*. Using these lessons, you can gain control of your life and live the way you want.

Most self-help books contain what we call *"fluff"* — extraneous details that don't contribute to the book's core ideas. To help you focus on what's most important, this book provides a filter that extracts the most critical principles from each topic. You can then decide which principles to implement in your life and move on to the next topic. By repeating this process, you can build a list of life principles to help you become your best version.

Rather than trying to absorb as much information as possible, focus on what's most important to you. Use this book to filter the information and prioritize what's most important to you. Changing how you think about these topics will require time and effort, but it's worth it if you want to achieve your goals and become the best version of yourself.

The Benefits of the Book

"The more that you read, the more things you will know. The more that you learn, the more places you'll go."

— Dr. Seuss

A s humans, we are naturally driven to improve ourselves and reach our full potential. However, the path to personal growth can sometimes be unclear or overwhelming. Fortunately, reading self-improvement books is a widely recognized and effective method for achieving this goal.

This book, in particular, offers a concise and comprehensive summary of some of the most significant concepts and ideas in the field of self-improvement and personal growth. By reading this book, you can save time and effort by accessing valuable knowledge and insights in one easy-to-read volume. The book's outline is as follows:

How to properly manage your money in the best ways.

Chapter 2 of this book delves into the timeless principles of financial management that have been passed down for centuries, offering invaluable insights into handling money more wisely. While the internet is a useful resource for obtaining quick tips on topics like index funds, debt reduction, and savings, it is unlikely to provide you with the depth of knowledge and nuanced understanding of these fundamental principles that a well-written book can offer. The subject of money management can be overwhelming, particularly as it is not typically taught in schools, leaving many people feeling ill-equipped to manage their finances effectively. However, by carefully curating the best books on money, finance, and investment, I have distilled the most promising principles and advice from the authors who have shaped our understanding of economics and revolutionized how we think about managing money. By learning from these experts, you can better understand how to build and manage your wealth sustainably and effectively, empowering you to achieve your financial goals and build a brighter future for yourself and your loved ones.

How to improve your communication and use proper body language.
Chapter 3 of this book is dedicated to helping you develop the skills necessary to engage in productive and effective conversations. Effective communication is a skill that is often undervalued and overlooked, but it can greatly impact your success in both your personal and professional life. In this chapter, you will learn how to use the right body language and attitude to communicate confidently, patiently, and effectively. Whether you're trying to close a sale, convince someone to invest in your business idea, or simply connect with others on a deeper level, knowing how to communicate effectively is essential.

How to increase your productivity and allocate your time.
In Chapter 4 of this book, I've curated some of the most effective strategies for increasing productivity and time management from the best books on the subject. In today's fast-paced world, it's more important than ever to be able to allocate your time wisely and make the most out of each day. You will learn the skills and concepts necessary to eliminate distractions and improve your focus, maximizing your productivity and achieving your goals. Whether you're a student, a busy professional, or an entrepreneur, the principles in this chapter will help you work smarter, not harder.

How to keep a balanced and healthy lifestyle.
Chapter 5 provides a comprehensive guide to understanding the fundamental principles of maintaining a healthy lifestyle. Applying the concepts laid out in this chapter will give you valuable insights into maximizing muscle growth during exercise. Moreover, this chapter delves into the intricate connection between the brain and body, emphasizing the profound impact of a healthy lifestyle on one's mood and overall well-being. By offering a comprehensive understanding of these essential concepts, Chapter 5 provides a solid foundation for anyone seeking to live a healthier and more fulfilling life.

How to Use the Book

"The journey of a thousand miles begins with one step."

— Lao Tzu

T o maximize the benefits of the valuable insights in this book, it is essential to develop effective strategies for utilizing and applying its contents. The following tips are designed to assist you in this reading adventure:

Use post-it stickers and markup pens.

To enhance your reading experience and facilitate effective retention of the concepts presented within this book, it is recommended that you equip yourself with post-it stickers and a markup pen. This simple but powerful approach will enable you to efficiently mark key passages, save time, and bolster your recall of the most important ideas. As you read, take note of the concepts that resonate with you and apply them to your personal circumstances. By doing so, you can create a personalized framework for applying the concepts contained within the book to your life, optimizing its value and relevance to your individual needs.

Pick a topic and read it twice.

One of the key benefits of this book is that it does not need to be read sequentially from chapter to chapter. Instead, readers can utilize various reading strategies, including browsing, skimming, and scanning, to efficiently navigate the content and identify the topics most relevant to their needs. To get the most value from this book, start by considering the areas in which you would like to improve. Once you have identified the relevant topics, you can quickly locate the corresponding chapters or sections and delve deeper into the material. It is often helpful to read these sections twice, allowing for a more thorough understanding of the concepts and a better chance of internalizing the ideas.

Speed-read.

Speed reading is a powerful practice that can help you absorb information much more efficiently, saving time and reducing the effort required to read and understand the text. One of the key benefits of speed reading is the ability to train yourself to read without vocalizing each word in your head, which can help increase comprehension, improve memory retention, and keep you focused on the material at hand. Consider the benefits of applying speed reading techniques to the material in this book. For example, imagine you could skim the entire chapter on personal finance before receiving your salary, allowing you to gain valuable insights on effectively managing your money. Or, before going on a date, you might want to review a section about communication and learn strategies for effective interaction.

Keep room for more.

To remain competitive in today's rapidly changing world of technology, we must embrace continuous learning as a way of life. While the knowledge and skills we acquire in school provide a strong foundation, they are often just the beginning of our educational journey. We must commit to a lifetime of growth and exploration to reach our full potential. This book aims to help you get started on this journey, providing you with the tools and insights you need to take your skills to the next level. By embracing the concepts presented within these pages, you will gain the knowledge and confidence necessary to navigate the ever-changing landscape of the modern world.

It is important to remember that this book is a collection of summaries of the most impactful and game-changing books encompassing the four key elements we encounter daily. The aim was to extract and filter out the most important concepts and principles from each of these books, and present them clearly and concisely. As a result, this book is designed to be comprehensive and to the point, with a focus on providing you with the key takeaways from each book. You can expect to find a lot of bullet points throughout the book, which is designed to make it easy to identify and remember the most important ideas. By reading this book, you can save yourself a lot of time and effort, while still gaining access to the most valuable knowledge contained within these books. ***Let the book begin.***

CHAPTER 2

MONEY

"Too many people spend money they haven't earned... to buy things they don't want... to impress people they don't like."

— Will Rogers

"Money is a guarantee that we may have what we want in the future. Though we need nothing at the moment, it insures the possibility of satisfying a new desire when it arises."

— Aristotle

"The lack of money is the root of all evil."

— Mark Twain

Your Money or Your Life

by Vicki Robin

"If you live for having it all, what you have is never enough. In an environment of more is better, "enough" is like the horizon — always receding."

T HE book aims to help individuals transform their relationship with money and achieve financial independence.

The author lays out a nine-step program for taking control of one's finances and changing one's habits and mindset about money. The steps include tracking expenses, creating a budget, and reducing unnecessary spending. The authors emphasize the importance of tracking every penny spent, which allows the reader to get a clear picture of their spending habits and areas where they can make changes.

It also stresses the importance of cutting down on unnecessary expenses, like subscriptions, memberships, and impulse purchases. The authors encourage readers to make changes gradually and focus on making sustainable changes rather than quick fixes.

In addition to providing practical advice on managing finances, *Your Money or Your Life* also explores money's psychological and emotional aspects. The book encourages readers to examine their beliefs about money and understand how they impact their financial decisions. The authors argue that by transforming one's relationship with money, individuals can achieve financial freedom and live a more fulfilling life.

Step 1 — Making Peace with the Past

This step involves reflecting on your past financial experiences and behaviors, examining the underlying beliefs and emotions that have influenced your decisions, and letting go of any guilt or shame associated with past financial missteps. This process of introspection is crucial in order to break free from negative patterns and establish a healthier relationship with money.

The chapter begins with a series of questions designed to help readers uncover their personal history with money, such as childhood experiences, past money mistakes, and current attitudes toward spending and saving. By reflecting on these experiences and emotions, readers can better understand their relationship with money and how it affects their lives.

Reasons, why this is important, are:

➤ Acknowledging past financial patterns and making conscious decisions to change them in the future.

➤ Releasing negative emotions and feelings associated with past financial experiences, freeing up energy and mental space for more positive and productive financial habits.

➤ Establishing a more positive relationship with money and taking control of their financial future by acknowledging and making peace with their financial history.

Step 2 — Tracking Your Life Energy

This step involves tracking all of your income and expenses for a full month to get a clear and detailed picture of where your money is going. This step aims to bring awareness to your spending habits and identify areas where you can make changes to improve your financial situation.

In this step, you are encouraged to record every penny you earn and spend in a ledger or a budgeting app. This includes all your fixed expenses, such as rent or mortgage, utilities, and insurance, as well as your discretionary spending on things like food, entertainment, and shopping. By the end of the month, you should have a complete picture of your cash flow and an understanding of where your money is being spent.

Reasons, why this is important, are:

➤ Gaining a clear and detailed understanding of your spending habits and cash flow.

➤ Bringing awareness to areas where you may be overspending and identifying areas for improvement.

➤ Providing a foundation for creating a budget and improving your financial situation in the future.

Step 3 — Where is it All Going?

This step involves analyzing the data collected in the previous step, *Being in the Present — Tracking Your Life Energy,* to determine where your money is being spent and identify areas for improvement. This step aims to gain a deeper understanding of your spending habits and find ways to reduce unnecessary expenses, so you can direct your money toward your goals and priorities.

In this step, you are encouraged to categorize your spending into housing, food, transportation, and entertainment categories and then evaluate each category to determine if the money spent is aligned with your values and goals. If you find areas where you are overspending or spending on things that are not important to you, you can make adjustments to your spending habits to redirect your money toward the things that matter most.

Reasons, why this is important, are:

➤ Understanding your spending habits and determining if your money is being spent in line with your values and goals.

➤ Improving your financial situation and progressing towards your financial goals by reducing waste and directing your money towards what matters most.

Step 4 — Three Questions that Will Transform Your Life

This step involves reflecting on your spending habits and making changes to align your spending with your values and goals. The three questions outlined in this step are designed to help you make more mindful and intentional decisions about using your money.

The first question asks, *"Did I receive fulfillment, value, and satisfaction from this purchase?"* This question helps you determine if a purchase was worth the money and energy you spent on it. The second question is, *"Did this purchase support my values and help me achieve my goals?"* This question helps you evaluate if a purchase aligns with your values and contributes to your long-term financial goals. The third question is, *"Would I be happy and proud to share this purchase with others?"* This question encourages you to consider your values and reputation concerning your spending habits.

Reasons, why this is important, are:

➤ Encouraging mindfulness and intentionality in your spending habits.

➤ Helping you make informed decisions about your spending that align with your values and goals.

➤ Improving your financial situation by reducing waste and directing your money towards what matters most.

Step 5 — Making Life Energy Visible

This step involves tracking all of your expenses, including both essential and discretionary spending, to make it easy to see where your money is going. This step is designed to help you better understand of your spending habits and identify areas for improvement.

In this step, you are encouraged to track your expenses using a budgeting tool or spreadsheet that allows you to categorize your spending and track your progress towards your financial goals. You are also encouraged to create a visual representation of your spending, such as a pie chart or bar graph, to help you see where your money is being spent and identify areas for improvement.

Reasons, why this is important, are:

➤ Gaining a deeper understanding of your spending habits and identifying areas for improvement.

➤ Improving your financial situation by reducing waste and directing your money towards what matters most.

➤ Making progress towards your financial goals by tracking your spending and making informed decisions about where to allocate your resources.

Step 6 — Valuing Your Life Energy (Minimizing Spending)

This step involves reducing your expenses and directing your resources toward what truly matters in your life. In this step, you are encouraged to prioritize spending on the things that bring you the most joy, fulfillment, and value and to minimize spending on things that do not align with your values and goals.

This step emphasizes the importance of being mindful and intentional about your spending and making conscious choices about allocating your resources. The goal is to minimize unnecessary spending and direct your resources toward what matters to you, such as your health, relationships, and personal growth.

Reasons, why this is important, are:

➤ Improving your financial situation by reducing waste and directing your resources towards what truly matters in your life.

➤ Enhancing your sense of well-being by prioritizing spending on the things that bring you the most joy, fulfillment, and value.

➤ Aligning your spending with your values and goals, making you more mindful and intentional about your financial decisions.

Step 7 — Valuing Your Life Energy (Maximizing Income)

This step involves increasing your income and maximizing the value of your time, skills, and resources. In this step, you are encouraged to explore ways to increase your income, such as taking on additional work, developing new skills, or starting a side hustle.

This step emphasizes the importance of valuing your time, skills, and resources and maximizing your earning potential. The goal is to create additional sources of income that will help you achieve your financial goals and live a more fulfilling life.

Reasons, why this is important, are:

➤ Improving your financial situation by increasing your income and maximizing the value of your time, skills, and resources.

➤ Enhancing your sense of well-being by creating additional sources of income that bring you joy, fulfillment, and financial security.

➤ Aligning your income with your values and goals, making you more mindful and intentional about your financial decisions.

Step 8 — Capital and the Crossover Point

This step focuses on building and managing your savings, investing your money wisely, and reaching a critical point in your financial journey, the *Crossover Point*. At the Crossover Point, your passive income from investments becomes greater than your expenses, allowing you to live off the interest and dividends from your investments without relying on a traditional source of income.

This step stresses the importance of saving and investing your money wisely to reach the Crossover Point and gain financial independence. The authors provide practical advice on investing your savings in low-risk, diversified assets and the importance of having an emergency fund for unexpected events.

Reasons, why this is important, are:

➤ Understanding the concept of passive income and the significance of reaching the *Crossover Point*.

➤ Providing practical tips for investing wisely and building your savings to reach financial independence.

➤ Highlighting the difference between *Capital* and *Income* and the benefits of building your *Capital* to achieve financial independence.

Step 9 — Managing Your Finances

This step focuses on establishing and maintaining a comprehensive and effective financial management system. The authors outline various methods for tracking your spending, budgeting and managing your finances, including simple tools like envelopes, spreadsheets, and personal finance software.

In this chapter, the authors emphasize the importance of being mindful and intentional about your spending, setting clear financial goals, and creating a budget that aligns with your values and priorities. They provide practical advice on controlling your spending, avoiding debt, and making the most of your money.

This step aims to help readers take control of their finances and establish a healthy relationship with money. By managing their finances effectively, readers can achieve their financial goals, reduce stress and anxiety, and increase their sense of financial security and well-being.

Reasons, why this is important, are:

➤ Providing practical and actionable advice on establishing a comprehensive financial management system that suits your needs and goals.

➤ Emphasizing the importance of being mindful and intentional about your spending and creating a budget that aligns with your values and priorities.

➤ Helping readers take control of their finances, reduce stress and anxiety, and increase their sense of financial security and well-being.

KEY LESSONS

1. **Evaluate the true cost of things.**
   This lesson emphasizes the importance of understanding the true cost of things, including the cost in terms of time and energy, and money. Considering the full cost, you can make more informed decisions about what you buy and how you spend your time and resources.

2. **Be aware of your spendings.**
   Tracking your spending is a key component of the book, and it helps you gain insight into where your money is going, identify areas for improvement, and make changes to your spending habits.

3. **Don't take on too much debt.**
   Debt can be a significant burden, and the book stresses the importance of paying it off quickly. This can free up more money each month to save or invest and reduce financial stress.

4. **Avoid *"Keeping up with the Joneses."***
   By living below your means, you can avoid overspending and focus on saving and investing. This helps you achieve financial stability and avoid the cycle of debt and overconsumption.

5. **Keep a healthy relationship with money.**
   The book emphasizes the importance of being mindful of how you spend your money and the impact that spending has on your life. This includes considering the true value of things and avoiding impulse purchases.

6. **Invest for the future.**
   The book encourages readers to invest for their future, including retirement savings and other investments. This helps to build wealth over time and prepare for the future.

ACTIONABLE STEPS TO TAKE

➤ **Track your spending.**

This step is crucial to gain an accurate understanding of where your money is going each month. You need to keep track of every cent you spend so you can identify areas where you can make changes and save more.

➤ **Create a budget.**

Based on the information you've gathered from tracking your spending, create a budget that outlines your income and expenses. This will help you see if you're spending more than you earn and identify areas where you can cut back.

➤ **Reduce monthly expenses.**

Look for ways to reduce your monthly expenses by canceling subscriptions, cutting back on eating out, and finding cheaper alternatives for essential items.

➤ **Pay off debt.**

Debt can be a significant burden, so it's important to work on paying it off as quickly as possible. This can free up more money each month to save or invest.

➤ **Build an emergency fund.**

An emergency fund is a crucial component of financial stability. Having money set aside for unexpected expenses is important to avoid going into debt or relying on credit cards.

➤ **Invest in your future.**

Once you've reduced debt and built an emergency fund, start investing for your future. This can include retirement savings or investing in stocks, bonds, or mutual funds.

➤ **Increase your income.**

Consider ways to increase your income, such as getting a side hustle, asking for a raise, or learning new skills to increase your earning potential.

➤ **Live below your means.**

This means spending less than you earn and avoiding lifestyle inflation.

This helps you save more, reduce debt, and build wealth over time. It's important to avoid overspending and focus on living within your means to achieve financial stability.

➤ **Evaluate your relationship with money.**
This step involves examining your beliefs, attitudes, and behaviors around money to identify negative patterns and make changes supporting your financial goals.

➤ **Embrace simplicity.**
The book advocates for a simpler lifestyle, which can reduce expenses, minimize waste, and increase happiness. By embracing simplicity, you can focus on what truly matters in life and avoid the trap of constantly chasing more things and experiences.

Rich Dad Poor Dad

by Robert Kyosaki

"The single most powerful asset we all have is our mind. If it is trained well, it can create enormous wealth."

M OST people don't know that an asset is something you own and a liability is something you owe. In this book, the author stresses that the only way to become financially independent is to build up assets that bring in money and can cover your costs. Still, many people would rather spend their money on a new car or an iPad than on stocks or real estate (assets). Fear of going off the generally accepted path of life greatly impacts how people make financial decisions. If you don't want money to run your life as it does for most people, you'll have to do things differently than the rest of the crowd.

The two dads in the book have two different ideas about how to get and keep the money. *Rich Dad* tells young people to make investments that make them money, learn about money, and practice thinking for themselves. *Poor Dad* says you should get a good job with benefits and then retire with a pension. In this book, you'll learn how to stop letting the things that keep you from getting rich get in the way of your goals and how to overcome the biggest mental barriers to getting rich and being financially independent.

Students don't learn about money in school; they care more about getting a good job than being financially stable. Because they don't know much about money, they don't understand that spending all the money you have is not a good way to live. So, they have no choice but to live from paycheck to paycheck.

6 Lessons from *Rich Dad*

Lesson 1 — Money is not what you make but what you keep.

Rich Dad believed that true financial success lies not in one's income but in the ability to manage that income effectively. In other words, it's not how much you make that determines your financial success but how much of it you keep. This idea challenges the traditional notion that earning more money is the key to financial freedom. Instead, it argues that it's more important to focus on developing sound financial habits that will help you keep more of the money you earn. This includes understanding the difference between assets and liabilities, learning to manage debt effectively, and developing a plan for investing in assets that generate passive income.

Lesson 2 — People of the middle and lower classes work for money. The wealthy have money to work for them.

This means that instead of relying solely on income from a job, the wealthy focus on creating multiple sources of passive income through investments, businesses, and real estate. By building these sources of income, they can put their money to work for them and generate wealth over time. This mindset shift is crucial for achieving financial independence and building lasting wealth. By focusing on creating passive income streams, individuals can break free from the cycle of trading time for money and start building a more secure financial future for themselves and their families.

Lesson 3 — Smart people don't always succeed, but those who take risks do.

Rich Dad argues that many highly intelligent people often fail to achieve success because they are too cautious and afraid to take risks. On the other hand, those who are willing to take calculated risks and step outside their comfort zones are often the ones who achieve the most success. This principle applies to all areas of life, including business, investing, and personal growth. It suggests that individuals who want to achieve financial independence and build lasting wealth must be willing to take risks and learn from their failures. While taking risks can be scary and uncertain, it is often the only way to achieve real growth and success in life. Embracing this mindset, individuals can break free from limiting beliefs and pursue their goals with courage and confidence.

Lesson 4 — A corporation is the biggest secret of the rich.

He proclaims that the wealthy understand the power of creating and using a corporation to build wealth over time. By creating a corporation, individuals can separate their personal and business assets, protecting them from lawsuits and other financial risks. In addition, a corporation can also provide numerous tax benefits and deductions that are not available to individuals. Individuals can build lasting wealth and protect themselves from financial risks by leveraging these benefits. While creating a corporation can seem intimidating, the author emphasizes that it is a crucial step for those looking to achieve financial independence and build lasting wealth.

There are significant differences between the two entities in the manner and order in which corporations pay their taxes.

➤ **Corporations:**

    1. Earn

    2. Spend

    3. Pay Taxes

➤ **Employees who work for Corporations:**

    1. Earn

    2. Pay Taxes

    3. Spend

There are four main types of financial intelligence that you need to learn if you want to be good with money. The author says that people should work on the following four areas to keep their financial knowledge up to date:

➤ **Accounting.**
The ability to read numbers is the essence of accounting. This is an essential skill when it comes to building a business or investing.

➤ **Investing.**
The act of investing involves the allocation of resources in the expectation of future gains. This is called the concept of money making money.

➤ **The Law.**
The law refers to the knowledge of state, federal, and corporate regulations. Knowing your tax advantages and protections is important.

➤ **Understanding markets.**
To understand markets, one should have a basic understanding of supply and demand.

Lesson 5 — Wealthy individuals focus on their asset columns, while most are concerned with their income statements.

Rich Dad introduces the idea that wealthy individuals focus on their asset columns while most are concerned with their income statements. It explains that most people focus on their income statements, representing their income and expenses. However, the wealthy understand that their financial success is determined by their income and the assets they own. Assets are things that put money in your pocket, while liabilities are things that take money out of your pocket. Types of assets are:

➤ Stocks.

➤ Bonds.

➤ Rental Properties (Real Estate).

➤ Businesses.

➤ Intellectual Property (Music, book, podcasts, etc.).

Most people can relate to this analogy because this is how most people live their lives. This shows how important it is to buy assets:

> *"Imagine playing **Monopoly** and never buying assets or investments that **generate** income.*
>
> *Imagine you just went around **collecting $200**, giving your money to the rich, and trying to stay out of jail.*
>
> *That is how **most people** live their lives."*

Lesson 6 — Avoiding failure also means avoiding success.

Rich Dad discusses how too many people are so afraid of failure that they never take the necessary risks to achieve success. He emphasizes that failure is a crucial part of the learning process and an inevitable part of any journey toward success. He suggests that those who are most successful have often failed numerous times before achieving their goals. By avoiding failure, individuals also avoid taking risks and trying new things, which limits their potential for growth and success.

We all have a lot of potential and are all born with unique traits. Even so, self-doubt and a lack of confidence keep us from reaching our goals and following our dreams. Fear, cynicism, laziness, and bad habits can also cause failure. Rich people, on the other hand, think about them differently than poor people do:

➤ **Fear.**

Most people feel more pain when they lose money than when they win money. To fix this problem, we have to accept that failure is part of the way. The author says that starting young may make people less afraid of losing.

➤ **Cynicism.**

Investors who have done this before know that when the economy is bad, it is often the best time to invest and make money. They know how to pull the trigger when no one else is willing to act. Don't let cynicism and predictions of the end of the world get in the way of your financial goals.

➤ **Laziness.**

Don't say, *"I can't afford it,"* repeatedly. Instead, you should ask, *"How can I pay for it?"* Most people have a fixed way of thinking when it comes to their own money. Take steps to improve your finances and adopt a growth mindset.

➤ **Bad habits.**

Stop paying yourself last and start paying yourself first. When the economy is bad, this way of doing things forces us to devise new ways to meet our financial obligations to others.

➤ **Arrogance.**

Find out what you don't know and learn it. Don't be afraid to try out new ideas or question the ones you already have.

MINDSET COMPARISON

Poor Dad	Rich Dad
Rich people should pay more taxes.	The tax system rewards those who produce.
Work for a reputable company.	Invest in a reputable company.
I am not wealthy because I have children.	Since I have children, I need wealth.
Dinner is not the time to discuss money.	Dinner conversation about money.
"Don't take risks."	"Learn to manage risk."
House is an asset.	House is a liability.
Pay your bills first.	Pay your bills last.
I'll never be rich.	"Because I am rich, I don't do this."

KEY LESSONS

1. **Don't join the rat race because you're afraid.**
   The main reason most Americans have money problems is that they don't play to lose.

2. **You shouldn't let your feelings affect the money decisions you make.**
   When fear or greed tells us how to spend our money, we make bad choices.

3. **Make learning about money a priority.**
   Because schools don't teach about money, many educated people make bad financial decisions.

4. **Taking risks is a must if you want to grow your money meaningfully.**
   Learn how to handle risk instead of being afraid of it.

5. **Figure out why you want to achieve your goals.**
   By writing down what you want and what you don't want, you can figure out the emotional reasons behind your goal.

6. **Being arrogant can lead to losing all of your money.**
   An arrogant person thinks that what he or she doesn't know doesn't matter, which causes them to make decisions based on what they don't know.

7. **Pay the bills with your job and build wealth with your business.**
   Build a business outside your 9-to-5 job to help you save money for your retirement until you can quit.

ACTIONABLE STEPS TO TAKE

➤ **Develop a financial education.**
Learning about money management, investing, and wealth building can help increase financial literacy and improve financial well-being.

➤ **Change your mindset about money.**
The author emphasizes the importance of creating multiple income streams, rather than relying on a single job or source of income. This can be achieved by investing in real estate, starting a small business, or earning money through a side hustle or passive income stream.

➤ **Take control of your finances.**
Taking control of your finances by creating a budget, reducing debt, and building an emergency fund can help improve financial stability.

➤ **Take calculated risks.**
The book encourages readers to take risks and learn from their mistakes. This means being willing to invest in assets and opportunities that may be considered unconventional or risky but potentially generate significant returns.

➤ **Invest in assets.**
Investing in income-generating assets, such as rental properties, stocks, or businesses, can help build wealth over time.

➤ **Be willing to learn constantly.**
Emphasizes that financial education is a lifelong process and that readers should be willing to continue learning and adapting their strategies as they gain more experience and knowledge.

➤ **Start a side hustle.**
Starting a side hustle or small business can help increase income and provide wealth-building opportunities.

➤ **Avoid lifestyle inflation.**
Avoiding lifestyle inflation, or increasing spending as income increases, can help increase savings and improve long-term financial stability.

The Science of Getting Rich

by Wallace D. Wattles

"You are the master of your destiny. You can influence, direct and control your environment. You can make your life what you want it to be."

T HIS book consists of action steps to add value for other people and become wealthy. It is a guide to acquiring wealth and success in life by following a set of principles and steps. The book's central message is that anyone can become rich by changing their thinking and acting toward their goals.

The author asserts that the primary reason people do not become rich is that they lack a clear understanding of the laws governing wealth accumulation. He states that there is a science to getting rich, and once understood and applied, anyone can achieve financial success.

The book outlines several key principles necessary to attract wealth into one's life. These principles include; the idea that wealth is not limited and that everyone can have abundance; the importance of a clear and definite purpose in life, the need to develop a positive mental attitude and cultivate gratitude; the power of thought and visualization in manifesting one's desires; and the role of action in turning one's desires into reality.

It also addresses the issue of wealth distribution and argues that wealth is not a zero-sum game and that an increase in wealth for one person does not necessarily lead to a decrease in wealth for others. He advocates for a more equitable distribution of wealth and argues that this can be achieved by creating wealth through honest means and sharing the benefits with others.

Take Advantage of What you Have

The book begins with understanding several truths so you can think and act in accordance with these truths to create massive wealth. The three most important concepts are:

Source

The *Source* is the infinite and unlimited source of wealth, prosperity, and abundance in the universe. He believes this *Source* is available to all individuals but that most people do not tap into it because they have to limit beliefs and negative thoughts.

According to the author, the *Source* represents the unlimited potential for wealth and abundance in the universe. By aligning one's thoughts, beliefs, and actions with this *Source*, one can attract wealth and success into their life. He emphasizes that wealth is not limited and that everyone has enough abundance to fulfill their desires.

The book argues that the key to accessing the *Source* is to develop a clear and definite purpose, cultivate a positive mental attitude, and take consistent action toward one's goals. He believes that by focusing on these principles and aligning oneself with the *Source*, one can attract wealth, abundance, and prosperity into their life.

Thoughts trigger creation

Each of our thoughts leaves an impression on the *Source*, and the *Source* is triggered to create whatever is contained in our thoughts. As you imagine a house, the shape of that house is imprinted within the *Source*. The *Source* then automatically begins to create that house. In this case, it could be the modification of the commerce or construction or the production of raw materials with which the house will be constructed. This process takes time. Imagine an oak tree, for example, and you immediately begin the process of creating it — even though it may take centuries for the tree to be fully developed.

The human brain is the thinking center

As humans, we can create thoughts; when we imagine something in our minds, we form it in our minds and imprint it on the *Source*. By doing so, creation is triggered. Everything you observe arises from an invisible thought. The same applies to all actions you take and everything you create with your hands. Wealth must be created from the inside out.

Be Precise with Your Thoughts

The author emphasizes the importance of mastering the art of thinking to create wealth. He argues that a person's thoughts, beliefs, and attitudes play a crucial role in attracting abundance and prosperity into their life. To achieve financial success, one must understand and apply the following key components of positive thinking:

➤ **Creativity is the key to success, not competition.**
Wealth is often perceived as a finite resource controlled or limited by others. To remain in harmony with the *Source*, we must seek riches in a way that creates more for ourselves and others.

➤ **Maintain a sense of faith and gratitude.**
As soon as you can impress your thoughts on the *Source*, you should be confident that it is already delivering the desired outcomes and grateful for it.

➤ **Maintain a clear and consistent mental picture.**
Having a vague idea of whether one wants to *live a better life* or *be rich* is insufficient. You must first produce a clear mental picture of what you want for the *Source* to deliver what you desire.

➤ **You should use your willpower for yourself and not for others.**
Attempt not to impose your willpower on others, e.g., do not take things from others, don't force them (mentally or physically) to comply with your wishes, or don't insist they do anything for their welfare. Concentrate all your willpower on clarifying your mental picture, sending it to the *Source*, and taking actions aligned with your mental picture.

Act with Responsibility

Based on the principle, taking action is essential in turning the gifts and opportunities the *Source* provides into wealth and prosperity. The following bullet points outline how one can take responsible and effective actions toward creating wealth:

➤ **Be proactive.**

Take initiative and seek out opportunities that align with your goals and purpose. Don't wait for opportunities to come to you; go out and create them.

➤ **Take consistent and persistent action.**

Consistent and persistent action is necessary to convert opportunities into wealth. Focus on taking small steps every day toward your goals.

➤ **Be helpful to others.**

By providing value and being of service to others, you create a positive impact in the world and attract abundance into your life.

➤ **Be ethical and honest in your dealings.**

Wealth should be created through honest means and with integrity. Building wealth through unethical or illegal means will not bring long-term prosperity.

➤ **Be open to new ideas and opportunities.**

Be flexible and open to new ideas and opportunities that may arise. This will allow you to adapt to changing circumstances and capitalize on new opportunities.

KEY LESSONS

1. **Under the power of thoughts.**
   Your thoughts can directly influence the life you lead and the physical reality you encounter.

2. **The importance of a positive mental attitude.**
   Cultivating a positive mental attitude attracts abundance and prosperity into your life.

3. **Embrace the power of visualization.**
   Visualizing your desired outcome can help you focus on your goals and attract positive energy into your life.

4. **Knowledge without actions is pointless.**
   Consistent and persistent action is necessary to turn opportunities into wealth.

5. **The ego is the enemy.**
   Giving to others positively impacts the world and attracts abundance into your life.

6. **Learn to create value.**
   Focus on creating value for others, and wealth will follow.

7. **The importance of honesty and integrity.**
   Building wealth through unethical or illegal means will not bring long-term prosperity.

8. **Be open, flexible, and adaptable.**
   Being open to new ideas and opportunities will help you capitalize on new ones and overcome challenges.

ACTIONABLE STEPS TO TAKE

➤ **Define your purpose.**

Identifying what you truly want in life will give you direction and focus. This is important because clearly understanding your goals will help you stay motivated and focused on what you want to achieve.

➤ **Cultivate a positive mental attitude.**

Focus on the positive aspects of life and cultivate gratitude. This is important because a positive outlook will attract abundance and prosperity into your life.

➤ **Visualize your desired outcome.**

Imagine what your life will be like once you have achieved your goals. This is important because visualization helps you focus on your goals and attracts positive energy into your life.

➤ **Take action.**

Consistent and persistent action is essential to convert opportunities into wealth. This is important because wealth is not created through thoughts alone but by acting toward your goals.

➤ **Be helpful to others.**

By providing value and being of service to others, you create a positive impact in the world and attract abundance into your life. This is important because giving to others is a key principle of the law of attraction.

➤ **Work hard.**

Hard work is essential to achieve your goals. This is important because effort and dedication are necessary to achieve your goals.

➤ **Be ethical and honest in your dealings.**

Building wealth through unethical or illegal means will not bring long-term prosperity. This is important because wealth should be created with integrity and honesty.

The Richest Man in Babylon

by George Samuel Clason

"Proper preparation is the key to our success. Our acts can be no wiser than our thoughts. Our thinking can be no wiser than our understanding."

T HIS book is a personal finance classic that offers timeless principles on how to build wealth and financial security. The book is written as a series of parables set in ancient *Babylon*, where ordinary people learn the secrets of acquiring wealth and financial freedom from the richest man in *Babylon, Arkad.*

The book covers a wide range of topics related to personal finance, including saving, budgeting, investing, and wealth creation. One of the key principles emphasized in the book is the importance of living below your means and saving a portion of your income, which should then be invested to grow your wealth.

Another important principle discussed in the book is the power of compounding, which emphasizes the need to let your money work for you over time. The book also emphasizes the importance of seeking wise counsel from knowledgeable and experienced financial advisors when making investment decisions.

The parables in the book are relatable and easy to understand, making it accessible to people of all ages and financial backgrounds. The book is written in a simple, engaging, informative, and entertaining style.

7 Cures for a Lean Purse

To establish a foundation for wealth creation, it is imperative to utilize your existing financial resources. Without taking proactive measures, your earnings will invariably be allocated towards essential expenditures. It is essential to differentiate between necessities and luxuries to develop a comprehensive budget. Below are seven steps that can facilitate your journey toward financial prosperity:

➤ **Prioritize to pay yourself first.**
Take out nine of every ten coins you put in your purse and keep the last

one. At some point, you'll notice that your purse has grown. This is because you get more money when you don't spend all of what you earn.

➤ **Be in control of your spending.**

Plan your income and outcomes with a budget to get the best results. Unless you make it otherwise, the amount of your income will always be equal to the amount of your necessary costs.

➤ **Invest in assets that can increase the value of your gold.**

Put your gold to work to produce more of the same. You can earn income whether you are at work or on the road. Passive income is the basis of real wealth and should go beyond the income you earn. Invest your money wisely, and take advantage of time and compound interest by making smart investments.

➤ **Protect your valuables from loss.**

Before you manage larger amounts, you should learn to protect the small amounts. Do your homework before investing.

➤ **Make the most of your residence as an investment.**

Every man needs to own a home. Thus, your cost of living is reduced, and you have more money available for other purposes.

➤ **As you age, take care of your needs.**

Make sure you will have a suitable income in the future, for when you get older, you are less capable of gaining an earning. This is the purpose of a retirement plan and insurance.

➤ **You will increase your income if you become more skilled and wise.**

To earn more, one must possess a strong desire. Remember this until you reach your fulfillment, and you will learn how to accumulate wealth. Your desires must be specific and clear. Put yourself in a position to earn more money by improving your skills and becoming more marketable. Take courses, attend classes, and work part-time.

The 5 Laws of Gold

➤ **Gold comes easily to those who save at least 10% of their earnings.**
"Gold cometh gladly and in increasing quantity to any man who will put by not less than one-tenth of his earnings to create an estate for his future and that of his family."
Lesson: You should set aside 10% of your income.

➤ **Gold labors diligently and multiplies for people who find this gold a profitable employment.**
"Gold laboreth diligently and contentedly for the wise owner who finds for it profitable employment, multiplying even as the flocks of the field."
Lesson: Spend your money wisely.

➤ **Gold clings to the people who invest their gold with wise people.**
"Gold clingeth to the protection of the cautious owner who invests it under the advice of men wise in its handling."
Lesson: Take the long-term view and be patient.

➤ **Gold slips away from people who invest in unfamiliar purposes.**
"Gold slippeth away from the man who invests it in businesses or purposes with which he is not familiar or which are not approved by those skilled in its keep."
Lesson: Don't invest in anything you don't understand.

➤ **Gold flees from people who force gold into impossible earnings.**
"Gold flees the man who would force it to impossible earnings or who followeth the alluring advice of tricksters and schemers or who trusts it to his own inexperience and romantic desires in investment."
Lesson: You should avoid get-rich-quick schemes.

How Can I Make My Money Multiply?

➤ You should strive to accomplish your goals and work hard. Working hard does not only help you earn money, but it also attracts good people and good opportunities.

➤ To achieve success, it's important to surround yourself with people who want, understand, and make a great deal of money. Utilize other people's pressure to your advantage.

➤ Only the best experts in the field should be asked for help with money. Don't ask family, friends, or coworkers for help with your investments.

➤ You should stick to your plan. Invest your money for the future and don't waste it on things you don't need. Invest wisely, and don't forget how much the compound effect can help. Don't invest based on what you see, but on what you know. Invest your money in things that will make you money, and let time do the rest.

KEY LESSONS

1. **Your most valuable asset is your passive income.**
   If you spend all the money you make, you will be poor in the long run. Put your money to work to make more money.

2. **You must not think you know more than you do.**
   A mindset that presumes complete knowledge is a hindrance to acquiring new information. Overconfidence is often a display of conceit, while true assurance speaks for itself.

3. **The only way to get rich is to try and fail.**
   Effective money management skills are typically acquired through trial and error, with individuals learning from their mistakes and persevering in their efforts.

4. **Think about the future when you look at your finances.**
   If you only worked for today, your only source of happiness would be your paycheck for today. How long you keep your money is a big factor in whether or not you become wealthy.

5. **A key to a person's success is not chance, but luck.**
   Although luck is inherently unpredictable, it can be cultivated and enhanced by seizing opportunities.

ACTIONABLE STEPS TO TAKE

➤ **Create a budget.**

One of the key messages in the book is the importance of living below your means and budgeting effectively. Start by listing your income and expenses and looking for areas where you can cut back on spending.

➤ **Pay yourself first.**

Set aside a portion of your income for savings and investments before spending on necessities and luxuries. This will ensure that you are consistently saving and investing for your future.

➤ **Invest in income-generating assets.**

The book encourages readers to invest in assets such as real estate and small businesses that can generate income. Look for opportunities to invest in assets that have the potential to generate cash flow.

➤ **Seek guidance from successful individuals.**

Look for advice and guidance from those who have already achieved financial success. Attend seminars, read books, and network with other investors to gain knowledge and insights.

➤ **Set financial goals.**

The book teaches that setting financial goals is the key to financial success. Determine what you want to achieve and create a plan to reach those goals.

➤ **Learn from mistakes.**

Be willing to take calculated risks and learn from your mistakes. Failure is a part of the process of achieving success.

➤ **Be willing to learn and adapt.**

The book stresses that financial education is a lifelong process and that readers should be willing to continue learning and adapting their strategies as they gain more experience and knowledge.

The Millionaire Fastlane

by M. J. DeMarco

"Somebody should tell us, right at the start of our lives, that we are dying. Then we might live life to the limit, every minute of every day. Do it! I say. Whatever you want to do, do it now. There are only so many tomorrows."

T HIS is a self-help book focusing on financial independence and building wealth. The author proposes that traditional methods of achieving wealth, such as saving, investing in stocks, and working a 9-to-5 job, are slow and ineffective. Instead, he offers the *Fastlane approach*, which involves creating a successful business that generates wealth quickly and sustainably.

The book begins by debunking common myths about wealth, such as the idea that it can be achieved through slow and steady savings or by winning the lottery. Instead, it argues that wealth is created by identifying a need or want in the market and providing a solution through entrepreneurship. He emphasizes the importance of creating a value-producing asset that generates income through a system or process that can be scaled.

The author divides the life approaches to wealth into three lanes: the Sidewalk, the Slowlane, and the Fastlane. The author emphasizes that the key to success is not just hard work but also creating a system that can generate wealth even while you're not actively working. He stresses the importance of identifying needs and wants in the market and creating a solution that can be scaled and automated.

The Sidewalk Wealth Equation

The Sidewalk wealth equation is:

$$Wealth = Income + Debt$$

Sidewalkers' way of life is directly related to how much money they make, and they borrow a lot to make up for it. People in the personal finance world often call these people those who are always trying to *"Keep up with the Joneses."* To summarize:

➤ **The Sidewalk doesn't think about the future. Instead, it lives for today.**
Because of this, they spend all the money they make on fun, consumption, gadgets, fashion, trips, shiny things, and endless entertainment. So, people who live on the Sidewalk usually live from paycheck to paycheck and have a lot of debt.

➤ **There is more to life on the Sidewalk than just being poor.**
People with a very high income may also live on the Sidewalk if they spend more than they make. Because of this, it's not unusual for celebrities who seemed to be on top of the world to go bankrupt a few years later.

The Slowlane Wealth Equation

The Slowlane wealth equation is:

$$\textit{Wealth = Job + Market Investments}$$

In this plan, money from a job is used to pay for living expenses and market investments. This is a problem because much of what affects your wealth is out of your control (for example, the stock market). In addition, there are only so many hours in the day. In other words, the two parts of the equation are controlled by things you can't change. To summarize:

➤ **In the Slowlane, they give up the present for the future.**
This means they read books about personal finance, save 10% of their income, invest in different funds, get compound interest, etc. Most people in our society, like parents, teachers, and financial experts, agree that this is the best way to do things. It's much better than the Sidewalk.

➤ **The Slowlane will take decades to complete.**
Because of this plan, they spend most of their lives cutting coupons, saving money, and not getting lattes so that they can retire someday. Sadly, by the time we get there, most of them will be old, bald, and maybe even in a wheelchair. This isn't the best case, is it?

➤ **There is no guarantee that the Slowlane will be a success.**

Even though it's shown as the safest way, nothing is certain here either. This plan is easy to get off track if something unexpected happens, like a health problem, a divorce, a market crash, or having kids.

➤ **The Slowlane experts don't follow their advice.**

The financial experts and authors who teach us about this strategy don't use it. They earn money by selling books, courses, seminars, radio shows, and other things. How funny!

The Fastlane Wealth Equation

The Fastlane wealth equation is as follows:

$$\textit{Wealth = Net Profit + Asset Value}$$

All business owners use this equation in their work. Fastlaners make money by giving their clients something of value. They can make more money by selling more units or making money on each unit they sell. Also, as a business makes more money, the value of its assets goes up as well. Because of this, it's possible to get rich quickly. If you want to get rich young, you must become an entrepreneur and start a business. To summarize:

➤ **The Fastlane is about how to start a business.**

Most people who get rich have done so by starting their businesses. When you own a business, you decide how much money you make and can potentially make much more than most people do in a year.

➤ **Retirement in the Fastlane is all about how to make the most of your retirement.**

Even though money can't make us happy on its own, it can help us get what we want, like freedom, good health, and close relationships.

➤ **On the Fastlane, there is no easy way to get rich. But it can be done in a short amount of time.**

In other words, if you think of quick as being less than ten years, then the answer is YES. In the book, the author often worked 12 hours a day, seven days a week, to build his business. Eventually, he only needed to work a few hours a week.

Developing a Successful Business

To develop a successful business, the author emphasizes the importance of identifying a need in the marketplace and creating a product or service that meets that need. He also stresses the need to constantly innovate and improve products and services to stay ahead of the competition. Additionally, he suggests that individuals must focus on creating value for their customers rather than just making a profit. The author outlines essential insights to empower entrepreneurs in building successful enterprises and achieving ultimate financial independence. The key factors are as follows:

➤ **The Commandment of Need.**
This principle emphasizes the importance of addressing a significant need or problem in the marketplace. *The Commandment of Need* encourages entrepreneurs to identify and understand their target's audience pain points and desires and to develop products or services that offer tangible benefits and address unmet needs.

➤ **The Commandment of Entry.**
This principle emphasizes the importance of identifying business opportunities with low barriers to entry. *The Commandment of Entry* encourages entrepreneurs to seek out industries or niches that are ripe for disruption, where there is a clear demand for innovative solutions that can be implemented without significant hurdles or barriers.

➤ **The Commandment of Control.**
This principle emphasizes the importance of retaining control over one's time, money, and resources in pursuing financial independence. *The Commandment of Control* encourages entrepreneurs to prioritize business models that offer scalability, leverage, and autonomy, allowing them to build sustainable and profitable enterprises without sacrificing their freedom or quality of life.

➤ **The Commandment of Time.**
This principle emphasizes the importance of valuing and maximizing one's time in pursuing wealth and fulfillment. *The Commandment of Time* encourages entrepreneurs to focus on high-impact activities that generate

disproportionate investment returns and eliminate time-wasting activities that offer little value or return. The author advocates for developing systems and processes that can operate independently of the entrepreneur's direct involvement, enabling them to create more free time for leisure, family, and personal pursuits.

The Law of Affection

The law of affection says that the more influence you have over something you own, the more money you will have. The principle emphasizes the importance of creating products or services that are genuinely beneficial to one's target audience. According to the author, building a successful business requires more than just identifying a profitable niche or industry; it also requires a deep understanding of the needs, desires, and pain points of one's customers. The *Law of Affection* encourages entrepreneurs to prioritize empathy, service, and value creation over self-interest or profit maximization. For the law of affection to work for your business, it must be able to make an impact on a large or small scale or both. The *net profit* variable in our Fastlane wealth equation has *scale* and *magnitude* as hidden variables.

➤ **The term *scale* refers to affecting a large number of people.**
   For example, *Stephen King* became a millionaire by selling books costing $10 each.

➤ ***Magnitude* refers to a significant impact on people's lives.**
   As an example, a local condo developer sells 100 units at $300,000 each. He has such a big impact on a few people that he could also become a millionaire.

When you want to build a successful business, you have to make your scale and/or magnitude impact bigger. The equation serves as a reminder that building a successful business requires a holistic approach that balances financial performance with long-term growth and sustainability. The following is the equation:

Net Profit = Units Sold (Scale) × Unit Profit (Magnitude)

KEY LESSONS

1. **If you think in the wrong way, it doesn't matter how much money you have.**
   You will fail if think you have no control over your success.

2. **People used the same way to get rich in the past, but that is no longer the right way.**
   People no longer know what it takes to live a good life step by step.

3. **Trading your time is the same as trading your life. So, college and getting a degree are not always the answer.**
   Some business ideas can be done without a degree.

4. **Not all definitions of wealth have to do with money.**
   How happy a person is with his or her life and things show how wealthy he or she is.

5. **Getting rich is not a goal, but a way to get there.**
   The key to getting rich is to keep working toward it.

6. **Wealth is created through value creation.**
   Wealth is created by providing value to others. Entrepreneurs who prioritize creating products or services that are genuinely beneficial to their target audience are more likely to establish trust, credibility, and brand loyalty.

7. **Persistence is key to achieving success.**
   Entrepreneurs who are willing to persevere through setbacks and failures are more likely to ultimately achieve their goals.

ACTIONABLE STEPS TO TAKE

➤ **Identify a *big idea*.**
A business or investment opportunity that has the potential to generate significant cash flow. The book emphasizes the importance of identifying a *big idea* that can create a significant income stream. This could be a new business or an unconventional investment opportunity.

➤ **Develop a business plan.**
Outline the steps needed to bring the idea to fruition. Once you have identified a *big idea*, it's important to develop a plan that outlines the steps needed to bring it to life.

➤ **Take action.**
Bring the plan to life by acquiring the necessary knowledge, skills, and resources. The book emphasizes the importance of taking action to bring the plan to life. This means acquiring the necessary knowledge, skills, and resources to turn the idea into a profitable venture.

➤ **Create income-producing assets.**
Focus on creating income-producing assets and businesses rather than relying on a steady salary or traditional investment strategies. Instead of relying on a steady salary or traditional investment strategies, the book encourages readers to focus on creating income-producing assets and businesses.

➤ **Take calculated risks.**
The book encourages readers to take risks and learn from their mistakes. This means being willing to invest in assets and opportunities that may be considered unconventional or risky but that have the potential to generate significant returns.

➤ **Continuously educate yourself and adapt to changes in your environment.**
Adapt your strategies as you gain more experience and knowledge. The book emphasizes that financial education is a lifelong process and that readers should be willing to continue learning and adapting their strategies as they gain more experience and knowledge.

The Automatic Millionaire

by David Bach

"In fact, what determines your wealth is not how much you make but how much you keep of what you make."

T AKE a moment to look at your current finances and figure out what assets you have. How much do you make and spend each month? How much do you owe in debt? The first step to making your financial situation better is to know where you stand. Everyone wants to be a millionaire, and there are many ways to get there. You might win the lottery or a popular game show, but that's not likely. You might also come up with a new idea and start a business.

You don't have to work as hard as you might think to become a millionaire. But you'll need to set up an automatic savings account so that your paychecks go straight into savings without you having to do anything else. Setting up this account is important if you want to be financially stable in the future. Also, the *Automatic Millionaire* plan doesn't require you to make a lot of money. In fact, all you need to do to succeed is agree to give yourself small payments every time you get paid.

This book provides guidance on how to eliminate debt, build credit, and protect assets through insurance and estate planning. The author's system is designed to be simple, effective, and adaptable to any income level or life stage.

The Automatic Millionaire Formula

No matter where we are in life, we all have our own goals that we want to reach. Creating an emergency fund, paying off our mortgage, paying off our credit card debt, and giving back to our communities are all goals that many of us share. The following formula is given in the book as a way to reach these goals:

➤ **Pay yourself first.**
   The first step is to automate your savings. This means setting up automatic transfers from your paycheck to a separate savings account, preferably a high-yield savings account. Aim to save at least 10% to 15% of your gross income.

➤ **Make it automatic.**

Set up automatic bill payments so you never miss a payment and incur late fees. This also helps you avoid the temptation of spending money that should go towards bills and savings.

➤ **Maximize your 401(k) or IRA contributions.**

The author suggests contributing the maximum amount allowed by law to your 401(k) or IRA. This not only reduces your taxable income but also helps you build wealth over time through compounding interest.

➤ **Buy a home.**

Homeownership is an important step in building wealth. He recommends buying a home that is affordable and within your means. A mortgage payment should not exceed 25% of your monthly income.

➤ **Pay off your mortgage early.**

One way to accelerate your path to wealth is to pay off your mortgage early. The author suggests adding an extra payment per year, which can save you thousands in interest over the life of your mortgage.

➤ **Invest in real estate.**

Real estate is another way to build wealth. It suggests investing in rental properties or REITs (Real Estate Investment Trusts) as a way to generate passive income.

➤ **Make charitable contributions.**

Giving back to your community is an important part of building wealth. The book suggests setting aside a portion of your income for charitable donations.

➤ **Build an emergency fund.**

Having an emergency fund is crucial to financial stability. He recommends having at least three to six months of living expenses saved in a high-yield savings account.

Avoid Credit Cards

The book highlights the dangers of credit cards and debt while emphasizing the importance of financial freedom. It strongly advises against carrying credit card balances and urges readers to pay off their credit card debt as quickly as possible. He argues that credit card debt is a trap that keeps people in a cycle of paying high-interest rates and never truly making progress toward their financial goals. The author also suggests cutting up credit cards as a way to avoid the temptation of overspending. He recommends creating a debt repayment plan and setting a timeline for becoming debt-free. This includes identifying the highest interest-rate debt and focusing on paying it off first while continuing to make minimum payments on other debts. He stresses the importance of developing healthy financial habits and learning to live within one's means. By avoiding debt and paying off credit card balances, individuals can achieve financial security and start building wealth for the future.

The following three practical steps can be taken to manage credit cards and debt:

1. **Pay off high-interest debt first.**
   Make a list of all debts, including credit card balances, and prioritize them by interest rate.

2. **Negotiate lower interest rates.**
   Contact credit card companies and negotiate for lower interest rates. A lower interest rate can save hundreds or thousands of dollars in interest charges over time.

3. **Use credit cards wisely.**
   Limit credit card use to essential expenses and pay off the balance in full every month. Avoid using credit cards to finance lifestyle expenses or impulse purchases.

KEY LESSONS

1. **To be rich, you don't have to make a lot of money all at once.**
   People's wealth comes from what they have saved, not how much money they make.

2. **First, you should put some money in your pockets.**
   First, put money into a pre-tax retirement account. Then, put money into the things you need.

3. **Automatic millionaires are made when savings are put into your account regularly.**
   Don't let yourself choose between spending and saving. Instead, make a promise to your savings account.

4. **Save money for rainy days to be prepared.**
   Automatic millionaires always have money set aside for emergencies.

5. **You should strive to own.**
   Viewing rent as a source of income is incorrect. Rather, it should be regarded as a cost or an expense.

ACTIONABLE STEPS TO TAKE

➤ **Create a budget and stick to it.**

One of the key takeaways from *The Automatic Millionaire* is the importance of having a budget and sticking to it. This means setting spending limits for different categories, such as housing, transportation, and entertainment, and making sure you don't overspend in any of these areas.

➤ **Automate your savings.**

Automating savings, such as through payroll deductions or automatic transfers, can help increase the likelihood of consistently saving and building wealth.

➤ **Start saving early.**

The book emphasizes the importance of starting to save as early as possible, and making it a regular part of your life so that it becomes automatic.

➤ **Utilize the power of compounding interest.**

The author highlights the power of compounding interest and how small amounts of money saved consistently over time can grow into significant sums.

➤ **Create multiple streams of income.**

Increasing income through a side hustle or asking for a raise can help improve financial stability and increase wealth-building potential.

➤ **Live below your means.**

Living below your means by spending less than you earn can help increase savings and improve financial stability.

➤ **Pay yourself first.**

Prioritizing savings by paying yourself first, before paying other bills, can help increase overall savings and improve financial stability.

➤ **Consider a mortgage acceleration plan.**

A mortgage acceleration plan, such as making extra payments towards the principal, can help reduce the total amount paid on a mortgage and increase wealth.

➤ **Reduce debt.**

Reducing debt, such as paying off credit cards and loans, can improve financial stability and reduce stress.

➤ **Be intentional with spending.**

Being intentional with spending, such as prioritizing needs over wants, can help reduce unnecessary expenses and improve financial management.

I Will Teach You To Be Rich

by Ramit Sethi

"The single most important factor to getting rich is getting started, not being the smartest person in the room."

RICH people don't just come from Ivy League schools, play in the NFL, or win the lottery. Anyone can become wealthy. All you have to do is figure out what it means to you to be wealthy. Step one is to start today. Instead of saving money on $3 lattes and coupons, you should focus on a few areas of your personal finances where you can make big gains. Then, you should set up an automatic money system and start investing without thinking about it. The book is aimed at young adults in their 20s and 30s who are looking to build wealth and become financially independent.

To accumulate wealth, it is crucial to take action and start early. Assuming responsibility for personal finances from a young age is vital, which involves steps such as enhancing credit scores, establishing automatic payments for bills, making wise investments, and developing plans for significant purchases. The book highlights three key lessons in this regard:

1. You are the only one who can fix your money problems.

2. If you know how much money comes into your business, you can set it up so that it goes where you want it to.

3. Don't delay. Even if it's only $1, invest now.

Many people feel emotionally drained when they have to deal with their finances. The author is telling you that you don't have to know everything before you start. For example, 99% of us only need to know two things if we want to lose weight: eat less and move more. Only the very best athletes have to work harder to keep their performance at a high level. We should just accept and act on these simple facts, but instead, we talk about trans fats and diet pills. The most important things the author wants you to learn from the book are:

➤ Don't worry about being an expert. It's more important to get started than to become an expert.

➤ If you do ordinary things, you will get ordinary results.

➤ Once your automatic system is set up, don't change it too often.

➤ Don't be afraid to spend a lot on the things you love and cut back on the things you don't.

The 6-Week Gameplan

In his book, the author talks about different ideas about money and finances, such as credit, banks, how banks work, different kinds of bank accounts and investment accounts, and asset classes. This book is a good way to learn about these terms for people who don't know them. After talking about how to set up your money so that it grows on its own and makes you rich, the author talks about how to actually make money. The author has made a plan called The *6-Week Gameplan* to help you start and carry out your plan to get rich:

1. Learn how to set up your credit cards and improve your credit score.

2. Set up your bank accounts properly.

3. Invest in a 401(k) and open a taxable investment account.

4. Determine how much money you are spending and what you are spending it on. Make a budget.

5. Your new infrastructure should be automated so that all your accounts are integrated.

6. Read about investing and how it's different from picking stocks.

Use Your Credit Cards Wisely

As you strive to achieve financial success, it's important to understand that building good credit is a crucial part of the process. However, many people tend to overlook this aspect because it can be complex and overwhelming. The truth is that your credit history can have a far greater impact on your finances than minor daily expenses like buying a cup of coffee. According to *Forbes*, millionaires set aside at least 20% of their income each year. One of the key differences between the wealthy and the average person is that the wealthy plan for the future before the need arises. To maximize your credit card benefits, it's essential to follow these guidelines:

➤ **If you pay off your credit cards regularly, you won't have to pay interest on them.**
One late payment can hurt your credit score, make your annual percentage rate of interest (APR) go up, and cause you to have to pay late fees.

➤ **Remove the fees from your credit card.**
Call the company that issued the card and ask about any fees that come with it. Talk about ways to lower the fees.

➤ **Lower the APR by negotiating.**
If you can't pay off your balance in full every month, your APR tells you how much more you'll have to pay in the long run. You can save a lot of money by talking to your credit card company about lowering your APR.

➤ **Keep your cards active for a period of time.**
Your credit history is a big part of what your credit score is based on. Your score will go up the longer you keep an account and make regular payments.

➤ **Utilize your rewards as you receive them.**
Take advantage of perks like extended warranties, airline miles, and insurance for rental cars.

Eliminate Your Debts

Getting out of debt has more benefits than just making you feel better. Not only does it alleviate the stress of living paycheck to paycheck, but it can also boost your credit score and save you thousands of dollars in interest payments. Follow these five steps to learn how to pay off your debt:

➤ **Step 1 — Make a list of all the debts you owe.**
Many people don't know how much debt they have, which makes it hard to make a good financial plan.

➤ **Step 2 — You need to decide where you want to start.**

Pay off each credit card individually. Start with the card with the highest interest rate if you have a small balance.

➤ **Step 3 — Negotiate the APR to lower it as much as possible.**

Your interest payments will be reduced as a result.

➤ **Step 4 — Consider how you can afford to make more aggressive payments each month.**

By looking at how you spend your money, you can find places where you can save money.

➤ **Step 5 — Take action now.**

The best thing to do is to start with a plan that is mostly solid instead of trying to come up with a plan that is 100% perfect right away.

KEY LESSONS

1. **Don't blame anyone else for the trouble you're having with money.**
Putting the blame on your education, the market, or the fact that you can't afford to invest is just an excuse.

2. **If you have good credit, you can save a lot of money on interest.**
Lenders look at your credit profile to figure out how much you will pay in interest on loans, mortgages, and credit cards. If you have a good credit score, you will pay less interest.

3. **Find out which banks have the best rates of interest.**
Online banks may be able to offer higher interest rates on savings accounts because they have lower operating costs than local banks. Find out who the best provider is and pick from the list of results.

4. **If you only have a small amount to invest, you should open an investment account.**
A 401k, Roth IRA, or ideally both, is the best way to grow your money.

5. **Think carefully about how your money is being spent.**
Set fixed amounts for each type of spending to help you plan your spending. Once you've spent the most you can for the month in that category, you can't spend any more.

6. **Create an automatic payment and transfer system.**
Set up a budget that moves money automatically every month so you can stay on track with your money.

7. **Don't listen to what the experts say. Instead, go with your gut and keep your investment plan simple.**
No matter how hard financial experts try, they can't predict the future. Follow the advice that is simple and sensible.

ACTIONABLE STEPS TO TAKE

➤ **Increase your income.**
The book emphasizes the importance of earning more money as the first step towards achieving financial success. Start by negotiating a raise or starting a side hustle to boost your income.

➤ **Create a budget and savings plan.**
The book provides tips on budgeting and saving and encourages readers to automate these processes so that they become a habit. Set financial goals and create a savings plan to put your money to work for you.

➤ **Diversify and invest for maximum growth.**
Diversify your portfolio and understand the different types of investment vehicles to make the most of your money.

➤ **Change your mindset about money.**
The author encourages readers to change their mindset about money and wealth, and to focus on acquiring assets and creating cash flow. Shift your focus from saving money to acquiring income-generating assets.

➤ **Take calculated risks.**
Take risks and learn from their mistakes and be willing to invest in assets and opportunities that may be considered unconventional or risky but that have the potential to generate significant returns. Be bold, and don't be afraid to take a risk.

➤ **Automate your savings and investments.**
Make it easy for yourself to save and invest with automation.

The Simple Path to Wealth

by J. Collins

*"Life choices are not always about the money, but you should al-
ways be clear about the financial impact of the choices you make.
Sound investing is not complicated. Save a portion of every dollar
you earn, or that otherwise comes your way."*

E VEN though money is one of the most important tools in our society, most
people have never been taught how to think about or use it well. Many
people find it hard to understand their own finances, especially when it comes
to investing. No matter how well-meaning and accurate the literature is from a
technical standpoint, it only makes us more worried, more confused, and less
able to understand money.

The Simple Path to Wealth is a must-read for anyone who wants to take
control of their personal finances and build a strong investment portfolio with
as little effort and thought as possible. The author, a seasoned investor with
decades of experience in the industry, has written this book specifically for those
who don't have the time or inclination to become experts in finance but who still
want to make smart investment decisions.

The author's approach is refreshingly straightforward and easy to understand, making it accessible to anyone regardless of their financial background.
Unlike other personal finance books that may overwhelm readers with complicated math, statistics, and technical terms, *The Simple Path to Wealth* offers a
simplified, common-sense approach to investing that is easy to follow and implement.

The book emphasizes the importance of understanding the fundamentals of
investing, including the power of compounding, diversification, and low-cost index funds. The author also stresses the importance of creating a solid financial
plan, including setting realistic goals, managing debt, and building an emergency fund.

A Guide to Financial Success

When trying to get rich and be financially independent, it's important to stop thinking of money as something you can buy and start thinking of it as something that can bring in money. Here are some tips on how to change your mind about becoming financially independent:

➤ **Understand money.**

- People often don't pay attention to the basics of personal finance because they seem too hard or boring. By spending a few hours learning the basics, you can make your money work for you instead of against you. This will give you the freedom to make decisions without thinking about money.

- Money is the most important tool we have for getting around in the complicated world, so it's important that we know how it works. Money is a great servant if you know how to handle it. But if you don't know how to work with it, it will definitely control you.

➤ **Don't invest in anything you don't understand.**

- The point of complex investments is to make money for the people who make them and sell them. They are also both more expensive and less effective for investors.

- Be wary of investment opportunities that seem complicated and appealing. The author shows that sometimes the simplest plan is the best one in the book.

➤ **This rule is all you need to know.**

- You can already be financially free if you spend less than you earn, invest the extra money, and stay out of debt.

➤ **Money is the key to freedom.**

- Financial freedom is a goal that most people strive for. The ability to make your own choices, live life on your own terms, and not be tied down by financial obligations is a priceless feeling. Money can buy many things, but the most valuable thing it can buy is freedom. With financial freedom, you have the ability to make decisions based on what is best for you, not based on what others say.

- Aspiring to become financially independent is a dream for many people. However, the path to achieving this goal is often filled with misconceptions about how much money is needed to live a fulfilling life. A person's wealth does not necessarily determine the quality of their life, as those who earn more may still struggle with bankruptcy, while those who earn less may have a deeper understanding of their values and live a more fulfilling life.

➤ **You shouldn't worry about how things turned out.**

- Spend your time on things you can change instead of worrying about things you can't change or people who won't make your life better.

Debt is Not a Standard

You will need to change the way you think about money if you want to be financially independent. To start, you have to realize that being in debt is not a normal thing. Since debt destroys wealth, it should be seen as a harmful and destructive way to ruin opportunities to build wealth. Your financial life shouldn't include debit.

In the western culture, debt has become a normal part of life. But it shouldn't be taken as a rule. A credit card that you use and pay off every month is a great way to avoid getting into debt, but buying things you don't need just to rack up debt is a waste of time and will make you feel bad.

Pitfalls of Investing in the Stock Market

➤ We believe we can time the market.

➤ We believe we are able to select individual stocks.

➤ We believe we can select successful mutual fund managers.

➤ In the process of proper investing to achieve success, we believe we can scratch the surface of the process.

It is important to understand that there are no guarantees when it comes to investing in the stock market. It can be tempting to try to predict which individual stocks will perform well in the long run, but even the most seasoned financial managers have a hard time consistently choosing winners. The good news is that you don't need to be an expert in the stock market to build wealth. In fact, it is often more effective to take a simple and passive approach to investing. Instead of trying to beat the market, you can invest in a diversified portfolio of low-cost index funds, which are designed to track the overall performance of the market. This approach has been proven to be an effective way to build long-term wealth without taking on unnecessary risks. By understanding that the market is unpredictable and by investing in a simple and passive way, you can take control of your financial future and achieve your long-term financial goals.

Become Familiar with the Stock Market

As an investor, it's essential to recognize and accept certain realities about the market to achieve success. Without acknowledging these facts, it's easy to make emotional decisions that can lead to poor investment choices. Here are some of the fundamental facts about the market that you should understand and accept to invest successfully:

➤ **Markets have proven to be the most effective way to make money.**
It's important to get your money into the market as soon as possible if you want it to work as well as possible for you. The author says that the VTSAX Total Stock Market Index Fund from Vanguard is a good way to take advantage of the market's ability to build wealth.

➤ **In the long run, the market always rises.**
It's likely to be higher in 10 to 20 years than it is now. This has been going on for a very long time. The Dow Jones Industrial Average, for example, started the 20th century at 68 and ended it at 11,497 (in 2010).

➤ **The market goes up and down, and market volatility is prevalent.**
Market crashes (drops of 20% or more) are inevitable. A big drop happens about once every 25 years, and there are also many smaller drops and several bull markets in that time (markets that are growing).

➤ **Being a successful investor means accepting risk and staying on course.**
When you invest, you need to be mentally and emotionally ready for bad
times and able to handle them. You will lose if you sell instead of getting
ready for bad times.

KEY LESSONS

1. **Stop spending money on things that aren't necessary.**

   ➤ You can save a lot of money if you have a good plan for how you will spend your money.

   ➤ Make a list of all of your monthly financial obligations and expenses, and get rid of anything you can't afford.

   ➤ Money saved is money earned, don't forget that.

2. **Strive to achieve long-term success.**
   Many investors say that they can beat the system and that they can do this over and over again. *Bill Gates* and *Warren Buffett* would be seen as average achievers compared to these people. So, don't take advantage of deals that sound too good to be true. Be patient and make long-term investments.

3. **Having money eliminates the need to do things you dislike.**
   We have to act in a certain way because we are afraid or maybe because our instinct to stay alive is strong. At this point, we feel a lot of stress and negative energy, but we don't have many choices left. On the other hand, money gives you the freedom to do what you want. There are limits, but they are much less of a problem than not being able to make your own money.

4. **Keep it simple.**
   Investing doesn't have to be complicated. Simple investment strategies, like investing in low-cost index funds, can be just as effective as more complex strategies. This is important because simplicity reduces the likelihood of making costly mistakes and allows you to focus on what really matters — building wealth over the long-term.

5. **Focus on what you can control.**
   There are many factors that can affect the stock market, like geopolitical events, economic indicators, and company news. You can't control any of these factors. Instead, focus on the things you can control, like your savings rate, investment strategy, and spending habits.

ACTIONABLE STEPS TO TAKE

➤ **Start saving and investing as early as possible.**
Commencing the process of saving, even a small amount, at an early stage is vital in taking advantage of the power of compound interest, which can result in significant wealth accumulation over time.

➤ **Live below your means.**
Adhering to a frugal lifestyle by spending less than you earn, can aid in increasing your savings and improving financial stability.

➤ **Invest in low-cost index funds.**
Investment in low-cost index funds can offer a straightforward and cost-effective approach to investing in the stock market and building wealth.

➤ **Avoid lifestyle inflation.**
The author cautions readers against lifestyle inflation, which is when people increase their spending as their income increases.

➤ **Be patient and disciplined.**
The book stresses the importance of being patient and disciplined in your investments and avoiding the common mistake of trying to time the market.

➤ **Eliminate high-interest debt.**
Avoiding high-interest debt such as credit card balances or personal loans is crucial in reducing the burden of interest payments, thereby improving overall financial stability.

➤ **Acquire multiple income sources.**
Expanding your income sources through additional sources of revenue, such as a side hustle or by requesting a raise, can significantly enhance financial stability and increase the potential for wealth accumulation.

➤ **Maintain discipline and patience.**
Maintaining discipline and patience with investments, as opposed to making impulsive decisions, is crucial in achieving better long-term results and increasing wealth-building potential.

CHAPTER 3

COMMUNICATION

"The quality of your communication is a reflection of the quality of your thinking."

— Dr. Linda Elder

"Communication — the human connection — is the key to personal and career success."

— Paul J. Meyer

"Good communication is the bridge between confusion and clarity."

— Nat Turner

The Fine Art of Small Talk

by Debra Fine

"Start thinking of strangers as people who can bring new dimensions to your life, not as persons to be feared."

THIS book provides practical advices and strategies for making small talk more effective and enjoyable. The book covers the basics of small talk, including how to start and maintain conversations, build relationships, and create positive social interactions.

The author argues that small talk is an important social skill that can lead to better relationships and opportunities. She stresses that small talk is not just idle chitchat but a valuable tool for building relationships and making connections. The book covers different types of small talk and provides advice on how to handle specific situations, such as meeting new people, networking, and small talk with acquaintances.

It provides tips on how to overcome shyness and anxiety in social situations, including advice on how to build confidence, control nervousness, and appear relaxed and at ease. The author emphasizes that small talk is a skill that can be learned and improved with practice and offers exercises and techniques to help readers build their confidence and become better communicators.

Throughout the book, she provides anecdotes and examples of successful small talk, as well as mistakes to avoid. She also provides guidance on how to steer conversations toward topics of interest and how to handle difficult or awkward moments.

The Importance of Small Talk

Effective communication is key to building successful relationships, and small talk plays a crucial role in this process. In his book, the author highlights the value of small talk in creating connections and opportunities, emphasizing that it is not simply idle chitchat. The following three lessons outline the importance of small talk in developing meaningful relationships:

➤ **Small talk can build relationships.**
   The book emphasizes the role of small talk in establishing a rapport with

others, breaking down barriers, and building trust and connection. It argues that small talk is a crucial component of relationship building and can lead to more meaningful and lasting connections.

➤ **Small talk can improve confidence and social skills.**
The ability to communicate effectively is an essential skill in both personal and professional contexts. In the book, the author discusses strategies for overcoming shyness and anxiety in social situations and provides practical tips on how to build confidence and appear relaxed and at ease. One of the key takeaways from the book is that developing good communication skills is not a fixed trait but rather a process that requires time, effort, and practice.

➤ **Small talk can create opportunities.**
The book highlights the potential of small talk in opening doors to new opportunities, both professionally and personally. For example, it can lead to new business contacts, job opportunities, or friendships. It stresses that small talk is a valuable tool for networking and expanding one's social and professional circles.

How to Break the Ice

Breaking the ice refers to the process of initiating conversation and establishing a connection with others. It is an important aspect of small talk and can be a challenge, especially in new or unfamiliar situations. However, with some guidance and practice, anyone can learn how to effectively break the ice and build meaningful connections. The following are three tips on how to get started in business, relationships, and social/general settings:

➤ **Business settings.**
In business settings, it is important to make a good first impression and establish a connection with others. To break the ice in a business setting, try commenting on the event or location, asking about the person's job or company, or finding common ground based on shared interests or experiences.

➤ **Relationships.**

When trying to break the ice in a personal relationship, it is important to be approachable and friendly. To get started, try asking about the person's interests or hobbies, commenting on a shared experience, or simply offering a compliment.

➤ **Social/general settings.**

In general social settings, it is important to be friendly and open. To break the ice in a social setting, try commenting on the event or location, asking about the person's interests or hobbies, or finding common ground based on shared experiences or interests.

Breaking is a critical aspect of small talk and an important step in building meaningful connections. By being approachable, friendly, and finding common ground, anyone can effectively break the ice and make new connections in a variety of settings.

Why Names are Important

The importance of names in social interaction cannot be overstated. In the book *The Fine Art of Small Talk*, the author highlights the significance of names in building relationships and establishing connections with others. The following are three key lessons about the importance of names outlined in the book:

➤ **Names serve as an identifier.**

A name is a critical aspect of identity and serves as a unique identifier for each individual. Remembering someone's name can make them feel valued and respected and is a critical first step in building a relationship.

➤ **Names create a sense of familiarity.**

Using someone's name in conversation can create a sense of familiarity and comfort and helps establish a connection with that person. The book stresses the importance of using names appropriately in conversation to create a sense of connection and build rapport with others.

➤ **Names can help build memory.**

Names are an important tool for building memory and recall and can be helpful in recalling information about a person and establishing relationships. The book highlights the importance of making a concerted effort to remember names and provides tips and strategies for improving name recall.

The Conversation

In *The Fine Art of Small Talk*, the author focuses on the art of conversation and how it plays a critical role in building relationships and making connections with others. Conversations are a crucial aspect of small talk and involve exchanging thoughts, ideas, and information. The following are practical lessons outlined in the book about the importance of conversation:

Lesson 1 — Identify a Target

➤ **Read the situation.**
The book emphasizes the importance of reading the situation and determining who would be a good target for conversation. This involves observing the dynamics of the group, the body language of individuals, and the tone of the conversation.

➤ **Be approachable.**
In order to identify a conversation target, it is important to be approachable and exude confidence and positivity.

Lesson 2 — How to Join an Existing Conversation

➤ **Be observant.**
Before joining a conversation, it is important to observe the dynamics of the group and the topic of discussion. This helps you to determine if it is an appropriate time to join and how to approach the group.

➤ **Show genuine interest.**
Joining a conversation requires showing genuine interest in the topic of discussion and being able to contribute in a meaningful way.

Lesson 3 — Take Advantage of Open-Ended Questions

➤ **Encourage dialogue.**

Open-ended questions are questions that cannot be answered with a simple yes or no, and they encourage dialogue and conversation. The book stresses the importance of using open-ended questions in conversation to encourage the other person to share their thoughts and experiences.

➤ **Show interest.**

Asking open-ended questions shows interest in the other person and encourages them to open up and share more information.

➤ **Avoid closed questions.**

The book emphasizes the importance of avoiding closed questions, which are questions that can be answered with a simple yes or no, as they can shut down conversation and limit the exchange of ideas and information.

Lesson 4 — Be Attentive and a Good Listener

➤ **Pay attention.**

Effective small talk requires being attentive and paying attention to what the other person is saying. The book stresses the importance of being present at the moment and focusing on the conversation.

➤ **Respond appropriately.**

Effective small talk also requires responding to what the other person is saying in an appropriate and meaningful way.

➤ **Avoid distractions.**

In order to be an effective listener, it is important to avoid distractions, such as checking your phone or looking around the room. The book emphasizes the importance of avoiding distractions and focusing on the conversation.

Lesson 5 — Avoid the Conversation Crimes

➤ **Be mindful of body language.**

The book stresses the importance of being mindful of nonverbal cues, such as body language, facial expressions, and tone of voice, in avoiding conversation crimes. This includes avoiding gestures that are negative, aggressive, or dismissive.

➤ **Avoid negative topics.**
Negative topics, such as complaining, gossiping, or discussing sensitive or controversial issues, can quickly bring a conversation to a halt and damage relationships.

➤ **Avoid bragging.**
Bragging can quickly turn off the other person and damage the connection. Instead, it's better to focus on having a conversation that is mutually enjoyable and engaging and to avoid talking about oneself too much.

Lesson 6 — The Graceful Exit

➤ **Timing is key.**
The book emphasizes the importance of timing when making a graceful exit from a conversation. Knowing when to leave a conversation can make a big difference in making a positive impression.

➤ **Being polite.**
Making a graceful exit requires being polite and avoiding any abrupt or rude behavior.

Conversation Starters for Singles

Conversation starters for singles can be an effective way to make connections and start building relationships. According to the principles and information outlined in the book, there are several strategies that can help make conversation starters more effective and engaging. Here are five conversation starters implied:

➤ **Ask about hobbies or interests.**
People are often passionate about their hobbies and interests, and asking someone about these can be a great way to start a conversation and get to know them better.

➤ **Talk about the environment.**

The surroundings, such as the weather, the venue, or the event, can be a great way to start a conversation and break the ice.

➤ **Comment on current events.**

Keeping up with current events and news can provide a great conversation starter as long as the topic is not too sensitive or controversial.

➤ **Share personal stories.**

Sharing personal stories and experiences can be a great way to start a conversation and build rapport.

➤ **Ask for advice.**

Asking for advice or opinions can be a great way to start a conversation and engage the other person.

In addition to the aforementioned conversation starters, the book also provides three important lessons about the use of conversation starters for singles. These lessons are designed to help individuals create engaging and meaningful conversations that can lead to more meaningful connections and relationships:

1. **Keep it light and positive.**

   It's important to keep the conversation light and positive, avoiding negative or sensitive topics that can quickly turn off the other person.

2. **Be genuinely interested.**

   In order to make the conversation effective and engaging, it's important to be genuinely interested in the other person and what they have to say.

3. **Be flexible.**

   Conversations can take many different directions, and it's important to be flexible and willing to adjust the conversation based on the needs and interests of the other person.

KEY LESSONS

1. **There is a lot of power in a smile.**
   A smile can break the ice and make it easier to start a conversation, helping to create a positive and welcoming atmosphere.

2. **Active listening is key.**
   Paying attention to what others are saying and responding appropriately can help you connect with others and build rapport.

3. **Be aware of your body language.**
   Using nonverbal cues, such as eye contact, nodding, and gestures, can convey your level of engagement and interest in the conversation.

4. **Don't try to be someone else than yourself.**
   Being genuine and authentic in your interactions will help you make more meaningful connections and establish stronger relationships.

5. **Practice, practice, practice.**
   The more you practice small talk, the more comfortable and confident you will become, allowing you to engage in small talk effectively.

6. **Take a moment to understand your environment.**
   Taking note of your surroundings and using them as conversation starters can help you build rapport and create common ground.

ACTIONABLE STEPS TO TAKE

➤ **Start with a smile.**
Smiling is a universal sign of friendliness and a great way to put people at ease. This is important because a smile can break the ice and make it easier to start a conversation.

➤ **Ask open-ended questions.**
Ask questions that require more than a one-word answer to encourage conversation. This is important because open-ended questions help people feel more engaged and connected.

➤ **Listen actively.**
Pay attention to what others are saying and respond appropriately. This is important because active listening shows that you are interested and engaged in the conversation.

➤ **Use body language.**
Use nonverbal cues, such as eye contact, nodding, and gestures, to show that you are interested in the conversation.

➤ **Be aware of your surroundings.**
Take note of your surroundings and use them as conversation starters.

➤ **Find common ground.**
Look for common interests, experiences, or backgrounds to build rapport and make the conversation more enjoyable.

➤ **Practice.**
The more you practice, the more comfortable and confident you will become with small talk. This is important because repetition and practice will help you develop the skills needed to engage in small talk effectively.

➤ **Be yourself.**
Be genuine and authentic in your interactions. This is important because people can tell when someone is being fake or insincere, and being yourself will help you make more meaningful connections.

Never Eat Alone

by Keith Ferrazzi

"It's better to give before you receive. And never keep score. If your interactions are ruled by generosity, your rewards will follow suit. Real networking was about finding ways to make other people more successful."

T HIS book is a personal development classic that offers practical tips on how to build a network of relationships and use them to achieve success in both your personal and professional life. The book is divided into four parts, with each section focusing on a different aspect of building and leveraging your network.

The first part of the book focuses on the importance of building your network by being proactive and reaching out to others. It emphasizes the need to be genuine and authentic in your interactions with others and to approach networking as a way to build mutually beneficial relationships.

The second part of the book explores the different types of networking that are available, from traditional in-person events to online networking and social media. The author provides tips on how to make the most of each type of networking opportunity and stresses the importance of being strategic in your networking efforts.

The third part of the book focuses on how to deepen your relationships with your network contacts. The book emphasizes the importance of being generous and giving to others and provides tips on how to stay in touch with your contacts and add value to their lives.

The final part of the book offers advice on how to leverage your network to achieve your goals and advance your career. It provides practical tips on how to use your network to find new opportunities, gain insights and knowledge, and build your reputation and influence.

The Network Mindset

In the world of business, building successful relationships is essential for long-term success. The author stresses the importance of collaboration over competition, emphasizing that the most successful businesses are built on strong networks of relationships. To cultivate a *Network Mindset*, the author provides several guiding principles for effective networking. By following these principles, individuals can build strong relationships with others, leading to greater opportunities and success.

➤ **Building relationships shouldn't be about keeping score.**
It's essential to recognize that relationships cannot be approached like a financial account. Viewing relationships as short-term investments can be detrimental to building and maintaining strong connections with others. Instead, a long-term approach is necessary, where relationships are cultivated and nurtured over time to strengthen and deepen their value.

➤ **Connect with people before you need their help.**
Individuals who struggle with networking often approach it in a self-serving manner, only reaching out to their network when they need something. Such behavior demonstrates a lack of consideration for others, as relationships are perceived solely as a means to an end.

➤ **There is no such thing as a limited amount of time. Instead, there is a limited amount of good time.**
Time spent well is more important than how much time is spent.

➤ **Take a deeper dive into the small talk.**
Instead of trying to pass the time by making small talk or talking about nothing, try to talk as honestly and openly as you can.

Networking Tips

Creating a strong network takes time and effort, and waiting until you need help or job opportunities to start building one is not a sustainable strategy. To be effective, networking requires consistent and deliberate action, where you actively seek out opportunities to connect with others and offer value. By doing so, you can build authentic relationships and establish a reliable support system that can assist you in achieving your goals when the need arises. The key is to approach networking with a long-term perspective, recognizing the value of cultivating meaningful connections over time. The author offers advice on how to network like a pro:

➤ **Get ready ahead of time.**
Make sure you know what they like and don't like before you meet them.

➤ **Keep in touch.**
Not the other way around, but you should remind them of what you can do for them.

➤ **Authenticity is key.**
The author says that vulnerability is one of the most underestimated traits.

➤ **Care for people who have a lot of power.**
They are valuable because they are easy for decision-makers to access.

➤ **Contribute to events.**
Organize events and speak at them so you can help and support them.

➤ **A relationship is like a muscle in that way.**
You can use them more often to make them stronger over time.

➤ **Make use of connectors.**
Make sure that you get in touch with people who know a lot of different people.

➤ **Exchange networks.**
Every person in your network is a door to a bigger network. If you help them with theirs, they will help you with yours.

➤ **Dig deeper into the relationships.**
What do they have to deal with? Most people care most about their health, their money, and their children. Hold more in-depth conversations to make your relationships stronger.

➤ **Maintenance is also very important for networks.**
If you don't keep in touch, the network will die. Checking your network every now and then may seem like boring work, but it's important to keep it running.

Avoid Being a Network Jerk

Networking is often misunderstood as only being useful when one needs something from someone else. In reality, those with the most successful networks understand that it is necessary to cultivate relationships long before they require assistance. The author of the book emphasizes the importance of being genuine, polite, and respectful when networking to avoid being perceived as pushy or opportunistic. To be an effective networker, one should follow these guidelines:

➤ **Avoid schmoozing.**
  If you have something to say, you should talk about it in a businesslike and convincing way. When you talk, try to be honest and give useful information.

➤ **Never talk about or believe what other people say.**
  As more and more people start to think that they can't trust you with any information, the source will become less reliable over time.

➤ **Bring something to the table at all times.**
  A successful person is someone who gives more than they get.

➤ **Think of everyone as the same.**
  There is a chance that one of your colleagues will become your boss in the future. Companies often do this.

➤ **Transparency is key.**
  Using stealth to meet people in a bar is a good idea, but you shouldn't do it if you want to get close to someone.

➤ **Sincerity is essential.**
  If you don't get along with the people you meet, it would be best to stop building the relationship. If two people don't like each other, all of the good things about their relationship are gone right away. Positive relationships with other people are a great foundation for business transactions.

How to Become a Person of Value

To establish a strong network, it is essential to demonstrate your value to others. When building your personal brand, there are key questions you should consider, such as what sets you apart from others, what skills and interests you possess, and how you want to be perceived by others. The author of this book emphasizes the importance of creating a personal brand, which can help you achieve three important goals. These goals include distinguishing yourself from others, creating a positive reputation, and establishing a clear message to others about who you are and what you can offer. By following the principles of personal branding, you can become more attractive to potential business partners, mentors, and clients and ultimately build a stronger network. Here are three ways to build your brand in, according to the author:

➤ **Opinions — Make your voice heard.**
When it comes to hiring, employers prioritize selecting individuals who possess the skills and abilities that will contribute to the success of their organization. Personal affability is not the sole determining factor in the recruitment process. It is commonly believed that candidates with diverse perspectives and a broad range of experiences are considered to be the most valuable assets to any team.

➤ **Expertise — Be able to express yourself uniquely.**
To be successful at anything, you need a deep passion and a set of beliefs that go beyond your self-interest. If you want to persuade people, you have to speak from your heart. It's important to be brave, but that's not always enough. As with anything else, there is a difference between getting noticed and being noticed for trying to make the world a better place.

➤ **Story — Describe yourself in an interesting manner.**
Capturing a listener's undivided attention requires an engaging narrative about either yourself or your organization, showcasing the ideas that it embodies. Once created, such content should be widely disseminated. Have you ever reflected on your passion for your work? Have you had the opportunity to articulate to a journalist why your work is vital? While public relations professionals handle countless communications daily, nobody can convey the importance of your work with more fervor and expertise than you. As one of the foremost authorities in your field, you are uniquely positioned to convey your message with clarity and conviction.

KEY LESSONS

1. **For your career to go well, you need to build a strong personal network.**
   When you act like a lone wolf, your chances of being successful aren't very good.

2. **Your strategy for networking should focus on being kind and loyal.**
   When you help and support other people, they are more likely to do the same for you.

3. **Build your network before you need it so that when you do, you will be ready.**
   When you network to get help right away, you don't build any trust.

4. **You can make the most of your networking skills and make them work for you by finding things you have in common with other people.**
   Quality is more important than quantity when it comes to building relationships. You should find something you have in common with someone else, like a hobby, a political view, a favorite food, etc.

5. **You need a unique message if you want to be able to network.**
   Take the lead and start talking to people to make sure they remember you.

6. **Use people who have already built up a large network of connections.**
   A *super-connector* is the best person to help you grow your network. This is someone who meets hundreds of new people every day and can put you in touch with the right people.

7. **Make a plan for how you will reach your networking goals.**
   To have a successful career, you need to find your inner drive and passion, which is where your skills and interests meet and set long-term, medium-term, and short-term goals.

8. **If you have the right brand and the right mentors, you will do well.**
   In a consumer-driven world, it's important to market yourself and surround yourself with people who have experience and can help get your brand in front of potential customers.

ACTIONABLE STEPS TO TAKE

➤ **Make a list of people you want to connect with.**
Maintaining regular contact with people in your network helps to build and strengthen relationships and helps you stay connected and informed about opportunities in your industry.

➤ **Be genuinely interested in others.**
The book emphasizes the importance of being genuinely interested in others and their lives to build genuine connections.

➤ **Attend networking events and conferences, and always bring business cards.**
Attending networking events provides opportunities to meet new people and expand your network, and having business cards makes it easy to exchange contact information.

➤ **Offer help and advice to others before expecting anything in return.**
Helping others establishes you as a trusted and valuable member of your network, and can lead to future opportunities and relationships.

➤ **Be generous with your time and resources.**
Offer help and support, such as making introductions, providing resources, and giving advice, to create opportunities for mutually beneficial relationships.

➤ **Find mutually beneficial opportunities.**
The book encourages readers to find opportunities that can benefit both themselves and the people they are connecting with.

➤ **Create a culture of connecting.**
The author encourages readers to build a culture of connecting and networking within their organizations by supporting and encouraging others to network and connect.

➤ **Seek out mentors and be a mentor to others.**
Having a mentor can provide guidance and support in your career, and being a mentor yourself helps to establish yourself as a leader in your industry.

Quiet

by Susain Cain

"Introverts, in contrast, may have strong social skills and enjoy parties and business meetings, but after a while, wish they were home in their pajamas. They prefer to devote their social energies to close friends, colleagues, and family. They listen more than they talk, think before they speak, and often feel as if they express themselves better in writing than in conversation. They tend to dislike conflict. Many have a horror of small talk but enjoy deep discussions."

T HIS book explores the nature of introversion and the impact of Western culture on the way introverts are perceived and treated. The book argues that while Western culture values extroversion, introversion is an important and valuable personality trait. It discusses how introverts process information and interact with the world differently from extroverts and how these differences can lead to misunderstandings and biases in education, work, and personal relationships. The book also provides practical advice for introverts on how to assert themselves and find fulfillment in a culture that often values extroversion. Additionally, it provides insights for extroverts on how to better understand and interact with introverts. Overall, the book is a comprehensive look at introversion and aims to help readers recognize and appreciate the strengths of introverts.

Introversion vs Extroversion

The concept of introversion and extroversion has been widely discussed in the field of psychology and has significant implications for our understanding of human behavior. The author sheds light on the impact of Western culture on the way introverts are perceived and treated. By exploring the fundamental differences between introversion and extroversion, she provides a compelling argument for why it is important to recognize and appreciate the value of introversion in a world that often prioritizes extroversion. In this subsection, we will delve deeper into the topic of introversion vs extroversion and examine the nuances of these two personality traits.

Introversion

Introversion is a personality trait characterized by a preference for solitude and inner reflection. Introverts tend to be more introspective, reflective, and reserved in their social interactions. They are energized by solitude and quiet activities and may become overwhelmed by too much stimulation in large groups or noisy environments. The book argues that the Western cultural bias towards extroversion has led to a misunderstanding and undervaluation of introversion. In reality, introverts have a unique set of strengths and qualities that can contribute to personal and professional success.

Some key personal traits of introverts include:

➤ **A rich inner world.**

Introverts tend to be highly imaginative, creative, and introspective, with a rich inner world of thoughts, feelings, and ideas.

➤ **A preference for deep thinking.**

Introverts often prefer to think deeply and critically about ideas, concepts, and problems.

➤ **A strong ability to focus.**

Introverts can concentrate well and are often able to sustain focus on complex or challenging tasks.

Extroversion

Extroversion is a personality trait characterized by a preference for social interaction and external stimulation. Extroverts are outgoing, talkative, and energetic in their social interactions. They tend to enjoy meeting new people, being in large groups, and engaging in activities that provide social stimulation. While Western culture has placed a high value on extroversion, it is important to recognize that both extroversion and introversion are valuable personality traits with their own unique strengths and weaknesses.

Some key personal traits of extroverts include:

➤ **A strong social orientation.**

Extroverts enjoy being around people and often derive energy from social interaction.

➤ **Confidence in social situations.**
Extroverts tend to be confident and comfortable in social situations and are often seen as natural leaders.

➤ **An optimistic outlook.**
Extroverts often have a positive outlook on life and are naturally optimistic and enthusiastic.

The Workplace

In the workplace, introverts may be overlooked or undervalued due to their more reserved and introspective nature, while extroverts may be favored for their confidence and sociability. However, introverts can bring unique strengths to the workplace, such as the ability to focus deeply on tasks, an aptitude for problem-solving, and strong critical-thinking skills. On the other hand, extroverts can bring energy, enthusiasm, and a talent for collaboration to the workplace. To sum up:

➤ **Different impressions.**
Introverts may be perceived as less confident or assertive than extroverts, but they often bring unique strengths such as focus, problem-solving skills, and critical thinking.

➤ **Energy-level.**
Extroverts can bring energy, enthusiasm, and a talent for collaboration to the workplace.

➤ **Finding the right balance.**
The book critiques the overemphasis on collaboration and group work and argues that the workplace should allow for both social interaction and solitude to support creativity.

➤ **Bigger paycheck doesn't mean better quality.**
Research cited in the book shows that charismatic leaders may earn bigger paychecks, but they do not necessarily have better corporate performance and that open office plans can hurt concentration and productivity.

Personal Relationships

In relationships, it is important to understand and appreciate both introversion and extroversion. Introverts may need alone time to recharge and may prefer more intimate and low-key social activities, while extroverts may enjoy larger social gatherings and may be energized by spending time with others. It is important for both introverts and extroverts to communicate their needs and preferences in relationships and to be understanding and respectful of their partner's differences.

To sum up:

➤ **Introverts are better listeners.**
Introverts may be perceived as reserved or shy, but they bring a strong sense of empathy and deep listening skills to their interactions with others.

➤ **Extroverts can offer an arrogant vibe.**
Extroverts tend to be outgoing and confident and often excel in social situations.

➤ **Importance of both.**
The book highlights the importance of understanding and valuing both introverted and extroverted personalities in personal relationships rather than assuming that one is superior to the other.

➤ **Again, the right balance is the key.**
The book suggests that both introverts and extroverts can benefit from learning how to communicate and interact with individuals of different personality types and that a balance of alone time and social time can support healthy relationships.

Find a Balance

The author highlights the importance of finding a balance between introversion and extroversion, recognizing that great ideas and leadership can come from both personality types. The key to maximizing one's potential is to be in the right level of stimulation for their personality. Finding the *"sweet spot"* means creating a balanced environment that suits both introverts and extroverts. For introverts, this could mean having quiet time to balance out a demanding social context in the workplace, and for highly sensitive people, it's about managing their intense emotional reactions to their surroundings. Over time, people can learn to deal with their personality traits and find a balance that works for them. *Eleanor Roosevelt*, who was both introverted and highly sensitive, is a great example of someone who learned to deal with her personality and use it to make a positive impact on the world.

KEY LESSONS

1. **Embrace your unique strengths.**
Understanding and accepting your introverted or extroverted nature is important for harnessing your unique strengths and using them to your advantage. It helps you recognize your natural tendencies, build self-awareness and make informed decisions.

2. **Solitude is valuable.**
Solitude is crucial for creativity and self-reflection. It allows you to recharge your batteries and helps you avoid burnout. By making time for quiet reflection and rejuvenation, you keep yourself motivated and productive.

3. **Communication is key.**
Knowing how to communicate effectively with people of different personality types can help build better relationships, reduce conflict, and increase collaboration. Understanding different communication styles and being aware of your preferred method can improve your interactions with others.

4. **Accept personality differences.**
Celebrate the diversity of personalities and resist the pressure to conform to cultural norms. Recognizing that introverts and extroverts bring unique strengths to the table can foster a more inclusive and productive workplace.

5. **Prioritize work-life balance.**
A balanced work-life schedule is essential for overall well-being and productivity. Make time for personal interests and relationships, prioritize self-care, and avoid overloading yourself.

6. **Create an inclusive environment.**
Encourage an inclusive environment that accommodates different working styles and personalities. Support solo time and quiet spaces, and give employees the option to work remotely when needed. This helps to reduce stress, increase creativity and create a more productive workforce.

ACTIONABLE STEPS TO TAKE

➤ **Embrace your introversion or extroversion.**
Understanding and accepting your personality type is the first step towards using your strengths to your advantage.

➤ **Create alone time.**
Solitude is crucial for creativity and self-reflection. Set aside time each day for quiet reflection and rejuvenation.

➤ **Seek out meaningful work.**
Pursue work that aligns with your values and interests, rather than just what is expected of you.

➤ **Manage your energy.**
Introverts and extroverts have different energy levels and need to recharge in different ways. Identify what recharges your batteries and make time for them regularly.

➤ **Communicate with others.**
Knowing how to effectively communicate with people of different personality types can help build better relationships and reduce conflict.

➤ **Manage group interactions.**
Group brainstorming can be overwhelming for introverts. Set up alternative ways to contribute and make sure that everyone's opinions are heard.

➤ **Work in an environment that suits you.**
If you work best in solitude, consider remote work or flexible schedules. If you work best in a collaborative environment, seek out opportunities to work with others.

➤ **Advocate for introverts.**
Challenge the cultural biases that favor extroversion and help others understand and appreciate the strengths of introverts. By doing so, we can create a more inclusive and diverse workplace and community.

The Four Agreements

by Don Miguel Ruiz

"There is a huge amount of freedom that comes to you when you take nothing personally."

THIS book is a transformative book that teaches readers how to live a happier, more fulfilling life. In this book, the author shares his personal insights and wisdom gained from a lifetime of spiritual study and practice, along with practical tools for personal growth and self-improvement. The four agreements that the book outlines are meant to help readers let go of limiting beliefs and negative thought patterns and cultivate self-awareness, compassion, and peace. It emphasizes the importance of living in the present moment and making conscious choices that align with one's true self rather than being driven by the expectations and beliefs of others. The book outlines four agreements that the author believes will lead to personal freedom and happiness:

1. **Be Impeccable with Your Word.**
   Speak truthfully, with kindness and integrity. Avoid speaking badly about yourself or others, and avoid taking things personally.

2. **Don't Take Anything Personally.**
   Realize that what others say or do is a projection of their own reality, and it has nothing to do with you.

3. **Don't Make Assumptions.**
   Communicate clearly and ask for clarification to avoid misunderstandings.

4. **Always Do Your Best.**
   Aim to do your best in every situation, but understand that your best may change from day to day.

Be Impeccable with Your Word

This agreement encourages individuals to be mindful of their language and to be conscious of their words. The author emphasizes that words have the power to create and shape our reality, and therefore it is important to be careful with what we say. The agreement suggests that people should aim to use words that are truthful, kind, and positive. The key lessons from this agreement are:

1. **Speak truthfully.**
   It is important, to be honest and truthful in our words. Speaking truthfully not only helps to build trust but also helps to avoid creating misunderstandings and conflicts.

2. **Avoid gossiping and speaking ill of others.**
   Negative speech can be harmful to both the speaker and the person being spoken about. By avoiding gossip and speaking ill of others, individuals can cultivate a more positive and harmonious environment.

3. **Choose words carefully.**
   Words have the power to shape our thoughts, feelings, and experiences. Therefore, it is crucial to choose words carefully and to use language that is aligned with our goals and values.

Don't Take Anything Personally

This agreement encourages individuals to let go of the belief that other people's opinions, attitudes, and behaviors are a reflection of their own self-worth. The author emphasizes that most people's negative words and actions stem from their own insecurities, fears, and limitations and have little to do with the person they are directed towards. The key lessons from this agreement are:

1. **Recognize that others' behavior is a reflection of their own limitations.**
   By understanding that others' negative words and actions stem from their own limitations, individuals can avoid taking these things personally. This can help to reduce feelings of hurt, anger, and frustration.

2. **Let go of the need for approval.**
   Seeking the approval of others can lead to a constant cycle of seeking validation and taking things personally. By letting go of the need for approval, individuals can become more confident and self-assured.

3. **Focus on your own happiness.**

By not taking things personally, individuals can focus on their own happiness, goals, and values. This can help to reduce stress, improve mental well-being, and increase overall life satisfaction.

Don't Make Assumptions

This agreement encourages individuals to break free from the habit of making assumptions about others, their intentions, and their behaviors. The author emphasizes that assumptions lead to misunderstandings and conflicts and that it is important to communicate clearly to avoid these issues. The key lessons from this agreement are:

1. **Ask questions.**

Rather than making assumptions, individuals are encouraged to ask questions to clarify their understanding of a situation or person. This can help to reduce misunderstandings and build stronger relationships.

2. **Practice active listening.**

To avoid making assumptions, it is important to practice active listening. This involves paying close attention to what others are saying, and understanding their perspectives.

3. **Be open-minded.**

Making assumptions often involves closing our minds to other perspectives and possibilities. By being open-minded, individuals can break free from limiting beliefs and see situations holistically.

Always Do Your Best

This agreement encourages individuals to strive for excellence and to make a consistent effort to improve their performance. The author emphasizes that by doing our best, we can avoid guilt and regret, and achieve our goals and aspirations. The key lessons from this agreement are:

1. **Set realistic expectations.**

It is important to set realistic expectations for what we can achieve, given our abilities, circumstances, and resources. By setting realistic expectations, individuals can avoid feeling overwhelmed and discouraged.

2. **Be kind to yourself.**

Doing our best requires a consistent effort, and it is important to be kind to ourselves when we make mistakes or fall short of our goals. By being kind to ourselves, we can avoid guilt and regret, and maintain a positive outlook.

3. **Strive for improvement.**

Always Do Your Best is not about achieving perfection, but rather about consistently improving. By striving for improvement, individuals can achieve their goals, grow, and live more fulfilling lives.

KEY LESSONS

1. **Understand the power of language.**
   Words have the power to shape our thoughts, beliefs, and experiences. By being impeccable with our word, we can positively influence our lives and those around us.

2. **The importance of detachment.**
   Taking things personally can lead to stress, conflict, and emotional turmoil. By detaching from our thoughts and emotions and not taking things personally, we can maintain our sense of peace and well-being.

3. **Never assume something.**
   Making assumptions about others can lead to misunderstandings and conflict. By avoiding assumptions and practicing clear and open communication, we can build stronger relationships and avoid unnecessary conflict.

4. **Consistency is key.**
   Doing our best requires a consistent effort, and by striving to improve our performance in all areas of our lives, we can achieve our goals and live more fulfilling lives.

5. **How our thoughts and beliefs are connected.**
   Our thoughts and beliefs shape our experiences. By becoming more aware of them and striving to replace negative thoughts with positive ones, we can increase our happiness and overall satisfaction with life.

6. **The importance of practicing mindfulness and presence.**
   By being mindful and present at the moment. By avoiding dwelling on the past or worrying about the future, we can reduce stress, increase our sense of well-being, and improve our quality of life. These lessons highlight the power of our thoughts, words, and actions, and the importance of being mindful and intentional in our daily lives.

ACTIONABLE STEPS TO TAKE

➤ **Be impeccable with your word.**
Practice speaking positively and truthfully, and avoid gossiping, lying, or speaking negatively about others. This will help to build trust and respect in your relationships and to maintain your integrity.

➤ **Don't take anything personally.**
Cultivate an awareness of your thoughts and emotions, and practice detaching from them when you might be tempted to take things personally.

➤ **Monitor your thoughts.**
Practice becoming more aware of your thoughts and beliefs, and strive to replace negative thoughts with positive ones. This will help to reduce stress and increase your sense of well-being.

➤ **Cultivate gratitude.**
Practice being grateful for the things and people in your life, and strive to focus on the positive aspects of your experiences.

➤ **Don't make assumptions.**
Practice clear and open communication, and avoid making assumptions about others' motives or behaviors. Ask questions when you need clarification, and practice active listening to understand others' perspectives.

➤ **Focus on the present moment.**
Practice being mindful and present at the moment, and strive to avoid dwelling on the past or worrying about the future.

➤ **Surround yourself with positive people.**
Seek out supportive and positive relationships, and strive to maintain healthy boundaries with those who are not supportive.

➤ **Always do your best.**
Set realistic expectations for yourself, and strive to improve your performance in all areas of your life. Be kind to yourself when you fall short, and remember that doing your best is about making a consistent effort, not perfection.

Start with WHY

by Simon Sinek

*"Working hard for something we do not care about is called stress,
working hard for something we love is called passion."*

T HIS book aims to determine why some organizations and people can inspire others while others can't. Leadership that inspires starts with WHY. Leaders figure out their reasons and beliefs first, before deciding WHAT and HOW to do something. A great book about why some businesses and people do better than others. If employers and employees learn to start with WHY, more people will go to work and feel good about what they do.

The book is divided into WHY, HOW, and WHAT. In the first part, the book introduces the concept of the Golden Circle, which consists of three concentric circles: WHY, HOW, and WHAT. He argues that most organizations focus on the WHAT and HOW, the tangible products or services they provide and how they deliver them, rather than the WHY, which is the underlying purpose, cause, or belief that drives the organization.

The author contends that organizations that start with WHY can inspire and motivate people to act, create loyal customers, and outperform their competitors. He provides several examples of purpose-driven organizations, such as Apple, Southwest Airlines, and the Wright Brothers, who succeeded by starting with WHY.

Throughout the book, he provides numerous insights and examples of the power of purpose-driven leadership. He emphasizes the importance of authenticity, transparency, and consistency in communicating one's WHY and provides practical strategies for identifying and articulating one's WHY.

The Golden Circle

This lesson centers on the idea that the most successful leaders and organizations all share one thing in common: they know their WHY. This is represented by a diagram of three concentric circles, each representing a different level of understanding. The outer circle represents the WHAT or the things that we do. This is the easiest to identify, as it's what we can see, touch, or measure. The middle circle represents the HOW, or what we do to accomplish our goals. This requires a deeper understanding, as it's not always immediately apparent. Finally, the inner circle represents the WHY or the reason why we do what we do. This is the most difficult to identify but also the most important. It's what drives us and motivates us and separates successful organizations from those that struggle to make an impact. Here is a much deeper understanding of the three circles:

➤ **WHY** — A belief.
Few people or groups can explain why they do what they do clearly. In this case, running a profitable business is not the goal but the result. The most important part of WHY is to know what your goal is. Why do you work for the company that you do? Why do you get out of bed every day to go to work? Why do you do what you do?

➤ **HOW** — Actions we take to realize that belief.
Some people and organizations know how to do certain things. Whether it's called a *differentiating value proposition* or a *unique selling proposition*, the HOW is a way to explain how something is different or better.

➤ **WHAT** — Results of those actions.
Undoubtedly, every company in the world knows what they are doing. This is true no matter how big or small the business is or what kind of business they are in. Everyone can easily name the products or services their company sells or their role in the organization.

Clarity, Discipline & Consistency

In the book, the author emphasizes the importance of having a clear sense of purpose and direction in any endeavor. However, simply having a WHY is not enough. Turning a WHY into a reality requires discipline and consistency. It's not just about setting goals or having a vision, but rather committing to a long-term strategy and having the discipline to follow through on that plan. This requires self-awareness, personal responsibility, and a willingness to make tough choices when needed. In this lesson, the author highlights the key components of Clarity, Discipline, and Consistency, and how these elements are essential to turning a WHY into a reality. Here is a deeper understanding of the key components that are essential to our WHY, HOW, and WHAT:

➤ **Clarity of WHY.**
The concept of clarity relates to having a clear understanding of your purpose, your why, and communicating it effectively to others. This involves articulating your vision and values in a way that resonates with others and inspires action.

➤ **Discipline of HOW.**
Discipline refers to the consistent effort and focus required to achieve your goals, even when faced with challenges or setbacks. It is important to remain committed to your purpose and take action every day, no matter how small the steps may seem.

➤ **Consistency of WHAT.**
Consistency is the practice of staying true to your purpose over time. It involves creating habits and routines that support your goals and avoiding distractions that take you away from your why.

When all three of these elements are in place, clarity, discipline, and consistency, individuals and organizations are better able to stay focused on their purpose, make meaningful progress toward their goals, and ultimately achieve success. We can live a more fulfilling and purposeful life by consistently reminding ourselves of our why, being disciplined in our actions, and maintaining clarity on our purpose.

Manipulation vs Inspiration

The book highlights the importance of genuine leadership and the dangers of manipulative tactics. It argues that while manipulation may produce short-term results, it ultimately undermines trust and damages relationships. On the other hand, inspiring leaders who communicate their vision and values clearly can earn the trust and loyalty of their followers, leading to long-term success. The author urges readers to reflect on their leadership style and consider whether they use manipulative tactics such as fear, incentives, or peer pressure to motivate their team. Instead, they should strive to inspire by connecting with their team on a deeper level, tapping into their shared purpose and values. The lesson emphasizes that inspiration cannot be manufactured or contrived. Still, it comes from a genuine belief in one's vision and a commitment to living by those values. Leaders can build strong, loyal teams that are committed to achieving their shared goals by focusing on inspiring rather than manipulating.

Here is how we differ them:

Manipulation Explained

There is no question that you can get people to do what you want them to do. Customers can be persuaded to buy a product by changing the price. You could give the customer a big discount to get them to buy, showing that they don't want to miss out on a good deal. This works! You might be able to get people to buy something once for a very low price, but it won't last. You can come to the same conclusion about cash-back deals, *2 for the price of 1*, and other short-term price changes. When customers get used to getting a discount, they will never pay full price again.

Fear is another way to get what you want. For our kids to not start smoking, we often show them pictures of people with blackened, clogged lungs or people who have to eat through a tube. Or, when we want our employees to work harder, we hold them accountable for their work. This has a short-term effect, but when employees rebel against the false pressure in the long run, it has the opposite effect.

Inspiration Explained

Inspiration is a powerful force that drives people to action. It's why people are willing to go above and beyond what's expected of them, push through adversity, and work tirelessly toward a goal. The power of inspiration lies in its ability to tap into something deep within us, to connect us to a higher purpose or cause that gives us a sense of meaning and fulfillment. We're more creative, focused, and committed to achieving our goals when we feel inspired. In business, inspiration is key to building a loyal customer base and a strong brand. When an organization's WHY is clear and compelling, it can inspire employees and customers. It's why companies like Apple, Harley Davidson, and Southwest

Airlines have been so successful — they're not just selling products, they're selling an idea, a vision, a way of life.

KEY LESSONS

1. **WHY is about figuring out what's important about an idea and why it exists.**

   Great leaders and people who develop new ideas know how important and valuable their ideas are.

2. **Long-term success depends on precise and fruitful outcomes, not short-term solutions.**

   A well-made product will last longer than a patch that only works for a short time. Businesses that can get this precise are good at what they do.

3. **To be a leader in any field, you have to know everything there is to know about it.**

   Even though Apple only has a few products, the values and beliefs of the company are unique to its customers.

4. **You will lose your integrity if you try to trick customers or force them to buy something.**

   When American car company General Motors had to compete with Asian car companies, it tried to trick customers with cash-back deals. This increased sales in the short term but hurt the company's reputation in the long run.

5. **The business starts to fail when people don't know WHY it's important or what it's worth.**

   If the company succeeds and loses sight of its core values, it will be a big mistake.

ACTIONABLE STEPS TO TAKE

➤ **Identify your WHY.**

The author encourages readers to discover their purpose or the reason behind their actions and decisions. It suggests that understanding this WHY can be a powerful tool for inspiring others and driving success.

➤ **Focus on serving others before yourself.**

Focusing on serving others helps to build trust and establish relationships, and provides a sense of purpose and fulfillment.

➤ **Lead with your WHY.**

Leading with purpose helps to inspire and motivate your team, and can lead to long-term success and sustainability.

➤ **Create a WHY-Driven culture.**

Surrounding yourself with like-minded individuals helps to create a supportive and productive environment, and can lead to future opportunities and collaborations.

➤ **Look for opportunities to inspire others.**

The book encourages readers to seek opportunities to share their WHY and inspire others. This can include speaking engagements, writing articles or books, or sharing their story on social media.

➤ **Measure success by impact.**

The author suggests that success should be measured by its impact on others and society, rather than by traditional metrics such as profit or revenue.

➤ **Continuously look for ways to improve.**

The book encourages readers to continuously look for ways to improve their WHY and make it more meaningful and impactful. This can include seeking feedback, conducting research, or reflecting on their experiences.

➤ **Communicate your WHY in a simple and inspiring way.**

Communicating your WHY in a simple and inspiring way helps attract and retain customers and employees, leading to increased engagement and success.

Getting to Yes

by Roger Fisher and William Ury

"The ability to see the situation as the other side sees it, as difficult as it may be, is one of the most important skills a negotiator can possess."

T HIS is a classic guide to negotiation and conflict resolution. The book presents a systematic approach to reaching mutually beneficial agreements in any negotiation.

The book is based on the premise that negotiations should focus on the interests and needs of both parties, rather than their positions or demands. The authors argue that by focusing on shared interests, negotiators can find creative solutions that benefit everyone involved.

One of the key takeaways from the book is the importance of preparation and planning in any negotiation. The authors stress the importance of setting clear goals and objectives, gathering relevant information, and considering the other party's perspective before negotiating. They also emphasize the importance of effective negotiation and active listening skills.

The authors introduce the concept of *principled negotiation*, which involves four key principles:

➤ **Separating people from the problem.**
The problem shouldn't be tied to the people who have it. Working together to solve a problem instead of trying to beat each other is a good way for participants to get closer to a solution.

➤ **Focusing on interests rather than positions.**
Put your attention on your interests, not your positions.

➤ **Generating a variety of options before settling on an agreement.**
Before making a big choice, you should consider all your options. This will help you and the other person.

➤ **Insisting that the agreement be based on objective criteria.**
Insist that the result be based on something that can be measured.

Separating People from the Problem

The author first wants you to understand that people are not the problem. People tend to think that the problems and positions of both sides are personal, and they often see answers to these problems and positions as attacks on them as people. By separating the people from the problems, the parties can better deal with the problems without hurting their relationship. The process also helps the people involved see the problem more clearly. People's problems can be broken down into three main categories:

➤ **Perception.**

- The ability to see things from the other side's point of view is one of the most important skills a negotiator can have.
- If they have a bad opinion of you, you could surprise them by showing them a different side.
- Give them a stake in the outcome by letting them help make decisions.
- Talk to each other about what you're thinking.
- Be careful not to blame them when you are having trouble.
- Let them save face by making sure your idea fits with what they believe in.

➤ **Emotion.**

- Know and understand how they feel as well as how you feel.
- Find out if their identity is being threatened and think about what role it plays.
- It's only natural to show how you feel.
- Give them a chance to let off steam or take a break if needed.
- Try not to react to emotional outbursts.
- Think about symbolic actions (like giving gifts) to show you care.

➤ **Communication.**

- Listen actively and show that you heard what was said.

- Talk clearly so that everyone can understand what's going on.
- Don't let your thoughts about them override what you think of them. Talk more about yourself than about them.
- Don't waste time with your speech; make it count.

Focusing on Interests rather than Positions

In negotiations, individuals often align with one side or the other, rather than focusing on what is best for their interests. To reach successful agreements, it is important to understand that positions merely reflect personal concerns, wants, and goals, while interests represent the underlying motivations driving these positions. In instances where interests clash, finding a mutually beneficial solution can be challenging if both parties remain focused on their positions. Instead, negotiating parties must focus on finding common ground based on shared interests rather than individual positions.

Identifying Interests

Effective negotiations are not solely about taking a side but understanding one's interests, wants, and goals. According to experts, successful agreements are founded on the interests of the parties involved, rather than their positions. It's crucial to recognize that the positions taken by each party are the result of their interests. When discussing an issue from the perspective of positions, there is a higher probability of one side losing the argument. Conversely, when a problem is approached from the standpoint of underlying interests, it's feasible to discover a mutually beneficial solution that works for all parties involved.

First, figuring out what each side wants from the situation is important. This can be done in several ways, including:

➤ Sort out the different things each side wants as they come to mind.

➤ This will let you improve your assessment as you learn more and put your interests in order of how important they are to you.

➤ Recognize what they're interested in. People are more likely to listen if they think you understand them. So, if you want the other side to care about your goals, you should show that you care about theirs first.

➤ Write down every interest.

Discuss and Engage in Interests

Once each party has identified their interests and objectives, the negotiation process can proceed to the next step. It is crucial for all parties involved to engage in a collaborative discussion to reach an agreement that satisfies all parties. Multiple topics can be discussed in one or more ways, depending on the circumstances of the negotiation:

➤ Make sure that both sides understand your important and specific interests and that the other side takes them seriously.

➤ Actively listen to the other side and consider what it wants.

➤ Tell us briefly what you want to know about.

➤ Pay more attention to what will happen in the future than what happened in the past.

➤ Stand up for what you think is right. Strongly talk about your interests, but be kind to those around you. Listen to them respectfully, serve them courteously, thank them for their efforts, and show that you care about meeting their needs. Two negotiators, each looking out for their best interests, will help each other come up with good solutions for both of them.

Mutual Options for Mutual Gain

In pursuing problem-solving and effective communication, it's important to recognize the common barriers preventing progress. While numerous factors can hinder creativity and collaboration, four key obstacles tend to arise frequently:

➤ There is a chance that parties will choose an option too soon and not look at other options.

➤ The parties may be trying to narrow down their choices so they can come to a clear decision.

➤ Parties may see a win-lose solution as their only choice if they think that only one party can win and the other must lose.

➤ The people involved may decide it's up to the other person to find a solution.

Negotiation is a complex process; developing effective options is crucial for successful negotiation. According to the authors, the first step towards generating options is to identify the available choices. Once both parties have discussed the problem and exchanged ideas, they can choose the most appropriate solution that benefits both sides. One of a negotiator's most valuable skills is coming up with new and creative solutions. Here are some tips for making options that work well:

➤ **Have a brainstorming session that is separate from the rest.**
Use a brainstorming session to develop ideas that will help everyone avoid being judged or criticized immediately. As the participants sit together and look at the problem, they are more willing to work together to solve it. After a brainstorming session, pick out the best ideas, rank them, and decide which ones should be taken into negotiations.

➤ **Make more choices.**
Analyzing ideas and identifying themes can be a powerful technique for generating more ideas and insights, as it can help you to view the problem from different angles or perspectives.

➤ **Try to help each other out.**
Find common interests and treat them as a shared goal to make the negotiation process go more smoothly and lead to more progress. Be open to and accepting of different interests if you want to reach an agreement.

Be Sure to Use Objective Criteria

People often have different goals in any negotiation, and it's not always easy to find a solution, especially when time is tight. Instead of relying on a battle of words or personal opinions to evaluate options together, you might consider using fair, objective criteria. Objective criteria should be used to settle disagreements between parties whose interests are at odds. When people fight over words, it hurts relationships, wastes time, and leads to agreements that don't work.

Before discussing an agreement's terms, it's often best to agree on the criteria or standards that should be used. So, we will be better able to convince the other side if we use the criteria they came up with. After the objective criteria have been made, there should be a talk between the people involved. The authors say that these rules should be followed:

➤ Think of it as a team effort to develop objective criteria for judging each issue.

➤ Be reasonable and open to reason when you choose and use standards.

➤ No matter how hard things get, stay true to yourself. No matter what, stay true to your values.

What if they are More Powerful?

In the world of negotiations, it's easy to get caught up in the moment and feel like every decision you make is of utmost importance. However, as the author points out, sometimes it's more effective to take a step back and reassess the situation. Just like catching the earliest airplane may not always be necessary, agreeing to a deal that's causing you stress and anxiety may not be the best course of action. It's important to keep a level head and evaluate each decision based on its potential long-term impact, rather than simply jumping at the first opportunity that comes your way.

They stress that while power is an important factor in negotiations, it does not necessarily dictate the outcome. Rather than focusing solely on power, the authors recommend shifting the focus to the interests of both parties. By understanding and addressing the other party's interests, even if they have more power, negotiators can often find mutually beneficial solutions.

Developing Your BATNA

One of the most effective ways to prepare for a negotiation is to develop a BATNA (Best Alternative To A Negotiated Agreement). By developing a BATNA, individuals can clearly understand their alternatives and identify the most favorable outcomes. The authors provide detailed instructions on creating a BATNA, emphasizing the importance of being realistic and identifying achievable alternatives. They have given instructions here:

➤ Prepare a BATNA, which you would do if you couldn't reach a deal. Use it as the standard to judge any agreement that is being proposed.

➤ Set up a safe space for the conversation. If you find one agreement that isn't perfect but is still better than your BATNA, that may be a sign that the content of the possible agreement isn't very good.

The Cost of Using a Bottom Line

The authors highlight that focusing solely on your bottom line, or your absolute minimum acceptable outcome, can be costly and limit the potential for creative solutions. By fixating on your bottom line, you may miss opportunities for mutually beneficial agreements or damage the relationship with the other party. Instead, the authors suggest focusing on your interests and needs and finding ways to meet the interests and needs of the other party. By doing so, you can potentially achieve outcomes that go beyond what you initially thought was possible.

But it may be hard to stand up to pressure once you have set your bottom line. Here are some of the obstacles once you have set your bottom line:

➤ You won't be able to use what you learn while negotiating. The bottom line is a position that can't be changed, no matter what the other side says.

➤ Also, it makes it hard to use your imagination. Because of this, there is less of a reason to come up with a solution that considers everyone's needs in a way that is good for everyone.

➤ It's important to remember that having a bottom line may keep you from agreeing to a bad deal, but it may also stop you from coming up with solutions that would be good for you to accept.

KEY LESSONS

1. **An open battle is something you should try to stay away from at all costs.**

   When two sides are in an open battle, they care more about winning than building a good relationship.

2. **Even if you win every negotiation, that doesn't mean you'll always be successful.**

   The main goal of negotiating is to reach a long-term agreement on fair terms and reduce bad feelings.

3. **It's important to figure out what each side wants.**

   To find the right solution, you must know why someone wants what they want.

4. **Find out what both sides can do before you agree.**

   Instead of getting the other person to agree to your terms, think of creative ways to help you find a solution that works for both of you.

5. **You'll be ready if you learn as much as you can about negotiating.**

   Spend time learning about all the details to make things more likely to go well.

ACTIONABLE STEPS TO TAKE

➤ **Understand the other party's interests.**
Getting to Yes emphasizes the importance of understanding the other party's underlying interests and concerns. This can help to identify potential areas of compromise and common ground, and to build a more effective negotiation strategy.

➤ **Separate the people from the problem.**
Separating the people from the problem helps to address the issue objectively and reduces the chance of personalizing the disagreement.

➤ **Focus on objective criteria.**
Using objective criteria helps to make decisions based on facts, rather than personal opinions, and reduces the chance of bias.

➤ **Generate a variety of options.**
The author encourages readers to generate various options for resolving the problem, rather than focusing on a single solution. This can help to increase the chances of finding a mutually acceptable solution.

➤ **Create a *package deal.***
The author suggests that readers can create a *package deal* that includes various elements, such as compromise, trade-offs, and shared benefits, to reach a mutually beneficial agreement.

➤ **Be prepared to walk away.**
The book advises readers to be prepared to walk away from a negotiation if the other party is unwilling to compromise or to meet their interests.

➤ **Know your BATNA.**
Knowing your BATNA helps you clearly understand what you will do if a negotiation fails, and provides leverage in the negotiation.

➤ **Be willing to compromise.**
Being willing to compromise helps to find solutions that benefit both parties and increases the chance of reaching an agreement.

Five Love Languages

by Gary Chapman

"Forgiveness is not a feeling; it is a commitment. It is a choice to show mercy, not hold the offense against the offender. Forgiveness is an expression of love."

T HE book is designed to help couples identify and understand their primary love languages, which are how they prefer to give and receive love. It emphasizes that everyone has a primary love language, which is the language that resonates most strongly with them. He explains that understanding your partner's love language is key to expressing your love in a way that they will feel most deeply. He also notes that it's important to communicate your love language to your partner so that they can reciprocate in a way that feels meaningful to you.

The book begins by explaining that people have different ways of expressing love, and that often, couples don't speak the same love language. This can lead to misunderstandings, feelings of unappreciation, and ultimately, relationship problems. The author introduces the concept of love languages to help couples better communicate their love to each other.

What are the 5 Love Languages?

Here is a summary of each of the five love languages that the book talks about:

1. **Words of affirmation** — Words that encourage others.

2. **Quality time** — The act of giving someone your full, undivided attention.

3. **Receiving gifts** — Objects that remind people they are loved.

4. **Acts of service** — Do what you know they want you to do.

5. **Physical touch** — A physical touch or request for full attention.

Love Language 1 — Words of Affirmation

Praise and encouragement are powerful ways to show that you care about someone. The best way to learn to speak this language is to compliment people often. You should tell them how much you like their laugh, new outfit, or smile. Some examples are given below:

➤ **Verbal compliments** — *"You look great!"*

➤ **Encouraging words** — *"You can do this!"*

➤ **Kind words** — *"I love you.", "I care about you.", "I forgive you."*

Love Language 2 — Quality Time

Our work and busy lives can make it hard for us to use this love language. We can be in the same room as our partner but still **not be** with them because of our phones and other devices. To have a good time together, we must give each other our full attention. You can spend quality time with your partner or do quality things with them, like going out on a date. Listed below are some examples:

➤ **Focused attention** — Spending time without thinking about anything else (e.g., phone).

➤ **Quality listening** — Allowing others to feel heard by listening to them.

➤ **Quality sharing** — The act of opening up and being vulnerable.

Love Language 3 — Gift Giving

Some people see gifts as a way for their partner to show them how they feel about them. Don't worry about how much the gift costs. How much you care about your partner will show how hard you worked to get it or make it. Some examples are given below:

➤ **Physical gifts** — Buy, make, or find a gift to show appreciation.

➤ **Remembered gifts** — Be sure to take note of anything they mention they enjoy.

➤ **Shared interests** — Share a quality book or activity that you both enjoy.

Love Language 4 — Acts of Service

In any relationship, whether romantic, familial, or platonic, it's essential to show your appreciation and support for your partner. How individuals prefer to receive help and support can vary greatly, ranging from doing their laundry to simply listening to their problems. In the book, the author emphasizes the importance of understanding your partner's needs and preferences to better assist. Some examples are given below:

➤ **Housework** — Paying bills, cooking, vacuuming, gardening, and fixing things.

➤ **Loved ones** — Look after the other person's family members or pets.

➤ **Interference** — While they are working, block interruptions and distractions.

Love Language 5 — Physical Touch

As social beings, humans have a basic need for physical touch and affection, regardless of age. While we often associate touch with infancy and childhood, it is equally important in adult relationships. Acts such as holding hands, cuddling, kissing, and sexual intimacy can all convey feelings of love and closeness. Understanding your partner's preferences for touch is key to building intimacy and strengthening your relationship. Some examples are given below:

➤ **Explicit (full attention)** — Massage someone, hold them when they cry, perform foreplay, or provide sex.

➤ **Implicit (in passing)** — Holding hands, touching shoulders, passing hands, sitting close together, exchanging a kiss or hug, or touching one's lower leg under the table.

➤ **Remote** — Wearing their clothing, giving tactile gifts, and sharing photographs.

KEY LESSONS

1. **How we feel about ourselves tells us how much love we need.**
   You can do better in a relationship if you figure out how much love you need.

2. **To love someone, you have to talk to them. The honeymoon phase won't last forever.**
   When the novelty factor of the relationship wears off, you will only have your partner and yourself. Learning to talk to each other is the key to having a good relationship.

3. **There are many ways to show that you love someone.**
   To ensure your partner feels the love you are trying to give them, you should first learn how they feel love.

4. **Love can be shown in many different ways.**
   Words of affirmation, quality time together, gifts, acts of kindness, and physical touch are all good ways to show love.

5. **Identify your love language.**
   To ensure your relationship lasts, you should know your love language and use it well.

ACTIONABLE STEPS TO TAKE

➤ **Understand your love language.**

The first step in improving your relationships is understanding your primary love language and how you express and receive love. This can be done through self-reflection and taking the love languages assessment provided in the book.

➤ **Learn to speak your partner's love language.**

Once you understand your love language, it's important to learn to speak your partner's love language.

➤ **Communicate effectively.**

Good communication is key to any relationship and the book emphasizes the importance of using *I* statements and active listening to express your needs and feelings in a way that is respectful and non-threatening.

➤ **Make time for each other.**

Quality time is a love language for many people, and it's important to be together and focus on each other. This can involve scheduling regular date nights or simply making a point to disconnect from other distractions and spend time together.

➤ **Show physical touch.**

Physical touch is an important love language for many people and it's important to make an effort to show affection through physical touch, whether it's through holding hands, hugs, or other forms of physical contact.

➤ **Give and receive gifts.**

Giving and receiving gifts is an important love language for many people, and it's important to make an effort to give thoughtful and meaningful gifts that show your love and appreciation.

➤ **Show acts of service.**

Doing things to help your partner and make their life easier is an important love language for many people, and it's important to make an effort to show acts of service that demonstrate your love and support.

Difficult Conversations

by Bruce Patton, Douglas Stone and Sheila Heen

"People rarely change without first feeling understood."

T HIS book discusses how communication is important in every part of our lives. Not only are great communication skills important for formal negotiations, but they are also important for everyday interactions. People have trouble with certain kinds of conversation more than others. This makes us avoid hard conversations, even if they are important to our success.

This book helps you understand why some conversations are hard. The book also discusses why people can't handle these conversations well. It shows how we can have more productive conversations by using certain techniques.

The authors begin by defining what they mean by difficult conversations — those that are emotionally charged, where there are differing opinions or perspectives, or where there are high stakes involved. They argue that these types of conversations are inevitable in personal and professional relationships, and avoiding them can ultimately lead to greater conflict and misunderstandings.

The Three Types of Difficult Conversations

Difficult conversations can be challenging to navigate, and it's essential to approach them with a clear understanding of their structure. According to the authors, difficult conversations can be classified into three types, each with unique limitations and complexities. Understanding these difficult conversations and their nuances can help you prepare for and manage them more effectively.

The *What Happened* Conversation

In these kinds of talks, people have different ideas about what happened or should have happened. A conversation like this can take many different shapes. This can be about who said what, who did what, who was right, what was meant, and who is to blame. Even though each of us thinks that our point of view is right, we are wrong in the following three ways:

➤ **Truth.**

We tend to think, *"I'm right and you're wrong,"* even though most diffi-cult conversations are about different values or points of view. For exam-ple, *"You don't have enough experience"* or *"You drive too fast"* are not facts; they are just opinions.

➤ **Intention.**

We assume that we know the real reason why someone does or doesn't do something. But we could be wrong about everything. For example, you might think your coworker is trying to make you feel bad by shouting at you, but he's just trying to be heard over all the other noise.

➤ **Blame.**

In many situations, our first instinct is to blame others for any problems that arise. This thinking can be counterproductive because it prevents us from looking inward and considering our role in the situation.

The *Feelings* Conversation

Everyone in a difficult conversation wonders if their feelings are real or not. Are you allowed to be upset? Do you think it's fair if the person you're talking to doesn't acknowledge your feeling? You might also wonder if your actions hurt the other person's feelings. To have a good conversation, you should talk about how you feel. The authors brought up 3 important points about the *Feelings* Conversation:

1. **Address the feelings.**

   Feelings are often at the heart of a difficult conversation. Recognizing and addressing emotions can prevent them from escalating and causing more conflict. Ignoring or dismissing emotions can worsen the situation and lead to a breakdown in communication.

2. **Validate the feelings.**

   People may have different emotional reactions to the same situation. It's important to acknowledge and validate each person's feelings, even if you don't necessarily agree with them. This can help build trust and lead to a more productive conversation.

3. **Be honest about the feelings.**

Understanding and expressing your feelings is just as important as acknowledging the feelings of others. Being honest and transparent about your feelings can create a safe space for others to do the same. This can lead to a deeper understanding of each other's perspectives and help find a resolution to the difficult situation.

The *Identity* Conversation

This is the kind of talk we have about who we are. The conversation will be about how you feel about this situation. During difficult conversations, many of us have second thoughts. Whenever we talk to someone, we consider whether we are smart, nice, and likable. During these talks, we are questioning who we are. Our biggest worry is that these conversations will hurt our sense of self and self-worth. *Identity* Conversations are mostly about being honest about ourselves and our beliefs. It's important to recognize that our identity is not fixed and can be influenced by the situation. This means that in an *Identity* Conversation, we must be willing to explore how the situation affects our self-perception and how we can adjust our identity in response. This conversation is mostly about three main questions:

➤ Am I competent?

➤ Am I a good person?

➤ Am I worthy of love?

The *Identity* Conversation can be difficult and make one feel vulnerable, but it's necessary for growth and understanding. We can gain valuable insight into our emotions and beliefs by addressing our sense of self and how it relates to the situation.

Learning Conversation

Initiating a difficult conversation can be daunting, but starting it off on the right foot can make all the difference. The authors of the book *Difficult Conversations* emphasize the importance of avoiding a judgmental approach, as it can make the other person defensive and derail the conversation. Instead, they suggest some alternatives to begin the conversation in a more positive light. When faced with a difficult situation, try one of the following:

➤ **Third Party.**

The authors give great advice on how to have this kind of conversation. Most of the time, people start by talking about the topic from their point of view, which makes the other person feel defensive. Start the conversation by telling about it from the point of view of a third person.

➤ **Be a good listener.**

A good listener knows that the key to being a good listener is to be genuinely interested in what the other person is saying. Ensure you understand what they tell you by asking questions, requesting examples, and rephrasing what they say.

➤ **Express yourself.**

Both sides must realize that their thoughts and feelings are their own and that there is no right or wrong. Also, the individual's thoughts and feelings are just as important as any other person's.

➤ **Difficult parties.**

The book's authors are right when they say the other person might not have read it. Because of this, the other person may try to find fault and argue about what is right and wrong.

➤ **Strive for mutual agreement.**

Remember that you both have to agree on the solution and that they have to convince you just as much as you have to convince them. Tell them what would convince you, and tell them what would convince them.

Preparing for a Difficult Conversation

Difficult conversations are often a source of stress and anxiety, but adequate preparation can make all the difference. The preparation should begin with identifying the purpose of the conversation, the other person's perspective, and any emotions that may arise during the conversation. Additionally, the authors recommend focusing on interests, rather than positions, to identify potential areas of agreement. This preparation can help to create a more productive and less confrontational atmosphere during the conversation, which is essential for achieving a positive outcome. Before having a hard conversation, you should always keep the following in mind:

1. **Identify your goals.**

   Before having a difficult conversation, it's important to identify what you hope to accomplish. This will help you stay focused and on track during the conversation. It's also important to consider the other person's goals and needs, and find ways to address both your goals and theirs.

2. **Consider your assumptions.**

   Our assumptions and beliefs can often influence how we interpret situations and conversations. It's important to reflect on your assumptions and consider alternative perspectives. This can help you avoid jumping to conclusions and making assumptions that may not be accurate.

3. **Plan your approach.**

   Consider the best way to approach the conversation, considering the other person's communication style and any potential communication barriers. Consider how you will frame the conversation and the language you will use. Plan to remain calm and focused throughout the conversation.

4. **Practice active listening.**

   Active listening involves hearing what the other person is saying, and paying attention to their body language, tone of voice, and other non-verbal cues. It's important to practice active listening during the conversation to ensure that you are truly understanding the other person's perspective.

KEY LESSONS

1. **Because of fear, people avoid having difficult conversations because they are afraid of what will happen.**

   Many people worry that the other person will get angry, say hurtful things, and then make things worse to the point where they can't work out their differences anymore.

2. **Communication is the key to getting things done well.**

   If you can figure out what's going on behind the scenes of an argument, you can make better decisions.

3. **You need to think about three things when having a hard conversation.**

   Individual differences in how they act, feel, and other people's actions can lead to conflict.

4. *Learning conversations* **are the best way to get things done.**

   Find out why the other person is angry so you don't have to blame them or imply they have bad intentions.

5. **Find your emotional footprint to find out how self-aware you are.**

   You can find out the truth and listen to your inner voice by asking yourself questions. This will put you in a good mood.

ACTIONABLE STEPS TO TAKE

➤ **Prepare yourself.**
Before the conversation, take some time to think about your goals, values, and priorities. Consider your emotions and what you want to achieve from the conversation.

➤ **Understand the other person's perspective.**
Try to understand the other person's perspective, feelings, and needs. This will help you to be more empathetic and open to different viewpoints.

➤ **Use *I* statements.**
Instead of blaming or accusing the other person, use *I* statements to express your thoughts and feelings. This will help keep the conversation focused on the problem, not the person.

➤ **Listen actively.**
Listen actively and try to understand the other person's perspective. Avoid interrupting or dismissing their feelings.

➤ **Explore different options.**
Look for creative solutions and options that can help to resolve the problem.

➤ **Find common ground.**
Find common ground with the other person and try to work together to find a solution.

➤ **Follow up.**
After the conversation, follow up to ensure that any agreements or decisions have been implemented.

➤ **Learn from the experience.**
Take the time to reflect on the conversation and learn from it. This will help you to handle difficult conversations more effectively in the future.

CHAPTER 4

PRODUCTIVITY

"Productivity is never an accident. It is always the result of a commitment to excellence, intelligent planning, and focused effort."

— Paul J. Meyer

"Productivity is less about what you do with your time. And more about how you run your mind."

— Robin S. Sharma

"Success is nothing more than a few simple disciplines practiced daily."

— Jim Rohn

Deep Work

by Cal Newport

"Who you are, what you think, feel, and do, what you love — is the sum of what you focus on."

T HIS book explores deep work, which the author defines as *"professional activities performed in a state of distraction-free concentration that push your cognitive capabilities to their limit."* The book argues that deep work is becoming increasingly rare in our modern economy and is essential for professional success and personal fulfillment.

The book begins by arguing that shallow work, which he defines as *non-cognitive, logistical, or minor duties*, has become increasingly prevalent in our economy due to technological distractions and the emphasis on constant communication. He argues that shallow work may be necessary but does not lead to true productivity or fulfillment.

The author argues that deep work is essential for professional success because it allows individuals to produce high-quality work and develop valuable skills. He suggests that to engage in deep work, individuals must create an environment that supports focus and concentration, and develop the ability to manage distractions.

Our world is full of things to do, and time is running out. For success, we need to learn new things quickly, focus for long periods without getting distracted, and learn new things quickly. We can do many things to change our lives and make them more focused on deep work. Deep work is a skill that can help us get ahead in the world today.

Deep Work vs Shallow Work

➤ **Deep Work** is a task that requires you to pay attention all the time and pushes your mind to its limits. To be successful, you need to be able to focus and not be distracted. The results can be valuable, help you improve, and are hard to copy.

➤ **Shallow work** comprises tasks that don't require much thinking and are more about logistics. These tasks are often done while someone else is talking or doing something else. Most of the time, these efforts don't add much new value and are easy to copy.

What makes Deep Work so Valuable?

The book highlights the importance of deep work for maximizing productivity and achieving success in today's knowledge economy. Deep work involves focused and uninterrupted concentration on cognitively demanding tasks over a long period, and it is increasingly rare in our age of constant distraction and shallow work. The author argues that deep work is valuable because it leads to higher quality output, faster skill acquisition, and increased creativity. Now let's examine how each of these approaches can aid us in accomplishing more:

➤ **Single-Tasking.**
Studies have shown over and over again that multitasking makes people less productive. Focusing on one task at a time is the best way to get the most done.

➤ **Get rid of distractions.**
This makes a lot of sense. The more time you have to focus on your work, the more likely you will get what you want.

➤ **Intense focus.**
You can get much more done in less time if you focus on the task and don't let anything else get in the way. The more focused you are, the more you will get done.

Deep work is becoming harder to do at the same time that it is becoming more valuable in our economy. Because of this, few people can develop this skill and make it a central part of their work lives. Deep work can be improved by working on two important things:

➤ **Concentration skills.**
Being able to give your work your full attention.

➤ **Beating the craving for distraction.**
You will never achieve deep concentration unless you overcome your brain's desire for quick distractions.

Change Your Habits to Encourage Deep Work

To develop lasting Deep Work habits, adding or eliminating habit triggers is easier when we make rapid external structural changes. This paves the way for creating new habits without relying on willpower to sustain them. Although the benefits of deep work are clear, the greatest challenge lies in discovering how to make the most of it. Thus, developing effective strategies to incorporate deep work into our routines is key to ensuring productivity and achieving our goals.

To change this, here are four ways to encourage and promote the deep work state:

1. **Turn off everything and work hard.**

   For deep work, we must be willing to put in the effort, which is the last thing most of us want to do. Combine this with a working environment and culture that make deep work hard and a limited amount of willpower that gets weaker as it is used, and you have a recipe for shallow work. To make deep work a part of our everyday lives, we need to set up rituals and routines that make it easier and more natural for us to do.

2. **Embrace boredom as a gift.**

   You have to learn how to concentrate very hard. You must take care of your focus when you're not doing deep work, just like athletes have to take care of their bodies when they're not training. To be able to concentrate deeply, you will have to be able to keep it up. This will be hard to do if you are easily distracted by even the smallest signs of boredom in your daily life.

3. **Stop using social media.**

   Using social media is a great example of living in a shallow way. Even though it can provide a small benefit, that doesn't mean we should spend much time on it. If you want to work hard, you can't feel like you have to check social media every minute. Due to this addictive quality, deep living and work cannot go together with social media.

4. **Drain the shallows.**

   The book *The Shallows* examines the impact of the Internet on our minds and daily routines. Shallow work, as described in the book, includes tasks such as replying to emails, attending meetings, making phone calls, and completing other necessary tasks that don't add much value in the long run. To engage in deep work, minimizing shallow work and creating dedicated time for focused, uninterrupted work is essential. It's crucial to prevent shallow tasks from interfering with deep work to achieve optimal results.

Utilize Routines to Adapt to Deep Work

According to the author, there are typically four methods for finding time to engage in deep work. As previously mentioned, relying on ad-hoc solutions is not the most effective approach, as it heavily relies on willpower and cannot be sustained over time. By choosing one of these methods, you can identify the approach that best suits your individual personality, lifestyle, and motivation:

➤ **Monastic Philosophy.**
This approach to work and productivity emphasizes the importance of deep work, concentration, and focus. The term *"monastic"* is used because it is inspired by the lifestyle of monks who live in seclusion, dedicating their lives to contemplation and focus on their spiritual practices. In a professional context, monastic philosophy involves creating an environment that supports deep work and minimizes distractions.

➤ **Bimodal Philosophy.**
This productivity approach involves dividing time between deep and shallow work. In this philosophy, a person would dedicate a specific period of time to deep work, focusing entirely on a single, cognitively demanding task, without interruption. The rest of their time would be spent on shallow work, such as answering emails or attending meetings. This approach allows individuals to make the most of their deep work sessions without sacrificing the necessary shallow work that must also be done.

➤ **Rhythmic Philosophy.**
This philosophy involves setting aside specific times each day or week for deep work and creating a predictable schedule around those times. Doing this can create a habit of deep work that becomes ingrained in your daily

routine. The key to success with the rhythmic philosophy is to create a schedule that works for you and is sustainable over the long term.

➤ **Journalistic Philosophy.**
This approach is inspired by the work habits of journalists who must fit in deep work around unpredictable schedules and deadlines. The idea is to seize every opportunity to work deeply when it arises. This means that when a journalist has a free hour between interviews, they will use that time to write an article instead of checking their email or social media. This approach requires flexibility and the ability to switch between different tasks quickly.

Build a Deep Work Routine

To cultivate a deep work habit, it's crucial to be intentional with your time. You must consider the optimal time and location for periods of undisturbed concentration. Developing a deep work ritual necessitates considering the following factors:

➤ **Location.**
Select a workspace that will provide you with a distraction-free environment and allow you to focus for long periods. You may use noise-canceling headphones without a dedicated space, allowing you to work without being disturbed by the outside world and letting your brain know it's time to concentrate.

➤ **Duration.**
Determine exactly how much time you will devote to the task at hand before you begin a deep work session. If you are uncomfortable with longer sessions, begin with 15 minutes and progress to longer sessions.

➤ **Structure.**
You should establish a structure for yourself and define deep work mode. For example, do you plan to turn your phone off while you work?

➤ **Requirements.**
You will learn how to support your commitment to deep work during a

few focused sessions. This might mean listening to a certain kind of music, drinking a drink, or using software. Make sure you have everything you need before you move on.

Make Room for Downtime

According to the principles of the deep work method, pursuing deep work goes beyond simply dedicating time during the workday. As the author emphasizes, working excessively long hours without breaks can hinder your ability to perform deep work. It is crucial, therefore, to prioritize and schedule downtime for yourself, as regularly giving your mind a break can significantly enhance the quality of your deep work. In other words, deep work is not just a matter of putting in more hours, but of taking intentional breaks to recharge your mental and physical energy. These are the benefits of downtime the author provides:

➤ **Downtime helps us think better.**
If you let your mind rest instead of trying to work yourself to exhaustion, you'll be better able to solve hard problems. As the author says, this gives your unconscious mind time to figure out how to deal with your most difficult work problems.

➤ **Downtime allows us to practice deep thinking.**
Spend time with family or friends, cook, or walk in the woods to let your mind rest. If you sneak in extra emails or group chats, your mind won't be able to truly rest.

➤ **Our ability to develop deep work is limited.**
Even though deep work has many benefits, it can't be done as much as you want. As our ability to pay attention grows, we find it harder to pay attention to the task at hand. Because of this, there will be plenty of time in the evening to use the downtime needed for deep work sessions the next day.

Eliminate Internet Entertainment

It is important to resist the temptation of mindlessly wasting time on the internet during your free time. Rather, you should engage in more meaningful and enjoyable activities that can rejuvenate your mind and body. The following list can serve as a helpful comparison guide in this regard:

Low-Quality Forms	High-Quality Forms
Watching television.	Playing an instrument.
Viewing your Facebook newsfeed.	Walking in nature.
Surfing the Internet for entertainment.	Taking time to read a good book.
Liking pictures on Instagram.	Spending time with friends and family.
Reading forums on the Internet.	Planting and gardening.
Watching Netflix shows regularly.	Exercising.

KEY LESSONS

1. **There is a difference between *being busy* and *getting things done*.**
   One of the most important things about high achievers is their ability to work deeply, which means they can focus on their challenges. Also, there is a difference between *hardly working* and *working hard.*

2. **Deep work is like a muscle that needs to be worked out regularly to stay strong.**
   We are not used to doing deep work because we always do shallow tasks and are distracted.

3. **To do deep work, you need to take a monastic approach.**
   By shutting yourself off like a monk, you can reach a deep state of concentration.

4. **When using a bimodal approach to deep work, you must give yourself time to meditate alone.**
   Focus on your most important tasks and do other things throughout the day to get your most important work done first.

5. **Working in a rhythmic way makes it a habit to focus very hard.**
   Set aside time every day for deep work. This will help you get used to it faster.

6. **You can get the most out of your free time if you take a journalistic approach.**
   You don't need to plan out a lot to do deep work. If you want to get some work done, it would help to take advantage of any free time, turn off any distractions, and get to work.

7. **The key to deep work is to be okay with boredom, avoid socializing, and do as little shallow work as possible.**
   Just sending emails or using social media is like being hooked on something. At first, it's hard to stop, and over time, it gets very uncomfortable.

ACTIONABLE STEPS TO TAKE

➤ **Identify your deep work goals.**

Clearly define what you want to accomplish through deep work and identify the specific projects or tasks to help you achieve these goals.

➤ **Schedule your deep work.**

Set aside dedicated blocks of time in your calendar for deep work and make it a non-negotiable commitment.

➤ **Eliminate distractions.**

Identify and eliminate sources of distractions, such as social media and email notifications, during your deep work sessions.

➤ **Use the Pomodoro Technique.**

Break your deep work sessions into 25-minute intervals, with 5-minute breaks, to increase productivity and prevent burnout.

➤ **Create a designated workspace.**

Establish a specific place where you will do deep work, making it free of distractions and comfortable. Regularly evaluate your progress and adjust your approach as needed to ensure you are making the most of your deep work sessions.

➤ **Make deep work a habit.**

Make deep work a regular part of your daily routine and develop the discipline to stick to your schedule.

➤ **Take time to disconnect.**

Be sure to disconnect from work and engage in activities that help you relax and recharge.

➤ **Learn to say *NO*.**

Avoid unnecessary obligations and distractions that can disrupt your deep work schedule.

Eat That Frog!

by Brian Tracy

"Every action you take is a vote for the person you wish to become. No single instance will transform your beliefs, but as the votes build up, so does the evidence of your new identity. Goals are good for setting a direction, but systems are best for making progress."

T HIS book is based on the premise that the key to success is prioritizing tasks effectively and focusing on the most important ones. The author uses the metaphor of *"eating the frog"* to describe tackling the most difficult or unpleasant tasks first, to increase productivity and minimize procrastination.

The importance of setting clear goals and prioritizing tasks is highlighted at the start of the book. The author stresses the need to focus on the most crucial tasks first, rather than being distracted by less important ones or absorbed in busy work.

Instead of trying to do everything, it's better to focus on the most important things, act on them, and do them well. The author says you should start your day by eating the scariest frog you have. But don't get the wrong idea — your frog is your most important task, the one you tend to put off the most but that can have the biggest impact on your results.

The Four Principles of Productivity & Achievement

In his book, the author emphasizes the importance of key principles essential to achieving success. Although simple, these principles are critical to ensuring that you get the desired results. The author repeatedly emphasizes these key ideas throughout the book as they are fundamental to the overall message. These four key principles are as follows:

1. **Select your most important task.**
   Stop doing things that aren't worth your time and start doing things that are. Determine your most important task and give it all your attention.

2. **Begin immediately.**
   To boost productivity, it is crucial to develop the habit of tackling the

most important task as soon as it is identified. According to experts, the human brain is wired to prefer straightforward tasks over difficult ones, causing many individuals to procrastinate or engage in busy work instead of tackling more pressing matters.

3. **Single-handedly execute.**
By focusing only on your most important task, you can avoid lengthy things like multitasking and attention residue.

4. **Complete what you have started.**
Achieving success requires discipline and the ability to prioritize essential tasks. Once you have identified the most critical task, it is essential to exercise self-control and avoid any distractions until it is completed.

Three Steps to Mastery in Your Field

➤ **Step 1 — Read a lot.**
Spend at least an hour a day reading about your field. Get a book or magazine with information that will help you be more effective and productive at what you do, and read for 30–60 minutes in the morning.

➤ **Step 2 — Participate in conventions.**
You should take all the courses and seminars on the key skills you want to learn. Take part in conventions and business meetings related to your job or profession. Go to sessions and workshops that are related to your job or profession. Write things down and pay attention. Audio recordings can also be bought. Decide to become one of your field's most knowledgeable and skilled people.

➤ **Step 3 — Listen to educational audios.**
Use the radio and other audio programs in your car. The average driver spends between 500 and 1000 hours a year behind the wheel getting from one place to another. Use the time you spend driving to learn something new. You can become one of the smartest, most skilled, and highest-paid people in your field just by listening to educational audio programs while you drive.

21 Ways to Stop Procrastination

1 — Set the table.

This is the first step towards effective time management and increasing productivity. Establishing the table is to plan and prioritize your tasks before you begin working. This ensures you don't waste time on unimportant tasks and helps you stay focused on the most important ones. The author provides two important lessons to take from this concept:

1. **Have a clear understanding of your goals.**

   By taking the time to identify your goals and break them down into smaller tasks, you can establish a clear action plan for achieving them. This makes staying focused and avoids getting sidetracked by less important tasks.

2. **Set realistic expectations for yourself.**

   You should be honest about how much time and effort each task will take, and prioritize them accordingly. This helps you avoid overloading yourself with too many tasks and becoming overwhelmed, which can ultimately lead to burnout.

2 — Plan every day.

To increase your productivity and accomplish your goals more efficiently, developing the habit of recording your ideas and thoughts in writing is essential. By planning and allocating specific time slots for each task, you can save up to 10-15 minutes during the execution phase. Prioritizing your tasks and placing the most important ones at the top of your to-do list is crucial. The author provides two important lessons to take from this concept:

1. **Reduced stress.**

   Writing down your ideas helps to clarify your thoughts and makes it easier to execute tasks: When you write down your ideas, you free up mental space and reduce the cognitive load on your brain. This clarity of thought makes it easier to execute tasks efficiently and focus.

2. **Improved time management.**

   Planning helps you to stay organized and prioritize your tasks: Planning your day helps you to avoid distractions and focus on your most important tasks. It also ensures you allocate your time effectively, maximizing your available resources.

3 — Implement the Pareto Principle (80/20 Rule)

The principle states that 80% of the outcomes come from 20% of the efforts. In other words, 20% of your tasks will give you 80% of the desired results. Focusing on these key tasks can maximize your productivity and achieve your goals more efficiently. The author provides two important lessons to take from this concept:

1. **Identify the 20% of tasks that will give you the most results.**
   This requires careful planning and prioritization. You need to determine which tasks are the most important and will impact your goals most.

2. **Avoid getting bogged down in the less important tasks that comprise the remaining 80%.**
   These tasks may be necessary, but they can also be distractions that prevent you from achieving your most important goals. By focusing on the key tasks that will give you the most results, you can avoid wasting time on less important tasks.

4 — Consider the consequences.

You should put your most important tasks in order of their importance to you. These tasks should be your top priority. The author emphasizes the importance of taking responsibility for your own life and being aware of the consequences of your choices. By understanding the impact of your actions, you can make more informed decisions and avoid negative consequences. The author provides two important lessons to take from this concept:

1. **Understand the long-term consequences.**
   It's important to think beyond your actions' immediate rewards or consequences and consider the long-term impact. This means considering how your choices affect your future goals and overall well-being. By doing so, you can make more strategic decisions that align with your long-term vision.

2. **Consider the Consequences of inaction.**

It's not just the consequences of our actions that we should consider, but also the consequences of inaction. Sometimes, avoiding a difficult or unpleasant task can have negative consequences in the long run. By recognizing the potential costs of procrastination, we can motivate ourselves to take action and avoid the negative outcomes of inaction.

5 — Procrastinate creatively.

The author believes that procrastination is not always a bad thing and that it can be used to your advantage creatively. One way to procrastinate creatively is to focus on other tasks that need to be done before starting on the most important one. This can be a form of productive procrastination, as long as those other tasks are still important and need to be done. The author provides two important lessons to take from this concept:

1. **Avoid overthinking.**

Procrastinating creatively can help you avoid overthinking and worrying about a task. Focusing on other important tasks or gathering more information can reduce your anxiety and gain more confidence in tackling the most important task.

2. **Increase efficiency.**

Procrastinating creatively can also increase your efficiency. By taking a little extra time to gather information or focus on other important tasks, you may be able to complete the most important task more quickly and with less stress. This can help you be more productive overall and free up time for other important activities.

6 — Practice the ABCDE method.

Set priorities and organize your tasks based on how important they are. When you've written down everything you must do on a certain day, use the ABCDE method to determine the most important.

➤ *A — are tasks you must do.*

Your most important tasks are the ones you have to do. Your life depends on these frogs, and you can make them even more important by sub-prioritize — putting A1, A2, etc. next to them.

➤ *B — are tasks you should do.*
You should do things that won't have too much of an effect on your life.

➤ *C — are tasks that would be nice to do.*
You could do things that would be helpful, like calling a friend or having lunch with a coworker, but that has nothing to do with your job.

➤ *D — are tasks you can delegate.*
Some tasks can be given to other people to do.

➤ *E — are tasks you can cut.*
You can get rid of these tasks without any trouble.

7 — Pay attention to Key Result Areas (KRAs).

The author suggests that if you want to be successful, you need to focus on the key result areas of your work. The KRAs are the few things you do that contribute the most to your success.

To understand KRAs, he recommends categorizing the tasks you are responsible for in your job into A, B, and C tasks. Tasks are the most important and contribute the most to your success, B tasks are moderately important, and C tasks are the least important. The author provides two important lessons to take from this concept:

1. **Focus on what matters.**
   By focusing on your KRAs, you can prioritize the most important tasks and ensure that they get done first. This allows you to make the most of your time and ensure that you are making progress towards your goals.

2. **Success requires effort.**
   To succeed, you must try to excel in your KRAs. By dedicating most of your time to your KRAs, you can work towards excellence and ensure that you do everything possible to achieve your goals.

8 — Apply The Law of Three

The book suggests that three key steps or activities usually lead to the successful completion of any task or goal. The author suggests identifying and prioritizing these three steps is essential for achieving maximum results with minimum effort. Here's how the Law of Three works:

1. **Identify the three most important steps.**
   Start by identifying the three key steps or activities most important for achieving your goal. These should be the three activities that will make the biggest impact on your success.

2. **Prioritize the steps.**
   Once you have identified the three most important steps, prioritize them in order of importance. Determine which one is the most critical and which one can be completed in a more flexible time frame.

3. **Take action.**
   Finally, take action on the most important step first. Once it is complete, move on to the second most important step, and so on. By focusing on the most important tasks, you'll achieve greater success in less time.

9 — Preparation is key.

This concept emphasizes the importance of planning and preparing before starting a task. The idea is that proper preparation leads to more efficient and effective work. To implement this concept, the author suggests that individuals should take time to gather all necessary materials, plan out the steps needed to complete the task, and anticipate potential challenges or obstacles. By doing so, individuals can work more efficiently and effectively. The author provides two important lessons to take from this concept:

1. **Saves time.**
   Taking the time to prepare thoroughly before starting a task can save time in the long run. Individuals can avoid unnecessary delays and interruptions by anticipating potential challenges and having all the necessary materials on hand.

2. **Reduces stress.**
   Proper preparation can also reduce stress and anxiety. Individuals can approach the task with greater ease and calm by having a clear plan of action and feeling confident in their ability to complete the task.

10 — Do your homework.

This concept focuses on breaking down big, overwhelming tasks into smaller, more manageable steps. By doing so, individuals can progress toward their goals and feel a sense of accomplishment. The author provides two important lessons to take from this concept:

1. **Promotes motivation and momentum.**
   When individuals see progress toward their goals, even if it's just a small step, they feel more motivated to keep going. Each small step builds momentum toward the larger goal, making it easier to stay on track and avoid procrastination.

2. **Allows for greater flexibility and adaptability.**
   When a task is broken down into smaller steps, individuals can adjust their plans more easily if circumstances change or unexpected obstacles arise. They can adjust their approach and continue progressing, rather than feeling stuck and unsure how to proceed.

11 — Utilize your special skills.

This step emphasizes the importance of continually developing and improving your key skills to achieve greater success in your personal and professional life. He suggests that consistently upgrading your skills can increase your value to your employer or clients, improve your earning potential, and enhance your personal growth and fulfillment. The author provides two important lessons to take from this concept:

1. **Identify your key skills.**
   To upgrade your key skills, it is important to first identify what they are. Take time to reflect on the skills essential for success in your current or

desired career. This could include technical skills, communication skills, leadership skills, or any other skills that are relevant to your field.

2. **Invest in your development.**
   Once you have identified your key skills, it is important to invest in your development. This could include taking courses, attending workshops or conferences, reading books, or finding a mentor. By investing in your development, you can stay up-to-date with the latest trends and best practices in your field, and continually improve your abilities.

12 — Leverage your special talents.

The principle focuses on the importance of leveraging your special talents to maximize your effectiveness and achieve success in your personal and professional life. The author argues that by focusing on your strengths and unique abilities, you can make a greater impact and achieve more significant results. The author provides two important lessons to take from this concept:

1. **Everyone has a unique set of skills and abilities that they can use to achieve their goals.**
   By recognizing and leveraging these talents, individuals can maximize their potential and increase their chances of success. This involves identifying your strengths, weaknesses, and areas of interest, and then developing a plan to build on your strengths while addressing any weaknesses.

2. **Focus on the areas where you excel, rather than trying to be good at everything.**
   This means setting goals that align with your strengths and prioritizing tasks that allow you to use your talents to the fullest extent. By doing so, you can work more efficiently and effectively, leading to greater satisfaction and success.

13 — Identify your key constraints.

This concept is about identifying the main obstacles preventing you from achieving your goals and finding ways to overcome them.

The author suggests it is important to identify the constraints that are holding you back, such as lack of time, money, resources, or skills. Once you identify these constraints, you can come up with a plan to overcome them and move forward toward your goals.

Here are two important lessons about why identifying key constraints is important:

1. **Helps you focus on the most important obstacles.**
   By identifying the key constraints, you can focus your attention and resources on the most important obstacles holding you back. This will help you avoid wasting time and energy on less important issues and focus on the ones most critical to your success.

2. **Boosts your confidence.**
   Overcoming constraints and achieving your goals can be a great confidence booster. By identifying your key constraints and finding ways to overcome them, you can develop confidence and self-efficacy that can help you tackle future challenges.

14 — Put the pressure on yourself.

It is based on the premise that setting high standards for yourself and applying pressure on yourself can help you achieve your goals and become more productive.

To apply pressure on yourself, you must set specific and challenging goals. This involves breaking down your goals into smaller, achievable steps and giving yourself strict deadlines for completing them. By setting challenging goals and deadlines for yourself, you will feel motivated to work harder and be more productive.

Two important lessons can be learned from the concept of applying pressure on yourself:

1. **Setting challenging goals can help you achieve more.**
   When you set challenging goals for yourself, you push yourself to work harder and achieve more than you would if you had set easier goals. You will feel motivated to work harder and take on more challenging tasks by applying pressure on yourself.

2. **Self-discipline is crucial for success.**

   To apply pressure on yourself, you must have a high level of self-discipline. You must stay focused on your goals, even when faced with distractions or setbacks. Self-discipline is a key characteristic of successful people, and it is something that can be developed through practice.

15 — Maximize your powers.

This concept is based on the idea that individuals possess unique strengths and abilities that, when maximized, can lead to greater productivity, effectiveness, and success.

Maximizing your powers involves identifying your strengths and leveraging them to your advantage. It requires a deep understanding of your skills, abilities, and passions, and a commitment to developing and utilizing them to their fullest potential. The author provides two important lessons to take from this concept:

1. **Know yourself.**

   The first step in maximizing your power is clearly understanding your strengths and weaknesses. Take some time to reflect on your skills, interests, and passions, and consider how you can leverage them to achieve your goals. Understanding your personal powers can help you make better decisions, set achievable goals, and stay motivated.

2. **Focus on your strengths.**

   Once you have identified your personal powers, focus on developing them further. Rather than trying to improve in areas where you are weak, focus on honing your strengths and becoming exceptional at them. This will help you stand out from the crowd and excel in your chosen field.

16 — Take action by motivating yourself.

The author stresses the importance of motivating oneself into action. He suggests that successful people are highly motivated and take action toward their goals with enthusiasm and energy. He provides practical strategies for individuals to increase their motivation and achieve success. The author provides two important lessons to take from this concept:

1. **Find your WHY.**

   Understanding the purpose behind what you want to accomplish is critical in motivating yourself. When you clearly understand WHY you want to achieve a particular goal, staying motivated and focused on the task is easier. It is important to be specific and clear about your WHY to help you stay on track.

2. **Visualize the result.**

   Visualization is a powerful tool that can help you to see your goals as already accomplished. When you visualize the result, you create a sense of excitement and enthusiasm that will help motivate you to take action. Visualization helps you to create a mental image of what you want to achieve and see yourself already there.

17 — Technology is a terrible master.

Technology has become an essential part of our daily lives in today's digital age. While it has made many things easier and more convenient, it can also be a significant source of distraction and time-wasting.

The author explains that while technology can be a useful tool, it can also be a major time-waster if not used correctly. He recommends several strategies to avoid technological time drain, such as setting specific times to check email, turning off notifications on devices, and using apps that help limit distractions. The author provides two important lessons to take from this concept:

1. **Technology can be both a blessing and a curse.**

   While it has made many things easier and more efficient, it can also be a significant source of distraction and time-wasting. It's important to recognize how technology can harm our productivity and take steps to minimize those negative effects.

2. **It's up to us to take control of our use of technology.**

   Setting boundaries and limiting our use of technology can help us be more productive. By setting specific times to check email or social media, for example, we can avoid constant interruptions and stay focused on important tasks.

18 — Slice and dice the task.

Break up big and complicated tasks into smaller steps that are easier to handle. After a small step, you can move on to the next. By breaking a large task into smaller, more manageable pieces, we can gain momentum and build confidence as we accomplish each step. The author recommends creating a list of small, concrete steps to achieve each task, which should be prioritized based on their importance. The author provides two important lessons to take from this concept:

1. **Helps to overcome procrastination.**
   Many people often procrastinate because the task seems overwhelming or intimidating. By breaking down a task into smaller, more manageable parts, we can reduce the sense of overwhelm and make it easier to get started.

2. **Improves focus and time management.**
   When we slice a task into smaller pieces, we can prioritize our work and focus on the most important steps. This helps us to manage our time more effectively and avoid getting bogged down by unimportant details.

19 — Create large chunks of time.

The author suggests it's important to identify your most important tasks and schedule dedicated time for them. This means setting aside large chunks of time, such as a half-day or a full day, to work on these tasks without interruption. The author provides two important lessons to take from this concept:

1. **Avoid multitasking.**
   Multitasking can be tempting when you're short on time, but it's counterproductive. By focusing on one task at a time, you can complete it more efficiently and effectively, ultimately saving time in the long run.

2. **Prioritization is key.**
   To create large chunks of time for important tasks, you must first identify what those tasks are. By prioritizing your to-do list and focusing on the most important tasks first, you can ensure you're using your time wisely.

20 — Develop a sense of urgency.

This concept emphasizes the importance of taking action quickly and efficiently to succeed. The author believes that a sense of urgency is essential for anyone who wants to be productive and achieve their goals. The author provides two important lessons to take from this concept:

1. **Time is a valuable resource.**
   Developing a sense of urgency helps you to appreciate the value of time and to use it more wisely. By focusing on what is truly important and urgent, you can accomplish more in less time and achieve greater success.

2. **Procrastination is the enemy of success.**
   Procrastination is the opposite of urgency and can be a major obstacle to achieving your goals. By developing a sense of urgency, you can overcome procrastination and take action to achieve your objectives.

21 — Single-handedly perform every task.

The concept focuses on the importance of focusing on one task at a time and completing it before moving on to the next task. The idea is to give full attention and effort to each task without distraction, leading to increased productivity and better results. Single-handling tasks involve setting clear priorities, eliminating distractions, and committing to completing each task before moving on to the next. The author provides two important lessons to take from this concept:

1. **Eliminate distractions.**
   Single-handling tasks require eliminating distractions, such as email notifications, social media, and phone calls, which can interrupt focus and decrease productivity. By turning off notifications and minimizing distractions, individuals can increase their ability to focus and complete tasks more efficiently.

2. **Stay committed.**
   To successfully single-handle tasks, individuals must commit to completing each task before moving on to the next. This requires discipline, focus, and a strong work ethic. Individuals can increase their productivity

and achieve better results by committing to completing each task fully and without distraction.

KEY LESSONS

1. **To reach an ambitious goal, you need to make a detailed plan.**
   If you can see exactly how you will get from point A to point B, you will be more likely to reach your goals.

2. **Make sure you understand what's important to you.**
   Using the ABCDE method, you can rank your tasks from most important to least important, with A being the most important.

3. **You will be more likely to reach your goals if you learn more about yourself.**
   As you become more aware of the skills you have, you will be able to see why other people value you.

4. **Do not forget the significance of your destination.**
   To achieve your goals, it is crucial to seize the opportunities that come your way, work diligently, and take responsibility for yourself.

5. **You should be ready for any problems that might come up.**
   Once you acknowledge that your obstacles are holding you back, you can overcome them.

ACTIONABLE STEPS TO TAKE

➤ **Prioritize tasks.**

Prioritizing tasks helps to focus on the most important and impactful tasks first, increasing efficiency and productivity.

➤ **Set achievable and specific goals.**

Setting achievable and specific goals provides a clear target to work towards and helps to measure progress.

➤ **Plan and organize.**

Planning and organizing help to manage time effectively and reduce the risk of forgetfulness or missed deadlines.

➤ **Break tasks into smaller, manageable chunks.**

Breaking tasks into smaller chunks helps avoid feeling overwhelmed, making it easier to get started and make progress.

➤ **Eliminate distractions.**

Eliminating distractions helps to stay focused and increase productivity.

➤ **Use the *two-minute rule*.**

The *two-minute rule* involves starting a task if it can be completed in two minutes or less, helping to avoid procrastination.

➤ **Focus on one task at a time.**

Focusing on one task at a time helps to avoid distractions and increase productivity.

➤ **Use the 80/20 rule.**

The 80/20 rule, also known as the Pareto Principle, states that 80% of results come from 20% of effort, and helps to prioritize tasks.

➤ **Set deadlines.**

Setting deadlines motivates to complete tasks and helps to manage time effectively.

➤ **Take breaks.**

Taking regular breaks helps to reduce stress, increase focus, and maintain energy levels throughout the day.

Atomic Habits

by James Clear

"You are the master of your destiny. You can influence, direct and control your own environment. You can make your life what you want it to be."

T HIS book is a comprehensive guide to understanding the science of habit formation and how to use it to make positive changes in one's life. The book provides practical strategies for developing good habits, breaking bad ones, and improving overall productivity and effectiveness.

The book begins by explaining the importance of habits, and how they are formed and reinforced through a cycle of cue, craving, response, and reward. It argues that by understanding this cycle, individuals can learn to create and reinforce good habits and break bad ones.

The author then introduces the concept of *atomic habits,* which he defines as small, incremental changes that are easy to implement and sustain over time. He argues that individuals can build momentum and achieve significant results by focusing on small, consistent changes.

The book also provides strategies for breaking bad habits, including identifying the triggers and rewards that drive them, and replacing them with healthier alternatives. The book emphasizes the importance of self-awareness and self-reflection, and suggests that individuals should develop a growth mindset and be willing to learn from their failures and setbacks.

Goals vs Systems

As you strive towards achieving your desired outcomes, evaluating whether your current habits are aiding or hindering your progress is crucial. Focusing solely on the outcomes you are currently achieving may distract you from the direction you're heading. Instead of fixating on specific goals, improving your systems to achieve better outcomes, in the long run, is essential. Adapting this mindset will ensure that your goals align with your actions, leading to more significant progress. The author presents some ways to differentiate between these two ideas:

➤ The point of goals is to get the results you want. Systems are meant to make sure that these results are reached.

➤ Having goals gives you direction, but systems help you move forward.

➤ The goals of winners and losers are the same.

➤ Getting a goal done is only a short-term change.

➤ Your goals keep you from being happy.

➤ Long-term progress conflicts with short-term goals.

➤ The point of setting goals is to win the game. Putting together systems is a way to keep playing the game.

➤ Your goals are not a good way to measure your performance. Your system tells you how you have to act.

The Three Levels of Behavior Change

➤ **Level 1 — Change your outcomes.**
This level focuses on attaining a specific outcome:

- Losing weight.
- Publishing a book.
- Winning a championship.

This level is usually associated with the majority of your goals.

➤ **Level 2 — Change the process.**
The goal of this level is to make you change your habits and ways of doing things:

- To establish new routines at the gym.
- Declutter your desk for improved productivity.
- To begin meditating.

Most of the habits you pick up come from this level.

➤ **Level 3 — Change your identity.**

In this level, your ideas and beliefs will change:

- Your worldview.

- Your self-image.

- Your verdicts regarding yourself and others.

This level describes most of your beliefs, assumptions, and biases.

The Habit Loop

Developing effective habits is essential for dealing with life's challenges swiftly and efficiently. A habit's foundation lies in the cue, as it triggers the brain to initiate a specific action that it perceives will lead to a reward. Subsequently, a desire emerges, driven by the positive feeling associated with the anticipated reward. The habit then forms as a response to the cue and the desire, which can be either a thought or an action. Ultimately, the reward serves as the reinforcement that reinforces the habit. Therefore, understanding the process of habit formation is crucial in developing effective habits that help you overcome life's obstacles.

How to Create a Good Habit

To effectively create a good habit, the book outlines several strategies one can employ. Here are some of the recommended guidelines:

➤ The 1st Law (Cue) — **Clearly state it.**

- Get the scorecard for the habit and fill it out. Write down your habits to help you become more aware of them.

- It's important to say what you plan to do: *"I will start doing [BE-HAVIOR] at [TIME] in [PLACE]."*

- Put the habits in this order: *"After I do [CURRENT HABIT], I'll do [NEW HABIT]."*

- Make sure that the place you live helps you form new good habits.

➤ The 2nd Law (Craving) — **Enhance its appeal.**

- Use temptation bundling to do both things you want to do and things you have to do.
- Join a group where the way you want people to act is the norm.
- Make a motivation ritual by doing something you enjoy right before you do something hard.

➤ The 3rd Law (Response) — **Make it simple for yourself.**

- Reduce friction and frictional barriers to make it easier to stick to good habits and reduce the number of steps you must take.
- By priming and preparing your environment, you can make it easier to do things in the future.
- Master the decisive moment and make the best of the small decisions with big effects.
- The two-minute rule says that you should change your habits so that they can be done in two minutes or less.
- Make your habits automatic and invest in technology that will keep you from changing in the future.

➤ The 4th Law (Reward) — **Ensure it's satisfying.**

- Reinforce yourself right after you do your habit by rewarding yourself.
- Make *"doing nothing"* fun and think of ways to show how good it is to avoid bad habits.
- Use a habit tracker to track your habits and ensure you don't break the chain.
- Make sure you never skip a habit twice, and if you do, get back on track as soon as possible.

How to Break a Bad Habit

To effectively break a bad habit, the book outlines several strategies one can employ. Here are some of the recommended guidelines:

➤ The 1st Law (Cue) — **Ensure it's invisible.**

- Find and eliminate the things in your environment that remind you of your bad habits.

➤ The 2nd Law (Craving) — **Don't make it attractive.**

- To stop bad habits, you need to change your thinking and focus on how good it will make you feel.

➤ The 3rd Law (Response) — **Ensure that it is difficult.**

- Increase the friction and number of steps between you and your bad habits to get further away from them.
- Buy a commitment device to make sure that the decisions you make in the future will be good for you.

➤ The 4th Law (Reward) — **Unsatisfy it or add penalties.**

- Consider getting a partner to hold you accountable and ask someone to watch your actions.
- Set up a habit contract and make it clear and painful what will happen if you don't change your bad habits.

KEY LESSONS

1. **We can make a difference if we develop good, reliable habits.**
   You can do many small daily things that will make a big difference in your life.

2. **The things that happen to us shape the habits we have.**
   Our habits are learned through trial and error throughout our lives.

3. **Signals keep telling us to do things in a certain way.**
   Even small things can turn into habits that are hard to break.

4. **If you make your habits fun, you'll likely stick with them.**
   Creating habits that make you feel good can encourage you to keep doing them.

5. **When making new habits, it's important to keep things simple.**
   In general, if something happens as a natural result, it is more likely that you will keep doing it as a habit.

ACTIONABLE STEPS TO TAKE

➤ **Identify your keystone habits.**
These are the habits that have the greatest impact on your life. Focusing on these keystone habits allows you to leverage small changes to create big results.

➤ **Make your habits obvious.**
Make it easy to see when you need to do your habit by putting reminders where you will see them.

➤ **Make your habits attractive.**
Make your habit more desirable by linking it to something you already enjoy.

➤ **Make your habits easy to perform.**
Reduce friction and increase accessibility so that your habit is easy to perform.

➤ **Make it satisfying.**
Create an immediate reward for your habit.

➤ **Create an implementation intention.**
Write down the habit you want to create, when you will do it, and where you will do it.

➤ **Use habit stacking.**
Stack a new habit on top of an existing habit.

➤ **Join a culture where your desired habit is the normal behavior.**
Surround yourself with people who already have the habit you want to create.

➤ **Create a system of habits.**
Build a collection of habits that support your goals.

➤ **Reframe your failures as feedback.**
Instead of seeing failures as a setback, use them as an opportunity to learn and improve your habit-forming process.

The 4-Hour Workweek

by Tim Ferriss

"What we fear doing most is usually what we most need to do."

T HIS book is the blueprint for figuring out how to live your life. Follow a simple step-by-step process to learn how to reinvent yourself, work more efficiently, start a business, and live a luxurious life that puts time and mobility first. The first goal of this book is to help anyone become more productive. The next goal is to help people spend less time at work, and the last goal is to help people quit their jobs and follow their dreams. This is a powerful book for people who want to put living before working.

The book guides achieving financial freedom and creating the lifestyle you want, by working smarter instead of harder. The author shares his personal experiences and gives practical advice on how to escape the 9-to-5 workweek, automate your income, and create a life filled with more free time, travel, and adventure.

The book emphasizes the importance of creating a *low-information diet* and minimizing distractions from emails, social media, and other time-wasting activities. He also provides practical advice on how to negotiate for more flexible work arrangements, and how to create a successful online business.

The Structure of the Book: DEAL

It's unnecessary to resign from your job, possesses youth, has a proclivity for risk-taking, or be unattached to apply the tactics elucidated in this book. Nor is it obligatory to come from a privileged background or attend an elite university to thrive in life. The deferred-life approach is a *fragile collection of socially reinforced illusions* that anyone can break away from.

The author has a deep-seated dread of achieving high comfort and living an unfulfilling life. Thus, we must question, *"How can one lead the life of a millionaire with absolute autonomy without having a million dollars?"* The author presents you with the book's framework that helps you start:

➤ **D is for Definition.**

A short explanation of the game and how to play it. In this section, you'll learn about the basics and recipes of the lifestyle design.

➤ **E is for Elimination.**

The old idea of how to manage time is eliminated for good. The best way to get ten times or more as much done in an hour is to be selective about what you don't know, eat less information, and ignore what doesn't matter. The first of the three parts of luxury lifestyle design that are emphasized are: **TIME.**

➤ **A is for Automation.**

Cash flow is automated by using geographic arbitrage, outsourcing, and rules for not making a choice. This is the second thing that makes luxury lifestyles possible: **INCOME.**

➤ **L is for Liberation.**

The mobile strategy is for people who look at the world as a whole. This part talks about how to break the chains that keep you stuck in one place. In the next part, we'll discuss the third and last part of luxury lifestyle design: **MOBILITY.**

Step 1 — D is for Definition

Stop working just to work. As discussed in the book, the ability to be flexible with time and location can lead to significant increases in income, ranging from three to ten times more than one's current earnings. However, the value of money extends beyond its monetary worth, as it can also afford individuals the power to make independent decisions regarding how, when, where, and with whom they choose to work. This concept is referred to as the *freedom multiplier,* and in the book, the author delves into the four W's that amplify the value of money:

➤ What you do.

➤ When you do it.

➤ Where you do it.

➤ Whom you do it with.

The Rules that Change the Rules

The author emphasizes the importance of breaking free from the traditional work mindset and developing a new set of rules to achieve success more efficiently and effectively. According to the book, the key to success is not simply following the established rules but creating your own rules that can change the game entirely. By developing a new set of rules prioritizing productivity, efficiency, and freedom, you can succeed in ways you never thought possible. This principle challenges individuals to question the status quo and think outside the box, ultimately leading to greater success and fulfillment in work and life.

The author provides a comprehensive list of ten ways in which individuals can transform and overcome the traditional path and they are:

1. **Retirement is a form of insurance for the worst case scenario.**
   The whole idea of retirement is based on the idea that we don't enjoy what we're doing when we're at our best physically. This is a horrible and unfair way to look at life. Given how things are in the current economy, most people can't save enough money to live above the poverty line in retirement. Only very ambitious and determined people could reach such a goal. If you're one of them, do you want to sit around and do nothing? You probably want a new job, so why did you wait so long?

2. **There is a cyclical relationship between interest and energy.**
   It is important to strike a balance between work and rest, just as it is necessary to alternate between different phases in one's career. Taking periodic mini-retirements at different points throughout one's life not only allows for increased enjoyment and relaxation but also ultimately leads to greater productivity and success in the workplace. By breaking from the traditional model of working non-stop for decades and instead incorporating rest and rejuvenation into one's life, individuals can achieve a more fulfilling and balanced existence.

3. **Less is not laziness.**

Traditional culture often places more emphasis on personal sacrifice and working long hours. The author argues that laziness is not equivalent to working less, but instead refers to a lack of control over one's life and passively watching opportunities pass by. The *New Rich* prioritize maximizing their time and effort, focusing on effectiveness rather than the appearance of effort, which allows them to achieve more in less time.

4. **Timing is never perfect.**

To achieve success in life, it is important to let go of the traditional approach of making a list of pros and cons before making any decision. Instead, one should take immediate action and start working towards their desired future. Waiting for the perfect time or making excuses with *"someday"* will only hinder one's progress and lead to unfulfilled dreams.

5. **Don't ask permission, ask forgiveness.**

Many people reject opportunities because of their initial feelings or doubts, but may eventually agree once the job is done. It's important to not let initial rejection discourage you. If the situation allows for it and the consequences aren't severe, it's often better to proceed with the task rather than to let the opportunity pass. Even if you have to ask for forgiveness later, taking action can often lead to positive results that wouldn't have happened if you had simply given up.

6. **Focus on strengths instead of weaknesses.**

Focus on one's strengths often yields greater benefits than attempting to improve on one's weaknesses. Building on one's natural strengths can lead to a compounding effect, whereas trying to fix weaknesses often results in incremental progress at best. Instead of spending valuable time and energy trying to fix weaknesses, individuals should focus on honing their strengths and leveraging them to achieve greater success in all aspects of their lives.

7. **Excessive things produce their opposite.**

You can achieve balance in your life by focusing on time and things. The book aims not merely to provide you with more free time, but rather to teach you how to use that time in a manner that aligns with your desires and aspirations, rather than being burdened by obligations that hold you back.

8. **The solution cannot be provided solely by money.**

Many people believe that increasing their income solves all their problems. However, this is not always the case. Focusing solely on earning more money can prevent us from addressing the root of the problem. Identifying and eliminating unnecessary expenses may be more effective rather than constantly striving for more money.

9. **The relative income of a person is more important than his or her total income.**

According to the author, measuring success based on relative income is a more effective way to evaluate time and money. For instance, an individual who works 10 hours a week and earns $10,000 could be considered wealthier than someone who works 80 hours a week and earns $100,000. By focusing on relative income, individuals can better appreciate the value of time and how to use it to achieve their desired lifestyle.

10. **Eustress is better than distress.**

Positive stress, which is also known as *"eustress,"* is the kind of stress that can help individuals grow and develop. Contrary to common misconceptions, stress can be good for individuals and should not be avoided simply because it is uncomfortable or challenging.

Dodging Bullets

The fear of the unknown often keeps people from trying new things, even if their current situation makes them unhappy. To overcome this fear, the author suggests imagining the worst-case scenario in detail and brainstorming ways to survive it. Doing this lets you identify your specific fears and develop a plan to face them. This process can help you overcome your fear and take steps to achieve your goals. Write down your answer to each question to help you figure out what you're afraid of:

1. **Identify the impact of the future.**
   What could go wrong, anyway? How bad would the situation be in the near future, on a scale of 1 to 10? How likely do you think these things are to happen?

2. **Damage control.**
   Would it be possible for you to fix what's broken? Could you get things back under control?

3. **Consider the upside.**
   What are the most likely results and possible short-term and long-term benefits?

4. **Correct mistakes.**
   How would you handle your money if you lost your job today? How could you return to the same career path if you quit your job to try something different?

5. **Identify your action.**
   Do you put something off because you're afraid? The thing we most fear doing is the thing we must do. Find the worst-case scenario, accept it, and do something about it. Do something you're afraid of every day.

6. **Be aware of the costs.**
   How much are you losing financially, emotionally, and physically because you aren't taking action? Think about the good about taking action. It is also important to measure the costs of doing nothing. Where will you be in a year, five, or ten years if you don't do what makes you happy?

7. **Identify your fears.**
   When will it be done? When you can only say *"timing,"* you are just scared, like everyone else. Think about how much it will cost you to do nothing, and realize that most mistakes won't be fixed. You should learn the most important habit of people who are good at what they do and love it: act.

Step 2 — E is for Elimination

The key to being efficient and effective is to do the right things in the least amount of time. The universe's default mode is to be efficient without caring about how well it works. Here are three important things to always remember:

➤ Even if you are good at something that isn't important, that doesn't make it important.

➤ Just because something takes time doesn't make it more important.

➤ What a person does is more important than how they do it.

Pay attention to what matters. Apply the 80/20 principle to everything. This principle applies to almost every aspect of life, from business to personal life. By focusing on the 20% that produces the most results, you can maximize your efficiency and productivity while minimizing wasted effort.

For example, in business, the 80/20 principle means that 80% of your revenue comes from 20% of your customers. This means you can increase your revenue by focusing on the top 20% of your customers, rather than trying to appeal to the entire customer base. In your personal life, the principle means that 80% of your happiness comes from 20% of your activities. This means you can increase your happiness by focusing on the activities that bring you the most joy, rather than wasting time on activities that don't significantly impact you.

The 80/20 principle is not just about focusing on the top 20%, it is also about eliminating the bottom 80%. This means identifying the 80% of the activities that produce only 20% of the results and either delegating or eliminating them. Doing so can free up time and resources to focus on the top 20%, which will produce the most results.

The Art of Refusal

Being assertive is an important skill to have, both in school and in life. Learning how to stand your ground when it counts can result in better treatment from others. However, this doesn't mean you must constantly beg or fight for what you want. Recognizing and eliminating interruptions hindering your progress toward important tasks is also important.

An interruption keeps you from doing a very important task from start to finish. Here are the three main things that cause interruptions:

1. **Time waste.**
   Things that won't hurt you if you ignore them.

2. **Time consumers.**
   Work that needs to be done but is boring or gets in the way of more important work.

3. **Empowerment failures.**
   When something small needs to be done, it needs to be approved.

The Art of Refusal is an essential skill that can help individuals reclaim their time and focus on their most important tasks. The book suggests that individuals should learn to say NO more often, especially to requests or tasks that don't align with their goals and priorities. Many people struggle with saying NO because they fear that it may harm their relationships or reputation. However, learning to decline politely can help individuals gain respect and preserve their time and energy. The author advises individuals to focus on their priorities and delegate or outsource tasks that don't require their specific expertise.

Step 3 — A is for Automation

Two of the most important skills for joining the *New Rich* are communicating and managing things remotely. The author suggests hiring a digital assistant to do this task so that you can get used to giving orders to others. One important part of being a *New Rich* is being able to replace yourself with a system.

The author is cautious against delegation without proper preparation. Before delegating any task, it's essential to ensure its purpose and importance are clear. Furthermore, it's essential to eliminate unnecessary tasks before the delegation. The author advises against automating tasks that can be accomplished without a computer and delegating tasks that can be automated. To get started with automating your life, the author provides several helpful tips:

➤ Employ an assistant, even if you don't require one.

➤ Start small but think big. Look at what's been on your list the longest, think about what makes you the most angry or bored, and give these tasks to someone else if necessary.

➤ Choose the five things you do outside of work that take you the most time and the five things you might do just for fun.

➤ Make plans and use calendars to keep in touch.

In the book, the author emphasizes the importance of creating a virtual architecture — a service-based business that can be transformed into a downloadable product. Developing new products is a key component of business architecture, as is managing cash flow and timeframes. Without these elements in place, achieving success is nearly impossible. The book provides practical guidance on how to join the *New Rich* by following these steps:

➤ **Step 1 — Choose a market segment that is affordable and reachable.** Filling demand is easier than generating demand. Find out who your customer is, and then make just the right products for them. You can't do business with everyone.

➤ **Step 2 — Invent new products and market.** To succeed in business, you must capitalize on your strengths and target markets that you know best. This might mean identifying magazines or other publications that cater to your niche and investing in full-page ads that cost less than $5,000. When pricing your product, aim for a range between 50 and 200 pounds, as this can attract higher-quality customers and lead to fewer questions and concerns.

➤ **Step 3 — Availability and distribution.** In business, products can take many forms, from tangible physical goods to digital services. The beauty of a product lies in its potential to be sold multiple times, licensed out to others, or even remade with improvements.

➤ **Step 4 — Testing your products on a small scale.** In the world of entrepreneurship, relying solely on intuition and experience to gauge the potential profitability of a product or business may not always lead to success. To effectively test the viability of a business idea, the author recommends creating a one- to three-page website with an offer that is more appealing than your competitors. This can be done using Google AdWords to test the offer's effectiveness for three hours to five days.

➤ **Step 5 — Focus on the end goal.**
Organizational charts have long been a staple of business planning, but their purpose can vary greatly depending on the desired outcome. Contrary to popular belief, the goal should not always be to scale a business as large as possible. Rather, the key is to create an organizational structure that minimizes potential problems and maximizes efficiency.

Step 4 — L is for Liberation

Be careful about how and when you try to get out of work. There are a few things you can do if you work for a company and want to live as the *New Riches* do, with no restrictions on where you live:

➤ **Make sure your employer puts money into you.**
You should persuade your boss to pay for your training to make yourself more valuable to the company.

➤ **Show that you can get more done when you're not at the office.**
If you get sick for two days in the middle of the week, you should work twice as hard.

➤ **Find the benefits that can be measured for the company.**
Write out what you have done outside of work in bullet points and explain each.

➤ **Recommend a temporary trial period.**
Offer to try out working from home one day a week for two weeks.

➤ **Consider expanding the use of remote time.**
Make the most of the days you work from home. Make it possible to work from home four days a week for a trial period of two weeks.

Ideas to Escape Normal

It's important to have a clear vision of what you want your life to look like, rather than just following the crowd. This is the essence of *Lifestyle Design*. However, many overlook this step and get stuck in a mundane 9-to-5 routine. To avoid this, the author advises planning out the life you want in the future and then making choices that align with your goals. It's important to question the norms of our society and understand why people follow them. Doing so lets you identify what matters most to you and create a lifestyle that aligns with your values and aspirations. This process requires introspection and self-awareness but can ultimately lead to a more fulfilling and purposeful life.

Using these simple tools for setting goals can help you stand out from the crowd and live the life you've always wanted:

➤ **Prepare a list of goals.**
Spend a few minutes writing down what you hope to become, have, and accomplish in the next year or two. Include skills, experiences, and possessions you hope to acquire.

➤ **The cost of the lifestyle design should be estimated.**
Find out how much each of these things costs each month. You will then be given a number called Target Monthly Income (TMI), which you should try to reach.

Ideas for Passive Income

Aspiring entrepreneurs often find themselves struggling to strike a balance between work and personal life. Many are forced to work long hours and handle copious amounts of stress, particularly if they have a business. However, some types of businesses offer the possibility of a 4-hour workweek. These businesses allow you to work on your terms and give you the freedom to create your schedule. Below are four types of businesses that have the potential to achieve this goal:

➤ **Information products.**
Books, audiobooks, courses, seminars, and other things are on the list. The author says this business is the best because it has low start-up costs

and product costs and is hard to copy later. Even if you don't know much about a subject, if you study it for a few months or weeks, you might be able to make something that beginners will find useful.

➤ **Physical products.**
You will need to contact manufacturers to make your product idea a reality. The process may seem hard and expensive, but it's not always that way. About $5,000 was how much the author spent on his first batch of supplements.

➤ **Re-selling.**
You can sell your products and products from other companies. For instance, dropshipping is when you sell products on your website and then send the orders to another company to fill. This can be a low-profit business that starts quickly but is also very competitive and low-profit.

➤ **Licensing.**
Royalties can be paid to people whose ideas are used by companies. Authors, musicians, and people who come up with new ideas can all get royalties. But you could look for people who already have a well-known brand and pay them a royalty to make products that are sure to sell.

Beyond Repair — Killing Your Job

In the world of work, some projects simply cannot be salvaged. Pouring more time and resources into them won't necessarily make them worthwhile. Successful individuals are adept at recognizing and letting go of what isn't working. To that end, here are some solutions to common anxieties related to quitting:

1. **Quitting is a permanent decision.**
   Think about what it would be like if you used fear-setting to go back to your chosen career path or start a business later on.

2. **The bills will not be paid.**
   Most expenses can be put on hold temporarily, and you can live off your savings for a while.

3. **The health insurance and retirement accounts will be eliminated.**
   Similar health insurance can be had for a few hundred dollars a month less than it is now. It's easy to move a 401(k) account.

4. **My resume will not look good.**
   Do something interesting that will make them want to be you.

New Rich Mistakes

The concept of the *New Rich* highlights a new way of thinking about wealth and work. While this lifestyle offers many benefits, there are also many mistakes that those pursuing it can make. Here are ten common mistakes that the *New Rich* often make:

1. Fall into the trap of being too busy to enjoy their newfound wealth and freedom.

2. Fail to create a system that allows them to effectively manage their time and resources.

3. Become too focused on increasing their income, which can lead to burnout and stress.

4. Failure to set clear priorities and goals can make it difficult to stay on track.

5. Underestimate the importance of building a solid support system, including a strong network of mentors, advisors, and peers.

6. Overlook the value of investing in their personal growth and development.

7. Don't always consider the long-term consequences of their decisions, especially regarding financial planning.

8. Fall into the trap of thinking that money is the only measure of success, neglecting other important aspects of life like relationships, health, and personal fulfillment.

9. Become too attached to their businesses or investments, making it difficult to let go of them when it's time to move on.

10. Fail to recognize the importance of giving back and positively impacting the world around them.

KEY LESSONS

1. **You don't have to be a millionaire to live like one.**
   The good things in life can now be enjoyed (traveling extensively, bold hobbies, and personal assistants). This goal is not impossible and can be reached right now.

2. **Consider what could go wrong and the worst-case scenarios when making big decisions.**
   When you look at the worst-case scenario, most big decisions don't seem nearly as risky as they did at first.

3. **You can live a free life if you set up your income to work for you.**
   If you want to live your life how you want, you shouldn't have to work to make money.

4. **Use the 80/20 rule to figure out how you should spend your time.**
   Most of your results come from 20% of your efforts, so set your priorities by spending most of your time on those 20% of activities that will give you the most results.

5. **Outsourcing work is the best way to get the most out of a business.**
   Outsourcing tasks you don't want to do or aren't good at is a good way to get more done and free up time.

6. **You need to remember that money has a relative value.**
   Think about how much money you make per hour and how much freedom that gives you.

7. **Make the most of mini-retirements and geoarbitrage.**
   By living in cheap countries for a while and making a passive income at a level similar to the US, you can make a big difference in your finances and quality of life.

8. **Get rid of information and interruptions that you don't need.**
   It can be hard to focus and waste time if you watch TV and go to meetings simultaneously. Keep your attention as narrow as you can.

ACTIONABLE STEPS TO TAKE

➤ **Define your ideal lifestyle and work backward to determine your income requirements.**
This step is important because it helps you set clear and realistic financial goals to guide your actions and decision-making. Knowing your desired lifestyle allows you to focus on creating a business or finding a job supporting it.

➤ **Eliminate or automate as many tasks as possible in your work life.**
By automating or outsourcing tasks, you free up time to focus on higher-income-generating activities. This step is important because it helps you prioritize your time and energy to achieve more with less effort.

➤ **Create multiple streams of income.**
Diversifying your income streams allows you to have a safety net in case one stream dries up and can also lead to increased income overall. This step is important because it diversifies your income and reduces financial risk.

➤ **Learn to sell and market effectively.**
Selling and marketing your products or services is crucial for any business or career.

➤ **Learn to outsource effectively.**
Outsourcing can assist in time-saving and allow you to concentrate on activities that generate higher income.

➤ **Learn to use technology to work more efficiently.**
Technology can help you automate tasks and work more efficiently. This step is important because it helps you find ways to work more efficiently and effectively.

➤ **Learn to master time management.**
By managing your time effectively, you can be more productive and accomplish more in a shorter amount of time. his step is important because it helps you make the most of your time and achieve your goals more quickly.

The Power of Habit

by Charles Duhigg

"Change might not be fast and isn't always easy or beautiful. But with time and effort, almost any habit can be reshaped."

THIS book explores the science behind habits and how they can be changed. The author argues that habits are the key to understanding human behavior and that we can make significant changes in our lives by understanding how they work.

Habits can turn a limited resource like willpower into an unlimited one by making it easy to use. By putting what you learn in this book to use, your results will change significantly.

The book's main idea is that habits are powerful and can be changed. It explains that habits are neurological patterns that can be rewired through intentional effort. By understanding the science behind habits and how they work, individuals, organizations, and societies can intentionally create new habits or change existing ones to achieve their goals.

The book aims to help readers understand the science behind habits and how they can be changed. The author provides practical tools and strategies for readers to identify and change their habits. He argues that we can change our lives and achieve our goals by changing our habits.

The Habit Anatomy

As outlined in the book, when a habit is formed, the brain stops playing an active role in decision-making. This occurs when the brain doesn't put in as much effort or turns its attention to something else. Therefore, unless one intentionally seeks to change a habit, or forms new routines, the pattern will continue to occur subconsciously. There are three fundamental steps to creating a habit:

1. **Cues.**
   This is the trigger or cue that initiates the behavior. It can be a time of day, a location, a specific sound, or any other stimulus that elicits the desired action.

2. **Routines.**

This is the behavior itself. It can be a physical action or a mental thought process.

3. **Rewards.**

This is the positive reinforcement that the brain receives after the behavior has been completed. It can be a feeling of accomplishment, relief, or a tangible reward, such as a treat or a break.

Keystone Habits

In pursuing changing our lives or businesses for the better, some habits hold more weight than others. These habits, referred to as *keystone habits*, can significantly impact our work, diet, lifestyle, finances, and even relationships. Keystone habits are key priorities that can trigger positive changes in other areas of our lives when given sufficient power and attention. The beauty of keystone habits lies in their ability to teach us that perfection is not necessary for success. Rather, we need to identify and prioritize a few critical habits that will have a cascading effect on other areas of our lives. Regular physical activity is often cited as a prime example of a keystone habit, as it can lead to better sleep, improved dietary choices, and reduced alcohol intake, among other benefits. Focusing on the right keystone habits can create a powerful ripple effect that leads to lasting and meaningful change.

The Golden Rule of Habit Change

Habit change is a complex process that involves developing new routines and replacing old ones. To successfully change a habit, it is important to understand the structure of the habit loop. This is how the process works:

1. Identify the cue or trigger that initiates the habit.

2. Establish a new routine or behavior that replaces the old habit.

3. Reward yourself for completing the new behavior.

How to Change Your Habits

Understanding your habits is crucial to making changes in your life, and to do that, you must identify the elements that make up your habit loop. By pinpointing the cue, routine, and reward that shape a particular behavior, you can start to explore new ways of replacing old habits with new, positive ones. This process involves four key steps:

1. **Identify the routine.**

   ➤ Choose the response that is already there that you want to change. Some of these are eating, surfing the Internet, smoking, sleeping, biting your nails, or stuttering.

2. **Experiment with rewards.**

   ➤ Think about it for a few days, a week, or even longer.

   ➤ Try different rewards to determine what drives your routine and how to change your response.

   ➤ Right after you answer, write down the first three feelings, thoughts, or sensations that come to mind.

   ➤ Set a 15-minute timer to give the reward and response time to work.

   ➤ You should review your notes and decide if you still have the same desire.

3. **Isolate the cue.**

   ➤ When you have a craving, think about the following:
   - Your location.
   - When it is.
   - Your feelings.
   - Who is present.
   - Your recent activities or thoughts.

   ➤ Look for patterns in your notes to figure out what makes you want to eat.

4. **Establish a plan or eliminate the cue.**

➤ We can control most of the cues we get.

➤ The fastest way to stop a response from happening is to get rid of the cue.

➤ Cue elimination can be very effective because it doesn't require willpower.

KEY LESSONS

1. **The first step toward making a change is understanding the habit loop: cue, routine, reward.**
   An outside cue starts a habit, leading to a routine that ends with a reward.

2. **Getting into a habit is hard because it makes you want a reward.**
   As we get the reward, our brains become hardwired to look forward to it.

3. **The habit should be changed into a new routine for the cue to work.**
   If something outside of you triggers a different routine, you can still give yourself the same reward.

4. **Figure out what your most important habit is.**
   As a keystone habit keeps you on track with other good habits, the cornerstone of a building is a keystone habit.

5. **You can train your willpower.**
   You can build up your willpower by practicing and imagining yourself in a situation where you will need to use it.

6. **Ultimately, it's up to each person to change their habits.**
   Bad habits and the lack of good ones can make us unhappy and less productive and even hurt us and others. But you can change your behavior by knowing the cues, routines, and rewards.

ACTIONABLE STEPS TO TAKE

➤ **Understand the habit loop.**
The habit loop comprises a cue, a routine, and a reward. Understanding this loop is the first step to changing your habits.

➤ **Identify the keystone habits.**
Keystone habits are the habits that have the power to change other habits. Identifying these keystone habits can help you make changes to your overall behavior.

➤ **Create an implementation intention.**
An implementation intention is a plan for when and where you will perform a habit. Creating an implementation intention makes you more likely to follow through with the habit.

➤ **Make it easy.**
Make it as easy as possible to perform the habit by minimizing barriers to entry.

➤ **Use a habit stacking.**
Habit stacking is the process of attaching a new habit to an existing habit. This can make it easier to form new habits.

➤ **Reward yourself.**
Rewards are an important part of the habit loop. Incorporating rewards into your habit routine can help you stay motivated.

➤ **Join a culture where your desired habit is the normal behavior.**
The culture we surround ourselves with can greatly impact our habits. Joining a culture where the desired habit is normal behavior can make it easier to adopt the habit.

➤ **Practice *Temptation Bundling*.**
Temptation bundling is the process of pairing an action you want to do with an action you need to do. This can help you overcome resistance to forming new habits.

The Power of Less

by Leo Babauta

"Limit yourself to fewer goals, and you'll achieve more. At the same time, we'll look at ways to narrow your focus on your projects, so that you can complete them more effectively and move forward on your goals. We'll apply limitations to our projects to increase our effectiveness. Doing many things doesn't mean you're getting anything meaningful done."

T HIS self-help book offers practical advice on simplifying your life by focusing on essential tasks and eliminating unnecessary distractions. The book is divided into two parts, with the first focusing on the theory of minimalism and the second offering practical strategies to implement minimalism in your life.

The book's main idea is that we can achieve more by doing less. Instead of trying to do everything, the author encourages readers to focus on a few essential tasks to help them achieve their goals. The book argues that limiting our options and removing distractions can increase our productivity and achieve greater success in our personal and professional lives.

The author uses a minimalist approach to productivity, emphasizing the importance of identifying and focusing on the most important tasks while eliminating distractions and time-wasters. He believes that by doing less, we can accomplish more, and by focusing on the essentials, we can create more time and space for the things that truly matter.

The Principles

The modern world is increasingly marked by a high level of consumption and production of goods, both real and digital. When we do more, we tend to do more of the things that are easy and, most of the time, not very important. When we decide to do less, we can do much more important and necessary things, even if they are more difficult.

The book outlines six principles that can help individuals achieve more with less. These principles are based on the concept of simplification and focus.

Principle 1 — The Art of Setting Limits

By limiting what we can do, we can focus on the most important things. Limiting things makes things easier, helps us focus, makes our efforts more likely to succeed, and makes it easier to reach our goals.

➤ **Putting limits in place makes many things easier.**
Life is less stressful and easier to deal with.

➤ **Concentration is improved.**
So, you can put your energy into a smaller number of things.

➤ **Focus on important things.**
This will give you more time to spend on the things that matter.

Principle 2 — Choosing the Essential

By focusing on only the most important things, we get the most done with the least amount of effort. You should always pick the most important tasks to get the most out of your time and energy. It's important to figure out what's important. These questions will guide you to find them:

➤ **What are your values?**
Make a list of the things that are important to you. You should make a list of the qualities you'd like to have and the rules you'd like to live by.

➤ **What are your goals?**
Identify your life goals.

➤ **What do you love?**
Think about the things you like to do and the people you like to be with when you are the happiest.

Principle 3 — Eliminate the Non-essential

In today's fast-paced world, many people believe multitasking is the key to productivity. However, according to experts, the opposite is true. The more we try to juggle multiple tasks simultaneously, the less efficient and productive we become. Instead, the principle of *"less is more"* can be applied to productivity.

This means eliminating all non-essential tasks and focusing solely on the most important and impactful ones. Figure out these steps will help you eliminate the non-essential:

➤ **What has the most impact long-term?**
Find the thing or work that will be worth the most in the long run.

➤ **Needs vs wants.**
You can eliminate most of what you want by figuring out what you need. The things that aren't necessary should be taken away.

➤ **Which items do you need?**
By figuring out what you need, you can get rid of many of the things you don't need.

Principle 4 — Aspects to Focus

To be more effective, you must focus on the task at hand. The focus should be on having a clear goal. It's important to stay in the here and now. Also, it's important to pay attention to the task at hand (single-tasking).

➤ **Focus on one goal.**
Staying focused on one goal at a time will help you reach all of your goals.

➤ **Focus on the now.**
Focusing on the present will make you feel less stressed and allow you to enjoy life to the fullest.

➤ **Focus on the positive.**
You will reach all of your goals if you think good thoughts instead of bad ones.

Principle 5 — Create New Habits

Developing new habits is key to achieving long-term changes in one's life. However, it's important to start small and gradually introduce new habits, rather than trying to implement all changes at once. It's also crucial to create new habits regularly, as habits drive our daily actions and can significantly impact our overall well-being.

> **Select a habit for the challenge.**
Choose any bad habit you want to break as your challenge.

> **Write down your plan.**
Your daily goals should be stated.

> **Report on your daily progress.**
Tell the same people every day if you have done well.

Principle 6 — Start Small to Ensure Success

As humans, we tend to see immediate results and changes in our lives. However, real progress and long-term success come from gradually changing and forming new habits. We are more likely to succeed in the long run when we take small steps toward creating new habits. By focusing on one habit at a time, we can simultaneously avoid overwhelming ourselves with too many changes. Slow, steady progress can lead to lasting changes that transform our lives. By recognizing that change is a gradual process, we can approach it with patience and perseverance, making small adjustments along the way that will ultimately lead to the transformation we seek. The benefits of this are:

> **Makes you more focused.**

> **Helps you keep your energy and enthusiasm for a long time.**

> **You'll be able to deal with it better and ensure you succeed.**

One Goal System

This is a productivity strategy outlined in the book. The system is based on the idea that focusing on one major goal or project at a time can help individuals achieve greater success and productivity. The system involves identifying the one thing that will impact your overall success and then prioritizing it above all other tasks or goals.

Here are the steps to execute the*One Goal System*:

1. **Choose one goal.**

   Select one specific, measurable, and achievable goal you want to focus on. This goal should be something you are passionate about and will significantly impact your life.

2. **Break it down.**

   Break your one goal down into smaller, actionable steps that you can take to achieve it. These steps should be specific and measurable.

3. **Create a plan.**

   Create a plan for how you will accomplish each step. This plan should include deadlines, resources, and any support or assistance you may need.

4. **Eliminate distractions.**

   Eliminate any distractions that may hinder your progress. This could include reducing your time on social media, avoiding certain people or situations, or setting boundaries with your time.

5. **Focus on one thing at a time.**

   Focus on completing one step at a time, without getting distracted by other tasks or goals. This will help you stay focused and motivated.

6. **Evaluate your progress.**

   Regularly evaluate your progress and adjust your plan as needed. Celebrate your successes and learn from any mistakes or setbacks.

7. **Repeat the process.**

   Once you have achieved one goal, choose another one and repeat the process. Over time, this system will help you achieve more and create lasting change in your life.

KEY LESSONS

1. **To simplify, you determine what is most important and eliminate everything else.**

   The modern world is getting more and more complicated. Because of this, you have to pay attention to more and more things. It's easy to feel stressed out by everything you must do every day.

2. **By focusing on what's most important, you can get the best results with the least amount of work.**

   Because you only have so much time and energy each day, focusing on what's most important lets you put much more of your time and energy into things that will give you the best results.

3. **You have to set limits — they don't do it on their own.**

   Most people don't like to set limits, which is a mistake. People tend to think that anything and everything is important.

4. **Don't think about more than one thing at a time.**

   Our minds can't pay attention to more than one thing at once. It's not true that you can do more than one thing at once.

5. **You shouldn't have more than three or four goals and projects going simultaneously.**

   If you've ever made a list of all the projects you want to finish, it likely has more than thirty items on it.

6. **Set your three Most Important Tasks (MITs) for each day and finish them before doing anything else.**

   Every individual is created equal, not every job holds equal importance.

7. **To stay on track, group tasks that are similar together.**

   Every time you switch your attention, you will lose a lot of time and effort.

8. **The best way to make good habits stick is to start small and build on your early successes.**

   When making good habits, people try to change too many things simultaneously. Take baby steps.

ACTIONABLE STEPS TO TAKE

➤ **Set clear and specific goals.**
Understand the power of having a clear and specific goal, as it helps you stay focused and motivated to achieve it.

➤ **Prioritize your tasks.**
Learn how to prioritize your tasks by identifying the most important and urgent ones, which will help you make the most of your time and energy.

➤ **Use the 80/20 principle.**
Learn how to apply the 80/20 rule to your life, which states that 80% of the results come from 20% of the effort. Identify the most important 20% of your tasks and focus on them.

➤ **Implement the *ONE thing rule*.**
Understand the power of focusing on one thing at a time, instead of trying to do multiple things at once, which will help you achieve better results.

➤ **Simplify your life.**
Understanding the importance of simplifying your life by reducing clutter and distractions will help you focus on what truly matters.

➤ **Create a routine.**
Learn how to create a routine that works for you, which will help you stay organized and on track toward achieving your goals.

➤ **Take regular breaks.**
Understand the importance of taking regular breaks to recharge and refresh your mind, which will help you stay focused and productive over time.

➤ **Reflect and evaluate your progress.**
Learn how to reflect and evaluate your progress regularly, which will help you stay motivated, adjust your approach, and make necessary changes to achieve your goals.

The ONE thing

by Gary W. Keller and Jay Papasan

"Extraordinary results are directly determined by how narrow you can make your focus. When you spread yourself out, you end up spread thin. Things don't matter equally. Success is found in doing what matters most."

T HIS book focuses on the power of focusing on ONE thing to achieve extraordinary results. The book argues that by identifying the ONE thing that matters most and focusing on it, individuals can achieve greater success in their personal and professional lives.

The book's main idea is that by focusing on the ONE thing that matters most, individuals can achieve extraordinary results in their lives. The authors argue that most people try to do too many things at once, and as a result, they spread themselves too thin and achieve mediocre results. The book provides a framework for identifying the ONE thing that matters most and provides practical strategies for focusing on it.

The book aims to help readers achieve greater success by focusing on the ONE thing that matters most in their personal and professional lives. The authors provide a step-by-step guide to help readers identify their ONE thing and provide practical strategies for focusing on it.

The Focusing Question

To achieve success, you don't need to be involved in endless activities. Instead, focus on a few things to help you attain your objectives. Avoid the temptation to multitask or spread yourself thin across several different goals. Apple and Intel, for example, are businesses that specialize in producing one product each, dedicating all their resources to excelling in their particular markets. Successful individuals prioritize a single relationship that propels them toward their desired destination, rather than attempting to learn everything at once.

Everything in life needs an answer to what the author calls *The Focusing Question*, which is a simple but powerful question:

"What's the ONE thing I can do such that by doing it everything else will be easier or unnecessary?"

By continuously asking and answering what the author refers to as *The Focusing Question,* individuals can make a series of informed decisions that ultimately lead them to their desired outcome. Instead of spreading oneself thin by taking on multiple tasks, narrowing down and concentrating on the ONE thing that will yield the best results is important. The idea is to dig deep and take the necessary actions that will get you closer to achieving your goal. By consistently prioritizing the most important task at hand, one can gradually work towards achieving success over time.

Six Lies We Believe about Success

Success is a term that holds different meanings for different people. Some may define success as having a high-paying job, others as a happy family life, while others may view success as achieving personal goals. Regardless of how one defines success, there are certain lies that people often believe about achieving it. The book discusses these lies, and identifying and overcoming them is essential to achieving success.

1. **All things are equal.**
   This is a common misconception; many people believe they should devote equal amounts of time and energy to all areas of their lives. However, the truth is that some tasks and goals are more important than others, and focusing on the most crucial ones can lead to greater success.

2. **Multitasking.**
   Many people believe they can achieve more by doing multiple tasks simultaneously, but research shows that this is not the case. Multitasking can decrease productivity and increase stress levels, making it harder to achieve success.

3. **Living a disciplined life.**
   Some people view discipline as something negative, but it is essential to achieving success. A disciplined approach can help individuals stay focused and achieve their goals more efficiently.

4. **There is always willpower at your disposal.**

   Many people believe they can rely on willpower to achieve their goals, but this is not always true. Willpower is a finite resource that can be depleted quickly, especially when faced with challenging situations or distractions.

5. **Living a balanced life.**

   Many people believe that they need to maintain a balanced life to achieve success, but this is not necessarily true. Instead, focusing on the most critical aspects of life can lead to greater success, even if it means sacrificing balance in other areas.

6. *"Shoot for the stars, aim for the moon"* **is bad.**

   Many people believe that success comes from achieving big goals, but this is not always the case. Small, consistent steps can lead to greater success than trying to achieve a big goal all at once.

Purpose-Driven Living

Your sense of purpose drives your life. The combination of where you want to go and what is most important to you ultimately determines your direction. Your priorities based on your purpose will dictate how effective your actions are in achieving your goals.

Without a clear goal, you may find yourself in a perpetual cycle of searching for, acquiring, and accumulating material possessions without experiencing true happiness. Genuine happiness is comprised of five essential elements:

➤ **Engagement.**

   When you are fully involved in activities that challenge and stimulate you, you experience a sense of flow and deep fulfillment.

➤ **Meaning.**

   You find a purpose that is greater than yourself and use your talents to contribute to the world around you.

➤ **Relationships.**

   You form meaningful connections with others, feeling valued and appreciated for who you are.

➤ **Achievement.**
You set and achieve goals aligning with your values and purpose, experiencing a sense of accomplishment and pride.

➤ **Positive emotion and pleasure.**
You seek out and enjoy experiences that bring joy, pleasure, and positive emotions into your life.

The most important things for your happiness are having a purpose and being involved in something. When you are interested in what you do and see the point in it, you can feel a strong and long-lasting sense of fulfillment.

When things don't go as planned, a person with a goal can better deal with the situation. If you're having trouble figuring out what your goal is, ask yourself:

"What's the ONE thing I can do in my life that would mean the most to me and the world such that by doing it everything else will be easier or unnecessary?"

Invest in Productivity

To achieve success, it is essential to prioritize and focus on the things that truly matter to you. Therefore, protecting your time and avoiding wasting it on activities that do not align with your goals is crucial. It is important to evaluate each request or opportunity and assess its importance. If the task does not align with your priorities, consider negotiating the timeline or delegating it to someone else. It is also important to recognize that productivity is critical to achieving success.

There are many ways to make yourself more productive. Some of the most important are:

➤ **Time off.**
Plan your vacation ahead of time so that it doesn't interfere with your work. This means a vacation won't just be a short break from work.

➤ **The ONE thing.**
Your goal for the day should be to get that ONE thing done. Give yourself

a few hours to do this when it suits you best. This usually happens early in the morning.

➤ **Time management.**
Make sure you look at your ONE thing every day, every week, every three months, and every year to ensure you are setting yourself up for success.

The Three Productivity's Thieves

1. **Not being able to say NO.**
The demands for your time are endless in life. Unfortunately, you cannot accept every invitation and should avoid doing so. All that you need to do is say yes to the ONE thing. Although there may be multiple reasons for your fear of saying NO, you should develop systems to learn how to say NO and become comfortable with it.

2. **Worrying.**
You must prioritize and focus on the ONE thing that matters the most to you. This may require you to let go of some other things that are not as important. It can be difficult for individuals who are accustomed to doing everything to give up control over certain tasks. They may fear the consequences of relinquishing responsibilities or worry about the impact on their workload. It is important to remember that saying YES to your ONE thing often means saying NO to other tasks or commitments. It is a trade-off that requires discipline and dedication.

3. **Unhealthy habits.**
If you want to do well, you must take care of your health. Remember that your body is the only house you'll live in, whereas the mind is the interior inside of it. Make sure you take care of them. Try things like meditation, exercise, taking a break, resting, etc. Do whatever you need to do to keep your health up. To get the most out of your energy management and productivity, plan your days around the following:

➤ Consider meditating or praying for **spiritual energy**.

➤ Eat well, exercise, and sleep enough to maintain a healthy lifestyle for **physical energy**.

➤ Enjoy the company of family and friends for **emotional energy**.

➤ Establish goals, a plan, and a schedule for **mental energy**.

➤ Set aside time each day for your ONE thing for **business energy**.

Living a Life with No Regrets

Living a life without any regrets is an ideal that many strive for. However, as human beings, we often make mistakes or miss opportunities, which can lead to feelings of regret later in life. According to the book, these are five common regrets that many people have:

➤ Permission to not be happy.

➤ Not being able to stay in touch with friends.

➤ They didn't dare to say how they felt.

➤ Overworking.

➤ The inability to live one's life based on one's values and beliefs instead of living based on what others want.

Avoid regretting your actions on your deathbed.

The Focusing Questions

The author writes:

> *"The Focusing Question can direct you to your ONE thing in the different areas of your life. Simply reframe the Focusing Question by inserting your area of focus. You can also include a time frame — such as 'right now' or 'this year' — to give your answer the appropriate level of immediacy, or 'in five years' or 'someday' to find a big-picture answer that points you at outcomes to aim for."*

To understand this, here are the questions the author recommends:

➤ **FOR MY KEY RELATIONSHIPS**

- What's the ONE thing I can do to improve my relationship with my spouse/partner?
- What's the ONE thing I can do to make my family stronger?

➤ FOR MY JOB

- What's the ONE thing I can do to ensure I hit my goals?
- What's the ONE thing I can do to improve my skills?

➤ FOR MY BUSINESS

- What's the ONE thing I can do to make us more competitive?
- What's the ONE thing I can do to make us more profitable?

➤ FOR MY FINANCES

- What's the ONE thing I can do to improve my investment cash flow?
- What's the ONE thing I can do to eliminate my credit card debt?

➤ FOR MY PERSONAL LIFE

- What's the ONE thing I can do to improve my skill?
- What's the ONE thing I can do to find time for myself?

➤ FOR MY PHYSICAL HEALTH

- What's the ONE thing I can do to achieve my diet goals?
- What's the ONE thing I can do to ensure that I exercise?

KEY LESSONS

1. **Building good habits is essential to achieving success.**
   By focusing on one habit at a time, we can develop a consistent routine that will help us achieve our goals.

2. **Focus on just ONE thing at a time.**
   This means identifying the most important thing we need to accomplish and putting all of our efforts into it.

3. **Time blocking is the practice of scheduling specific time for specific activities.**
   This helps ensure that we focus on the most important things during specific periods of the day.

4. **Make sure you don't try to get everything done all at once.**
   The idea that you can do more than ONE thing at once is wrong and keeps you from doing well at all of them.

5. **Don't be afraid to tell people NO.**
   Don't let everything get in the way. Learn to say NO to things that don't help you reach your bigger goals.

ACTIONABLE STEPS TO TAKE

➤ **Identify your ONE thing.**
Understand the importance of focusing on ONE thing at a time to achieve success and prioritize your efforts towards that ONE thing.

➤ **Create a clear goal.**
Clearly define and write down your specific, measurable, and time-bound goal for your ONE thing.

➤ **Eliminate distractions.**
Identify and eliminate any distractions that may keep you from fully focusing on your ONE thing.

➤ **Time block your day.**
Set aside a specific time each day to work on your ONE thing and create a schedule to keep yourself accountable.

➤ **Seek out knowledge.**
Continuously educate yourself on your ONE thing through books, courses, and mentorship to stay updated and improve your skills.

➤ **Surround yourself with like-minded people.**
Seek out individuals who share similar goals and passions to help keep you motivated and on track.

➤ **Measure your progress.**
Regularly track and measure your progress to stay motivated and adjust as needed.

➤ **Stay committed.**
Stay committed to your ONE thing even when faced with challenges and obstacles, as it takes time and consistent effort to succeed.

➤ **Take action every day.**
Consistently take small steps towards your ONE thing daily to build momentum and progress.

The Lean Startup

by Eric Ries

"A startup is a human institution designed to create a new product or service under conditions of extreme uncertainty. If you cannot fail, you cannot learn."

I N this book, the author offers a new approach to starting and managing a business based on lean manufacturing principles.

The key concept of the Lean Startup is the *Build-Measure-Learn* feedback loop. This involves creating a Minimum Viable Product (MVP) that allows you to test your business idea with customers and receive feedback. Based on that feedback, you can iterate and improve your product or service, leading to a better fit with the market.

The book also emphasizes the importance of continuous innovation and testing to avoid the common pitfalls of traditional business models. He argues that businesses must remain agile and flexible to adapt to changing market conditions and customer needs.

Another key aspect of the book is the use of data-driven decision-making. Rather than relying on intuition or guesswork, it encourages entrepreneurs to use data to guide their decisions and measure their progress. This involves setting measurable goals and using analytics to track progress toward those goals.

Vision — How to Get Started

Because of technology, startups are more likely to succeed than they were in the past. So, there are more entrepreneurs around us now than ever before. One of the most important skills for entrepreneurs to learn is how to run a business. As startups grow quickly, it can be hard for new entrepreneurs to switch from working alone to managing busy teams.

Define

To achieve success, leadership must move away from traditional management models and create a build-measure-learn cycle that encourages all employees to be entrepreneurial and try new things.

With all the different ways to describe it, what do we mean when we say *startup?* A startup is a young, ambitious company seeking to develop and deliver innovative products or services. These companies often operate in high-growth industries such as technology, healthcare, and finance. They are driven by a desire to disrupt traditional business models and create new value for their customers. *The Lean Startup* provides a framework for startups to build and test their ideas quickly and efficiently, aiming to achieve sustainable growth. Here are a few important aspects of a start-up provided by the book:

➤ One important aspect of a startup is its focus on experimentation. Startups often work with untested ideas and unproven business models, so they must be able to quickly and cheaply test their hypotheses and learn from the results. By using a process of iterative experimentation, startups can refine their ideas and develop a deep understanding of their customer's needs and preferences. This enables them to build products that are truly valuable and marketable.

➤ Another key aspect of startups is their emphasis on agility and adaptability. In today's fast-paced business environment, it is essential that startups can respond quickly to changing market conditions and customer demands. This means they must be willing to pivot their strategy or product offerings in response to customer feedback or changes in the competitive landscape. By staying nimble and flexible, startups can remain relevant and competitive over the long term.

➤ Finally, a successful startup must have a strong culture of innovation and collaboration. Startups are often founded by small teams of passionate individuals who are united by a shared vision for the future. To achieve their goals, these teams must be able to work together effectively, sharing ideas and collaborating on new initiatives. This requires a culture that values creativity, risk-taking, and open communication.

Experiment

Startups are driven by the desire to learn as much as possible and make sustainable business models that fit the company's vision faster. This is done by testing their main ideas and using build, measure, and learn cycles.

The Lean Startup method says that a startup's actions should be seen as experiments that test its strategy to see if it works. When a real experiment is done, the scientific method is used. The first step of a hypothesis is to make predictions about what is expected to happen. Then, these predictions are tested in the real world. The book says that the team building their startup used the following strategies:

➤ Developed an early prototype of low quality.

➤ From the start, started to charge customers.

➤ Low-volume revenue goals were used to make people take responsibility.

Like a scientific experiment, a new product's launch should also be thought of. As with any scientific experiment, it is suggested that hypotheses be made and then tested to ensure the predictions are correct. Here are two of the most common assumptions entrepreneurs make when launching a new product:

➤ **Value hypothesis.**
Once a customer uses a product or service, does it still give them value? Set up experiments to prove that it works. Try not to use survey methods.

➤ **Growth hypothesis.**
How can a product or service best get more people to buy it?

Build-Measure-Learn Feedback Loop

The feedback loop that *Lean Startup* is based on is called Build-Measure-Learn. Start with the Minimal Viable Product, a product with just enough features to test a startup's hypothesis about its product or service in the market, so you can move forward. Entrepreneurs should build a minimum viable product as soon as possible so they can start learning. Even though it may not be the biggest product possible, it is the quickest and easiest way to move through the Build-Measure-Learn feedback loop. The current version is the simplest and can be used to follow the build-measure-learn loop. After this evaluation, changes will likely need to be made. Planning can be a good strategy as long as you can figure out what will happen. As the world continues to change and become more unstable, those who can change direction when they need to have an advantage.

Build — Develop an MVP

Startups are in the business of creating products and services that customers will buy and use. When customers use a product, they provide valuable information, feedback, and data that can be used to improve the next version of the product. Customer feedback is often more valuable than the money made from early sales. This is the central idea behind the Build-Measure-Learn feedback cycle, which is a key concept in the *Lean Startup* methodology. Although one part of the feedback loop may be more familiar to some than others, it is essential to view the process as a whole, as all the parts are critical to the success of the startup. Feedback loops should be closed as quickly as possible to enable rapid iteration and learning. To analyze the startup's vision, it is important to break it down into its component parts and focus on pattern recognition to test the underlying assumptions:

➤ **Analogs.**
   Patterns from other products or services can be used to test an assumption.

➤ **Antilogs.**
   Anti-patterns are things from other products or services that can be used to prove an assumption wrong.

Measure — Obtain Data

It's important to show that a new business can grow into a successful one over time. For a business owner to reach his or her goal, he or she must keep track of how things are going. Standard accounting methods can't be used to measure how well a startup is doing. Accounting for innovation is important for industries that change quickly. Here's how the process works:

➤ Establish a baseline with an MVP.

➤ Improve the product.

➤ For the product to improve, turn around and set a new baseline, then start the process over.

Three key considerations should be taken into account when reporting on metrics related to the MVP. Firstly, focusing on metrics relevant to the specific assumptions being tested is important. This ensures that the startup gathers the right data to make informed decisions about the product or service. Secondly, metrics should be tracked consistently over time, enabling startups to identify trends and patterns that may be relevant to their business model. Finally, metrics should be presented easily, both for internal stakeholders and external investors or partners.

By providing clear, concise reports on metrics, startups can demonstrate progress towards their goals and build confidence in their ability to execute their business plan. Three things should be considered when reporting on metrics:

➤ **Actionable.**
   A clear link between the metric and the result must be established. You'll have to experiment to see how an experiment changed your metric.

➤ **Accessible.**
   You should make your metrics easy to understand for everyone in the company. It should be explained in simple terms and use group-based metrics that are easy for the audience to understand.

➤ **Auditable.**
   You should be able to *"drill down"* into the data to determine how a certain metric is made. So, employees don't have to argue about how the metric was made, and they can focus on making progress instead.

Learn — Incorporate Validated Learning

For lean startups, validated learning must be the main way to measure progress. Each business decision should be thought of as an experiment to test, with the goal of figuring out if the product could be made and if the business model would be able to last. So, if the main point of entrepreneurship is to build an organization when there is a lot of uncertainty, the most important thing it does is to learn. We need to find out which parts of our strategy are helping us reach our vision and which are just not working. Validated learning is a process in which the team has to show through experience that they have learned something useful about a startup's current and future business prospects.

If an idea isn't working, you might need to try something else. It's not smart to keep fighting for something that can't be fixed. The point of pivoting isn't to throw everything away and start over from scratch, but to build on what you already know.

To be good at pivoting, you need to know what's going on. If product experiments and product development don't work, that could be a sign that something needs to change. There are different kinds of pivot tools to use:

➤ **Zoom-in.**
The product should be changed to focus on one part of the bigger picture.

➤ **Zoom-out.**
Putting your product in a new place as a part of a bigger product line.

➤ **Customer segment.**
The way it works hasn't changed, but the people it's meant for have.

➤ **Customer need.**
Realizing that the problem you're trying to solve for a customer isn't as important as another one and moving on to the more important one.

➤ **Platform pivot.**
Rather than selling your product directly to customers, make it available as a self-service platform.

➤ **Value Capture.**
Getting hold of the value that your product creates in new ways.

➤ **Channel.**
Think about different ways to sell and distribute the solution to make it work better.

Grow — Maintaining Customer Loyalty

In the context of the Lean Startup methodology, a startup's growth engine is the mechanism that enables sustainable, long-term growth. This growth is achieved by avoiding reliance on one-time sources of growth that may not be sustainable in the long run.

To achieve sustainable growth, startups can leverage a range of factors that enable them to build a robust growth engine. These factors may include:

➤ **Word of mouth.**
Customers recommend your product to friends, colleagues, and family.

➤ **Reviews and observation.**
How customers of the company see the product being used.

➤ **Traditional advertising.**
This kind of advertising ensures the costs are less than the extra sales profits.

➤ **Repeat purchasing.**
As long as the new company's product isn't too expensive, repeat business is a key part of their business plan.

Five Key Concepts For a Lean Start-up

1. **Entrepreneurs are everywhere.**
Anyone can start a business, no matter how old they are or where they come from. All you have to do is let your imagination run wild. If you want to start a business, all you have to do is follow the advice of *Vivek Kundra*, who said, *"Think big. Start small. Scale fast."* With this method, you need to be creative and have big goals if you want to start small but quickly grow your business.

2. **Entrepreneurship is management.**
"A startup is an institution, not just a product, so it needs management and a new kind of management that fits its situation. This is the process of getting your startup up and running." This means that a new business needs to be carefully run to succeed. Taking notes and learning from mistakes is important, which will help the business grow.

3. **Validated learning.**
Startups don't try to make goods or services, and they also don't try to make money. Their main goal is to learn how to build a lasting business. During each step of the process of making a lean startup, experiments are done to test the startup's parts. With this method, we can determine what a good practice will be.

4. **Innovation accounting.**

   During this stage, entrepreneurs need to look at how well their startup is doing so they can improve it. By keeping track of how well they do, they will be able to improve the startup vision. Their main focus is tracking their progress, making plans for the future, and balancing and organizing their work.

5. **Build-Measure-Learn.**

   As part of these three steps, the startup builds on what it has learned in the past. After going through the above four steps, a new business must learn from its mistakes and move on to get better. Measure how customers respond to determine if they should change direction or keep going. The new company must use a feedback loop to improve its work to become a successful business.

KEY LESSONS

1. **Most of a startup's success depends on how flexible it can be.**
When you start from scratch, making a plan and setting specific goals can be hard. Entrepreneurs don't always have the chance to use what they've learned in the past.

2. **The main goal of a startup should be to find a good business model.**
Don't let your complicated milestone plans distract your attention from getting customers in your doors and making sure they pay for your services.

3. **Optimize your business model using what you've learned that has been proven by science.**
You will hypothesize about your product and customers, which you will then test with real customers.

4. **Before you put money into your Minimum Viable Product, you should test it.**
Most founders spend way too much time making products that haven't been tested. Instead of making prototypes or finished products, you should make mock-ups or pictures early to get feedback.

5. **Watch and repeat the Build-Measure-Learn process.**
A startup needs real-world feedback to get real-world experience. The only way to get real-world feedback is to build a product, see how customers react, and learn from those experiences.

6. **By running split tests, startups can find out which features their customers want and which ones they don't.**
Test the product with and without the feature to find out which features are useful and which are not.

7. **Entrepreneurs will likely have to change their business models a few times before they find the best one.**
When entrepreneurs are forced to stick to an old way of doing business, they can go out of business. Successful entrepreneurs often change their minds about what they initially thought they knew.

8. **Find one way to grow and put all your efforts into that.**

   There are three main growth engines:

   > **The sticky engine.**
   > Keeping the customers you already have and getting them to buy more.

   > **The viral engine.**
   > Marketing products and services to customers who have already bought them.

   > **The paid engine.**
   > Investing in a marketing strategy.

9. **Focus on important metrics instead of useless ones.**

   To figure out how well your business model works, you need to come up with real metrics, not just vanity metrics, to measure its success.

ACTIONABLE STEPS TO TAKE

➤ **Validate your idea.**

Test the viability of your product idea by talking to potential customers, understanding their needs and pain points, and creating a hypothesis about how your product will solve their problems.

➤ **Build an MVP.**

Create a minimal version of your product to test your hypothesis and get feedback from early adopters.

➤ **Measure and analyze feedback.**

Gather data on how your MVP is being used and gather feedback from customers. Use this information to refine and improve your product.

➤ **Pivot or persevere.**

Based on the feedback and data, determine whether to pivot (make significant changes) or persevere (continue with small improvements) with your product.

➤ **Continuously experiment and iterate.**

Incorporate a culture of experimentation and continuous learning into your startup. Use your MVP and customer feedback to make informed decisions and improve your product over time.

➤ **Embrace uncertainty.**

Recognize that startup success is uncertain and embrace the process of experimentation and learning. Be flexible and adaptable to changes in the market and customer needs.

➤ **Focus on creating value.**

Stay focused on creating value for your customers and solving their problems, rather than just building features.

➤ **Build a strong team.**

Assemble a team of dedicated individuals who share a common vision and work together towards a common goal.

CHAPTER 5

HEALTH

"There's no excuse to not be the hardest motherfucking worker in the room, whatever it may be, your job, the gym, your relationship. Your name's attached to it, and that has to mean more than anything."

— Gregg Plitt

"Take care of your body. It's the only place you have to live."

— Jim Rohn

"The mind and the body are not separate. What affects one, affects the other."

— Socrates

Bigger Leaner Stronger

by Michael Matthews

"You are the master of your destiny. You can influence, direct and control your own environment. You can make your life what you want it to be."

T HIS book aims to help you get in shape and lose weight. The book aims to provide readers with a science-based approach to building muscle, losing fat, and achieving a strong, lean physique.

Throughout the book, the author emphasizes the importance of science-based methods for achieving fitness goals. He draws on research studies to support his claims and provides practical advice for incorporating these methods into your own fitness routine.

The main idea of *Bigger Leaner Stronger* is that building muscle and losing fat are complementary goals that can be achieved through strength training and proper nutrition. The author presents a compelling case for utilizing a science-driven methodology to attain a robust and lean physique, all the while avoiding the pitfalls of trendy dietary regimes or arduous workout regimens

This book aims to offer readers an all-inclusive manual for effectively constructing muscle mass, shedding excess fat, and attaining a robust, slender figure. It hopes to educate readers on the science behind fitness and empower them to control their health and fitness.

The Concept of Fat Loss

One of the most widely held beliefs in the fitness world is that all cardio makes you lose muscle. The author thinks that doing too much cardio can make you lose muscle. But he also says that a moderate amount of cardio that is done right can also help build muscle. Cardiovascular exercise, for example, can help repair muscle fibers by bringing more blood to the areas that need it. During this blood flow, minerals and waste products that are needed for muscle recovery are moved through the body. Because of this, recovery times get shorter and muscle growth gets better. Since running and cycling are cardio exercises that use the legs a lot, these benefits tend to help the legs more than the upper body.

Imagine that you burn an average of 2,000 calories per day and decide to only eat 1,500 calories per day. This will help you burn fat; if you keep doing this, you'll lose weight. This claim is backed up by scientific evidence. To lose weight, you must ensure you eat fewer calories than you burn (if you are trying to lose weight). If you use this method, you will lose weight no matter how much you eat. The main point is that you should only be in a caloric deficit if you want to burn fat and lose weight. On the other hand, if you are already thin but want to gain muscle, you should eat between 2200 and 2500 calories per day.

The author delves deeply into a plethora of misconceptions and pitfalls that individuals encounter when attempting to shed weight. Additionally, the author expounds upon the three fundamental principles of wholesome fat reduction, while also debunking five commonly held myths regarding weight loss:

Three Laws of Healthy Fat Loss

1. You can lose weight by eating less than you burn.

2. Set up a schedule for eating that works for you.

3. Use cardio exercises to burn fat.

Five Myths of Fat Loss

1. You don't have to count calories.

2. Do cardio exercises to lose weight.

3. Going after the trends.

4. Do exercises with low weight and many repetitions to get your body in shape.

5. Burning calories at a certain spot on the body.

The Concept of Muscle Gain

The author thinks that the best way to build and keep muscle is to do progressive overload. Progressive overload could be thought of as gradually adding more weight to what you are lifting. As your muscles get bigger, the same amount of weight will put less stress on your muscle fibers. To keep building your muscles, you should keep this level of tension by adding more weight to your weights.

In this book, the author stresses that even if you do everything else right, you won't be able to build muscle if you don't overload your muscles gradually. In this case, you should always do more reps or lift more weight than you did in your last workout.

The author gives a full summary of the most common myths and laws about building muscle. He also talks about the four rules of building muscle in a healthy way:

Laws of Muscle Gain Based on Science

1. Muscles only get bigger when they are forced to.

2. Muscles grow when they are overworked, not when they are tired or *"pumped."*

3. Muscles can also grow in places other than the gym.

4. Muscles can only grow if they are given the proper fuel.

Muscle Gain Myths & Mistakes

1. A greater number of sets will lead to greater growth.

2. To grow, you must *"feel the burn."*

3. Time wasted with the wrong exercises.

4. Being a complete fool when you lift.

5. Taking the lift like a weakling.

6. Eating to remain thin or gain weight.

The Bigger Leaner Stronger Weight Training Method

FORMULA

1-2	4-6	9-12	2-3	45-60	5-7	8-10

1. Train 1-2 Muscle Groups Per Day.

2. Do Sets of 4-6 Reps for Nearly All Exercises.

3. Do 9-12 Heavy Sets Per Muscle Group.

4. Rest 2–3 Minutes in Between Sets.

5. Train for 45-60 Minutes.

6. Train Each Muscle Group Once Every 5-7 Days.

7. Take a Week off Training Every 8-10 Weeks.

Recommended Exercise Types

1. The Bench Press

2. The Military Press

3. The Squat

4. The Deadlift

Macronutrients

Maintaining a healthy diet is important for achieving a healthy body composition. Failing to pay attention to what you eat can result in unwanted weight gain or loss. Insufficient protein can lead to muscle loss rather than gain during a cutting phase, while insufficient carbohydrates can negatively impact training and muscle recovery. Additionally, inadequate fat intake can significantly drop testosterone levels and other negative health consequences.

To ensure a balanced intake of macronutrients, paying attention to the types and amounts of foods you eat is essential. This will help you maintain your energy levels, build muscle, and regulate hormone levels and cellular functions. For individuals seeking to gain muscle mass, consuming more calories than your body needs to support muscle repair and growth is important. This kind of energy is important for fixing damaged muscles and building lean muscle.

➤ **Protein.**

Your diet should have a lot of protein in it. Getting enough protein is all about choosing the right foods. Protein that comes from natural sources is what is meant by the term *"whole food protein."* Whole food proteins like chicken, turkey, lean red meat, fish, eggs, and milk are some of the best.

➤ **Carbohydrates.**

Sugar is a carbohydrate that comes from plants, fruits, grains, and other things. Sugar is bad for you because it is quickly absorbed and makes you hungry again soon after. As a natural sugar, glucose is found all over the world. It's an important way for living things to get energy. glucose is a part of many carbohydrates. You should eat carbs with a glycemic index between 70 and 90 30 minutes before your workout and 30 minutes after your workout.

➤ **Fats.**

When you are in a caloric deficit to lose fat, it is hard to build muscle. On a diet to lose fat, your main goal should be keeping your muscles from weakening. Most of your fats should come from unsaturated sources, like olive oil, nuts, peanut oil, avocados, flaxseed oil, safflower oil, sesame oil, or cottonseed oil.

KEY LESSONS

1. **Many men and women have trouble losing weight and getting the body they want because they follow fad diets, exercise plans, and take supplements.**
   Supplement companies pay for most health and fitness magazines, so their information may be biased.

2. **Progressive overload is the key to building impressive muscles and a solid body shape.**
   Progressive overload means lifting more weight over time, making the muscle fibers tighter.

3. **The best way to get a masculine body is to gain weight and muscle, then lose fat. These steps are called *bulking* and *cutting*.**
   Men or women can build muscle and lose fat without losing muscle mass if they follow the right steps.

4. **A good workout plan for building muscle requires free weights and compound weightlifting.**
   Compound exercises are good because they produce more anabolic hormones than isolation exercises.

5. **Cardio can make you lose muscle if you do it too much. But if you do cardio in the right way and in small amounts, you can build muscle.**
   How often and for how long a person should do cardio exercises depends on many things, but most people know that some are necessary to get the best results.

6. **You must keep track of your progress to get the best results from the *Bigger Leaner Stronger* program.**
   With the help of technology, like fitness apps and wearable fitness bands that are getting better at collecting data, you can keep track of your diet and exercise progress.

ACTIONABLE STEPS TO TAKE

➤ **Start with the basics.**
Gain a solid understanding of anatomy, physiology, and nutrition fundamentals, and learn how they apply to building muscle and strength.

➤ **Focus on compound exercises.**
Include compound exercises, such as the squat, bench press, and deadlift, in your workout plan as they are the most effective for building muscle and strength.

➤ **Use progressive overload.**
Progressively increase the weight you lift to continue challenging your muscles and making progress.

➤ **Eat a balanced diet.**
Focus on eating a balanced diet with sufficient protein, carbohydrates, and healthy fats to support muscle growth and fat loss.

➤ **Calculate your calorie and macronutrient needs.**
Determine your daily calorie and macronutrient needs based on your fitness goals and use this information to guide your diet.

➤ **Plan your meals.**
Plan your meals in advance and have healthy food options available to make it easier to stick to your diet.

➤ **Stay hydrated.**
Stay hydrated by drinking enough water throughout the day to support muscle growth and overall health.

➤ **Get enough rest.**
Get sufficient rest and recovery between workouts to allow your muscles to recover and grow.

➤ **Supplement wisely.**
Consider taking supplements, such as protein powder, if necessary to meet your protein needs and support muscle growth.

No Excuses!

by Brian Tracy

"Your ability to think, plan, and work hard in the short term and to discipline yourself to do what is right and necessary before you do what is fun and easy is the key to creating a wonderful future for yourself."

THIS book focuses on the importance of taking responsibility for one's life and achieving success through hard work, dedication, and discipline. It argues that successful people do not make excuses for their failures but instead take responsibility and learn from their mistakes.

The book is divided into 21 chapters, each exploring a different aspect of personal responsibility and success. Some of the key topics covered in the book include goal-setting, time management, self-discipline, positive thinking, and overcoming obstacles.

The author emphasizes the importance of setting clear and specific goals and creating a plan of action to achieve them. He also stresses the need to manage one's time effectively and to prioritize tasks based on their importance and urgency.

Throughout the book, he provides numerous examples of successful people who have overcome challenges and achieved their goals through hard work and perseverance. He also provides practical advice and exercises to help readers develop the habits and mindset necessary for success.

One of the main strengths of *No Excuses!* is its focus on personal responsibility. The book argues that individuals have the power to shape their own lives and that success is not determined by external factors such as luck or circumstances. By taking responsibility for their actions and decisions, readers can achieve their goals and live a more fulfilling life.

The Laws of Resistance

Developing oneself is essential to achieve success beyond the average level. The journey towards reaching one's goal is not just about the destination, but also about the experience and lessons learned along the way. Having a strong character who can overcome challenges and stay committed to personal growth is crucial. To quote *Albert Hubbard*:

> *"Self-discipline is the ability to do what you should do when you should do it, whether you feel like it or not."*

— *Albert Hubbard*

Self-discipline is a vital ingredient for success, as it plays a crucial role in shaping our behavior and determining the outcomes of our actions. Without self-discipline, we may make excuses and give in to our impulses, which can hinder our progress and prevent us from reaching our full potential. On the other hand, when we cultivate self-discipline, we are better equipped to make the right choices and pursue our goals with determination and focus. Two of the biggest things that stop people from being successful and happy with their lives are:

➤ **The Path of Least Resistance.**
Most of the time, people who go down this path choose the easy way out. Most people take this route when they're looking for a quick way out of almost any situation. These are the people who are always late to work and leave as soon as they can. Also, people here seek ways to get rich fast and make more money without working hard. When people do this, they always look for an easier and faster way to get what they want. This keeps them from reaching the level of success that they need and want.

➤ **The Expediency Factor.**
People always look for the fastest and easiest way to get what they want now, with little or no thought for how their actions will affect them in the long run. This is a side effect of the expediency factor. The Expediency Factor is the tendency to prioritize short-term pleasure over long-term benefit. Essentially, people tend to choose the easiest or most convenient option available to them at the moment rather than working towards a larger, long-term goal. This factor is a common barrier to success, as it prevents people from taking the necessary steps to achieve their goals.

Seven-Step Method to Achieve Your Goals

As human beings, we are wired to respond to both success and failure in different ways. Failure often results from taking the path of least resistance and avoiding hard work, while success is achieved by setting a goal and working towards it with determination. By setting a clear goal, you can switch off the failure mechanism and begin to focus on success. Successful people can offer valuable advice on achieving your goals, from how they dress to the books they read and the classes they take. To achieve your goals, it is essential to follow a step-by-step process that includes the following seven key steps:

1. **Identify your goals and objectives.**
   Make sure to get specific. Instead of just saying *making more money,* decide on a specific amount of money you want to make.

2. **Note it down.**
   When goals aren't written down, they drift away and disappear like cigarette smoke. They don't say much and aren't clear. They don't mean anything or have any real importance. On the other hand, written goals can be seen, touched, read, and changed as needed.

3. **Decide when you will achieve your goal.**
   Set a date for when you want to reach your goal and choose a reasonable time frame. When your goal is big enough, set a final deadline and then set smaller deadlines or steps between where you are now and where you want to be.

4. **Identify all the possibilities that you can think of to achieve your goal.**

   ➤ Find out what problems you will need to solve.

   ➤ Find out what skills and knowledge you need to reach your goal.

   ➤ Think about the people who can help you get where you want to go.

   ➤ Make a list of the steps you need to take to reach your goal.

5. **Sort your list based on both order and importance.**
   From an ordered list of activities, you have to choose which one to do first, which one to do second, and which one to do last. Also, a ranked list lets you determine what is more important and less important.

6. **Implement your plan as soon as possible.**

Start with the first step, then move on to the second, third, and so on. Begin now. Do something. Do it now. Stop wasting time. Procrastination steals more than just time; it also steals your life.

7. **Make sure that every day you take steps toward your main goal.**

You must do something every day, seven days a week, 365 days a year, to succeed. Any action that moves you closer to the goal you are most focused on at the moment.

Self-Discipline and Leadership

To achieve success in life, focusing on personal development and character building is crucial rather than material possessions or professional accomplishments. Developing self-discipline is the foundation of becoming a better person, which involves integrating discipline into your personality and character.

Effective leadership entails taking charge and being accountable for meeting that goal. Leaders must always be aware of the expectations placed on them and act accordingly. They should constantly gather information, ask questions, make quick decisions, and follow through with actions. The behavior of leaders sets the tone for the entire organization, and it is their responsibility to establish a culture of discipline that brings out the best in employees. To be an effective leader, it is important to adhere to the following seven principles:

➤ **Clarity.**

A leader should know who he is, what he stands for, and the organization's mission, goals, and values.

➤ **Competence.**

Setting high standards for performance is part of being a leader.

➤ **Commitment.**

For an organization to do well, its leader must give it his or her all.

➤ **Constraints.**

To make sure the organization is successful, the leader must figure out what is holding it back and come up with plans to fix it.

➤ **Creativity.**

As a leader, you must always look for new and different ways to solve problems, make products that work well, and give great customer service.

➤ **Learning.**

Leaders need to keep learning and getting better at what they do, and they also need to create an environment that encourages their employees to do the same.

➤ **Consistency.**

Leadership should always be reliable, not just when things are really important.

21 Ways to Achieve Lasting Happiness & Success

In life, it's easy to get caught up in negative thinking and self-doubt. We can always find a reason or excuse for failing or losing, but this type of thinking is ultimately our biggest enemy. We must remove these limiting beliefs and start fresh to achieve success and happiness. It's important to embrace adaptability and learn to navigate any situation confidently and resiliently.

To achieve long-term success and happiness, there are some key principles to keep in mind:

1. **Be prepared to work hard and for a long time.**
   To be successful in life, you need to be able to see what you want. Set up a clear definition of success and use it at every level to get a full picture.

2. **Integrity and character are the hallmarks of a person.**
   How a person becomes who they are depends on what's going on in their lives. It is very important to be able to keep going through hard times and resist the urge to use unethical methods to get what you want.

3. **Own your life and take responsibility for it.**
   The author learned at a very young age that he is the only one who can change how his life turns out.

4. **Every day, make sure you are working towards your goals.**
   Without clear goals, your vision doesn't mean anything. Setting goals is

an important part of being successful. Set both long-term and short-term goals that are important to you.

5. **Build up your ability to learn more steadily.**
The most valuable thing in your life is deep inside you. Investing in yourself will make you more successful and have more wealth.

6. **Identify your fears and doubts, and overcome them.**
People will always be afraid, but many are too afraid to invest their money, making them poor in the long run.

7. **Persistence is self-discipline in action.**
Whether you are an insurance broker or a pilot, you should have a certain amount of stubbornness. To be successful, you have to keep going.

8. **Prioritize the most important tasks.**
The Pareto Principle, as explained by the author, highlights that a majority of your professional achievements, roughly 80%, can be attributed to a relatively small portion, around 20%, of your professional activities. This principle serves as a reminder of the importance of focusing your efforts on the tasks that truly matter to achieve the greatest impact and maximize your professional potential.

9. **Climb the ladder of success by becoming a leader.**
Leadership inside and outside of the office shows how much you care and how hard you work.

10. **Deliver great solutions to your customers.**
For your product or service to be successful, it needs to meet your customer's needs.

11. **Remember that sales are an important part of any business.**
There are a lot of people who think it's possible to go too far with *sales*. Still, this question lies at the heart of every professional project: Could this lead to a sale?

12. **Spend less and save more.**
We often have trouble with money because we don't have enough self-

control. You should take your time, think about what's happening, and then go through with your plan.

13. **Make the most of your life by taking charge of your time.**
    The author says this part is about choosing the order of events that works best for you.

14. **Improve your problem-solving skills.**
    Most people don't have the skill of being able to easily solve hard problems. Every journey starts with figuring out the problem and then moving toward a solution.

15. **Do what you like to do to make yourself happy.**
    Many parts of a person's life, including happiness, depend on others. So, being around others, talking to them, and sharing your thoughts will greatly improve your health.

16. **Maintain a healthy lifestyle.**
    Avoid eating too much junk food to keep your health healthy and save energy. A person can be happier if they are healthy and live longer.

17. **Maintain a healthy lifestyle by exercising and training.**
    To be successful, you need to make time for physical activity. The training doesn't have to be specific; it just needs to be something interesting.

18. **Be married to a strong and stable partner.**
    When people say *healthy relationship,* they don't always mean marriage. It could also be a relationship where both people are completely committed to each other.

19. **Educate your children well.**
    It's hard to find love that doesn't change. You should give your children your full support and love them no matter what.

20. **Develop deep friendships and relationships.**
    Before you try to make a real friend, consider whether someone like you would be a good friend.

21. **Get a real feeling of peace.**

    Not everything in life is about money. The key to success is keeping your mind in a good place. Spend time and effort on developing your spirituality and your career.

KEY LESSONS

1. **Take charge of your life and learn from experts to do well.**
   If you want to learn from the experts in your field, you should go to conferences, read their books, and listen to their podcasts.

2. **The Seven-Step Method is a powerful way to reach your goals; successful people will tell you to use it.**
   If you write down your goals, you are more likely to reach them.

3. **If you want to overcome your fears, you need to face them immediately and give the Disaster Report.**
   The first step to overcoming your fears is to figure out what they are and deal with them as soon as possible.

4. **Self-discipline is important no matter what you do for a living.**
   If you work for a company, you should try to do the job as well as possible. This rule applies to every part of a person's life. There is no reason not to try your hardest.

5. **By utilizing both the ABCDE Method and the *1% Rule*, achieving financial freedom is possible, which has become increasingly essential in our contemporary society.**
   Putting together a list of everything you need to do will help you get more done. You should never give out less important tasks before finishing more important ones. You only need to follow that rule.

6. **If you want to live a longer, healthier life, you might want to work out and avoid the *three whites* in your diet.**
   To live a long and healthy life, you should avoid sodium, sugar, and refined grains at all costs.

7. **Spend time with your family, and if someone has hurt you, forgive them.**
   We can start by promising to spend more time with our families.

ACTIONABLE STEPS TO TAKE

➤ **Set clear, specific, and measurable goals.**
Define your goals clearly and specifically, so that you have a clear direction and focus for your actions.

➤ **Create a powerful vision.**
Visualizing your goals and imagining yourself achieving them helps to provide motivation and drive toward your objectives.

➤ **Prioritize tasks.**
Prioritizing tasks based on importance and urgency helps to ensure that you focus on the most important tasks and make the best use of your time.

➤ **Break down large goals.**
Breaking down large goals into smaller, more manageable tasks helps to make them more achievable and less overwhelming.

➤ **Overcome procrastination.**
Overcoming procrastination helps increase productivity and ensure that you progress toward your goals.

➤ **Stay focused.**
Staying focused helps to avoid distractions and maintain focus on your goals, leading to increased productivity and success.

➤ **Develop healthy habits.**
Developing healthy habits such as regular exercise, sufficient sleep, and healthy eating habits helps to support physical and mental well-being, which is essential for sustained success.

➤ **Manage stress.**
Managing stress helps prevent burnout and maintain focus on your goals, allowing you to stay motivated and progress.

➤ **Avoid temptations.**
Avoiding temptations such as social media or junk food helps you focus on your goals and avoid distractions that can derail progress.

Psycho-Cybernetics

by Maxwell Maltz

"A human being always acts and feels and performs following what he imagines to be true about himself and his environment. Imagination sets the goal 'picture' which our automatic mechanism works on. We act, or fail to act, not because of 'will,' as commonly believed, but because of imagination. The greatest mistake a man can make is to be afraid of making one."

THIS is a groundbreaking self-help book that explores the relationship between the mind and the body, providing practical techniques for achieving success and happiness. The author discovered that many of his patients were unhappy with their appearance after surgery. This led him to explore the idea that true happiness and success come from within, and that how we think about ourselves can profoundly impact our lives.

The book is based on the idea of *self-image psychology*, which suggests that our thoughts and beliefs about ourselves determine our behavior and ultimately our success or failure. It argues that our self-image is largely formed in childhood and is influenced by our environment, experiences, and feedback from others. However, he also stresses that our self-image is not fixed and can be changed consciously.

One of the book's key takeaways is that our minds are like a guidance system, and we can use this system to direct our lives in a positive direction. The author uses the metaphor of a guided missile, which adjusts its course based on feedback from its surroundings, to explain how we can use our minds to achieve our goals. He suggests that we must set clear goals, visualize them regularly, and adjust our behavior based on feedback from our environment.

The Importance of Self-Image

Even if you're unaware of it, your past experiences have changed how you see yourself. Because of this, you tend to believe this picture of yourself and live your life based on it. So, this may explain why some people always reach their goals and others never do. The things they do and see in the future will add to their image of themselves. From what the author says:

"Whether we realize it or not, each of us carries about with us a mental blueprint or picture of ourselves. It has been built up from our own beliefs about ourselves. But most of these beliefs about ourselves have unconsciously been formed from our past experiences, successes and failures, humiliations, triumphs, and how other people have reacted to us, especially in early childhood."

The brain is very powerful, and there is evidence that your brain can access knowledge in your subconscious that is not related to your own experiences. We can access universal knowledge by analyzing, thinking about, and looking for answers. The book suggests that people use the following ideas in their daily lives to connect with a higher power:

➤ **Your success mechanism needs to be tied to a goal.**
You have to have a lot of faith in the plan you make for yourself.

➤ **You care more about the END RESULT of your mechanism than the PRESENT.**
When you give your mechanism a goal, it will find a way to get there.

➤ **To reach your goals, making mistakes along the way is important.**
"Failure is success in progress," Albert Einstein once said. You have to realize that making mistakes is part of reaching your goals.

➤ **Redirecting your mistakes until you are going in the right direction helps you improve.**
Once you've made the right choice, you have to FORGET what came before and focus on the last, right choice that got you there.

➤ **Once you've set your END goals, you have to trust the process and not try to change things as you go.**
According to many successful people, success is not something that can be forced or manipulated. It cannot be achieved by simply wanting it badly enough. Instead, success results from taking action and allowing it to manifest naturally. Attempting to force success or expect it before taking any action is unlikely to lead to success in the long run.

Success Mechanism

Happiness, kindness, willingness to help, and not caring about yourself all affect positive behavior. Unfortunately, you must learn how to be happy to get there. As the author says, learning to be happy means getting out of the habit of reacting badly to things around us. To be happy, you must also be able to distinguish between facts and opinions. Another important way to make people happy is to set and reach goals. Your outlook on things has a lot to do with how happy you are, so you should try to see setbacks as challenges instead of failures on the way to your goals.

To challenge yourself, try to be happier, friendlier, less critical, more tolerant, focused on your success, differentiating between opinions and facts, smiling, and responding calmly throughout the day. Do these things for at least 21 days.

The author gives tips that readers can use to figure out what success means to them:

[S]ense of Direction.
In *Albert Einstein's* words, *"Bikes and people are alike. As long as they keep moving, they can stay on their feet."* In fact, we are always trying to do and become things that are even better than we are now. Because of this, you need to have goals and dreams if you want to do well.

[U]nderstanding.
It's important to communicate well. A person with good social skills is able to understand the problems and goals of others, feel what they are feeling, and even admit their own mistakes and flaws and find ways to fix them.

[C]ourage.
If you can act on your goals and beliefs, you can make them come true. Taking a few steps daily, like starting a conversation with a stranger, is a good way to practice courage.

[C]harity.
Successful people always think about what others need because they know

that everyone is different and deserves to be treated with respect and dignity. In this way, respect is shown by not being angry or hateful toward other people and by noticing and thinking about their feelings, emotions, and needs.

[E]steem.

Doubt is like a poison that hurts both your physical and mental health. Since you are made of flesh and bones like everyone else, you deserve the same respect and admiration as everyone else. Stop thinking of yourself as a loser or a victim. You are much better than that.

[S]elf-Confidence.

Success gives you more confidence. If you can remember the things you've done well in the past, you'll feel more confident that you can do the same things in the future. How many times you have tried to do something well is more important than whether or not you have succeeded in the past. Most important is to keep your eye on the goal.

[S]elf-Acceptance.

You shouldn't try to be someone else to get a better idea of who you are. Instead, you should accept yourself exactly as you are: flawed, always changing, and worthy of respect. In fact, no one is perfect, and those who think otherwise are just fooling themselves.

Failure Mechanism

Just as there is a mechanism for success, there is also a mechanism for failure, which can manifest in various ways and must be avoided to live a content and satisfying life. The author provides readers with a list of reminders to distinguish between success and failure. These reminders can assist individuals in achieving their goals and avoiding potential pitfalls:

[F]rustration.

There is always going to be some disappointment and shame. We should learn to accept these things and not judge ourselves too much. On the path to becoming the best version of ourselves, we often become victims when we let a temporary failure define our emotional state for too long.

[A]ggressiveness.

When people don't know what to do, they act out incorrectly. Also, knowing the difference between successful and unsuccessful aggressiveness is important. Positive aggression looks like pure determination and lets you face life's challenges without fear. On the other hand, negative aggression is a sign of anger and can't lead to anything good.

[I]nsecurity.

Insecurity is the feeling that you're not good enough for something bigger. You're not good enough to get a girl's attention, rich enough to quit your day job, or unhealthy enough to start working out. No matter how you look at it, insecurity is just a mental block we can build or break with our thoughts.

[L]oneliness.

We've all felt lonely at some point, but we shouldn't try to be alone on purpose. It's no secret that feeling like you belong to a group is one of life's greatest joys. Interacting with other people makes us more interesting and less anxious. It also helps us learn more about the different kinds of people in the world, which gives us a better understanding of how people see the world.

[U]ncertainty.

Fear of making mistakes can hold you back in life. This fear can leave you uncertain about which direction to take. However, it is important to remember that making mistakes is a natural part of life and can serve as valuable learning experiences. In fact, it is through these mistakes that we can become our best selves. It can be tempting to remain comfortable, but this can lead to regret later in life when we realize we missed out on opportunities for growth and change. So instead of being afraid of making mistakes, embrace them as a necessary part of the journey towards achieving your goals and becoming the best version of yourself. Accept failures and learn from this quote by *Randy Pausch: "It's not the things we do in life that we regret on our death bed, it is the things we do not."*

[R]esentment.

An individual who consistently displays anger and sadness towards others not only negatively impacts those around them, but also tends to adopt a victim mentality. In most cases, anger does not arise from external sources, rather it is generated from within. Holding onto resentments only reflects how we feel about something that has occurred externally. Holding the belief that the world owes us something is a sure way to end up with nothing, which can perpetuate a cycle of never-ending anger. The path to a fulfilling life involves finding joy within ourselves through self-exploration and personal growth. It is important to remember that relying on others to fulfill our expectations is not the answer.

[E]mptiness.

Emptiness is similar to discouragement in that it describes a person who can no longer enjoy life for various reasons. Getting out of this state of mind can be helped by setting goals. A person who is morally, mentally, and physically committed to a cause doesn't worry about feeling empty on the inside because he knows how to pick his battles and do his best for the cause.

KEY LESSONS

1. **How we feel about ourselves shows up in how we live.**
   How we think about ourselves affects how our lives turn out.

2. **Instead of looking at the good things about ourselves, we focus on the bad things.**
   We are doomed to fail when we think we are doomed to fail. To get out of this state, we must change how we think about ourselves.

3. **Our nervous system doesn't know the difference between what we think and what is real.**
   Whether the success is real or not, the body will do what it needs to do to make it happen.

4. **You outline the path to success.**
   To have a successful personality, you need direction, understanding, courage, kindness, self-respect, self-confidence, and acceptance of yourself.

5. **Take care of your emotional health to be your true self.**
   You should care for your heart, mind, and spirit if you want to ensure you're working for your true self.

ACTIONABLE STEPS TO TAKE

➤ **Visualize success.**
Visualizing your desired outcomes can help boost confidence, motivation and increase the likelihood of achieving your goals.

➤ **Reframe negative self-talk.**
Reframing negative thoughts and replacing them with positive self-talk can improve self-esteem and overall well-being.

➤ **Practice gratitude.**
Focusing on what you are grateful for can help shift your focus away from negative thoughts, increase positive emotions, and improve overall satisfaction with life.

➤ **Set realistic goals.**
Setting realistic, attainable goals helps build confidence, increase motivation, and can lead to greater success.

➤ **Embrace failure.**
Embracing failure as a necessary part of the learning process can help build resilience and increase motivation to try again.

➤ **Practice self-care.**
Engaging in activities that promote physical and emotional well-being, such as exercise, meditation, and sleep, can improve overall health and reduce stress.

➤ **Cultivate a growth mindset.**
Adopting a growth mindset, where challenges and failures are seen as opportunities for growth, can increase resilience and overall well-being.

➤ **Seek out positive relationships.**
Building and maintaining positive relationships with others can provide support, increase feelings of connectedness and improve overall well-being.

The Body Keeps the Score

by Bessel van der Kolk

"Learning how to breathe calmly and remaining in a state of relative physical relaxation, even while accessing painful and horrifying memories, is an essential tool for recovery."

T HIS book is a comprehensive look at the impact of trauma on the human body and mind. The book explores the ways in which trauma affects a person's mental and physical health, and the various treatments available to help individuals overcome their traumatic experiences.

He argues that trauma is not just a psychological issue, but also a physical one. He explains that traumatic experiences activate the body's stress response system and alter the brain's structure and function. This can lead to a range of symptoms such as anxiety, depression, hypervigilance, and chronic pain.

The author highlights the importance of addressing the body in addition to the mind when treating trauma and explains how traditional talk therapy may not be enough for some individuals. Instead, he promotes the use of techniques such as Eye Movement Desensitization and Reprocessing (EMDR), yoga, and somatic experiencing, which involve engaging the body and helping individuals to process their traumatic experiences in a safe and controlled way.

The Body Keeps the Score also covers the impact of trauma on society and the importance of addressing it in public health and policy. The book sheds light on the need for a better understanding and recognition of trauma and its effects, as well as the development of more effective treatments for individuals who have experienced trauma.

The Effects of Trauma

The effects of trauma go beyond just psychological distress. Recent advancements in neuroscience and psychology research given in the book have shown that trauma can cause physiological changes in the brain, including an alteration of the brain's alarm system, heightened stress hormone activity, and modifications to the information filtering system. Despite traditional beliefs that discussing traumatic experiences can lead to resolution, trauma often impedes this process. The emotional brain can become stuck in its reality, making it difficult for individuals to integrate new experiences and move forward in their growth. The survival mode triggered by trauma consumes an individual's energy and focus, leaving no room for nurturing relationships, learning, and attention to others. This reduction in abilities can have a lasting impact on an individual's daily life.

In the author's words, trauma is:

> *"We have learned that trauma is not just an event that took place some-time in the past; it is also the imprint left by that experience on mind, brain, and body. This imprint has ongoing consequences for how the human organism manages to survive in the present. Trauma results in a fundamental reorganization of the way the mind and brain manage perceptions. It changes not only how we think and what we think about, but also our very capacity to think."*

Brain on Trauma

The author argues that trauma can cause changes in brain structure and function, leading to alterations in the way individuals process and respond to information. This can result in heightened stress hormone activity, re-calibration of the brain's alarm system, and modifications to the information filtering system. These changes can have long-lasting effects on an individual's behavior, emotions, and relationships.

Body on Trauma

Trauma can result in physical symptoms such as headaches, chronic pain, sleep disturbances, and changes in how the body responds to stress, such as increased stress hormone activity. The effects of trauma on the body can be complex and multifaceted and may vary from person to person depending on a variety of factors. However, it is clear that trauma can significantly impact physical health, and may require specialized treatment or interventions to mitigate its effects.

Relationships on Trauma

The book highlights the impact of trauma on relationships and how it affects an individual's ability to form and maintain connections with others. The author argues that trauma can change how an individual perceives and responds to social cues and relationships, leading to difficulties in forming and maintaining healthy relationships. Trauma can also impact an individual's ability to trust others, leading to feelings of isolation and disconnection.

How Trauma Effects Children

According to the book, childhood trauma can have a profound impact on the development of children. Children who experience trauma, such as child abuse and neglect, are more vulnerable to its effects compared to adults. During the early years of life, healthy development depends on a parent's ability to meet a child's needs and form a secure attachment, but trauma can disrupt this process. On the attachment spectrum, trauma can result in disorganized attachment where a child experiences constant feelings of threat and distrust towards their caregiver.

The chronic stress of trauma can cause children to disconnect from their bodies and shut down emotionally, leading to long-term consequences such as mental, emotional, and physical problems. The author's research found that most child mental health issues stem from trauma and that these children are constantly dealing with triggers in their daily life. He also advocates for the diagnosis of Developmental Trauma Disorder to replace most childhood diagnoses in the DSM V (which is a comprehensive classification system and guidebook used by mental health professionals to diagnose mental disorders), as he believes that current diagnoses only describe the behavioral and emotional symptoms of trauma and not the underlying cause.

To understand the effects trauma has on children the author wants the reader to understand these three key lessons:

1. Childhood trauma can have lasting effects on the development of children and should be taken seriously.

2. The experience of trauma can disrupt the formation of a secure attachment, which is critical for healthy development.

3. Trauma-informed diagnoses and interventions are needed to address the root cause of child mental health issues.

Pathways to Recovery

The book presents the findings of several decades of research into the nature of trauma and its effects on the brain. This research draws on the fields of neuroscience, developmental psychopathology, and interpersonal neurobiology, which have all shown that trauma leads to actual changes in the brain, such as a recalibrated alarm system, increased stress hormone activity, and alterations in information filtering. As a result, trauma results in a fundamental reorganization of the way the mind and body manage perceptions, leading to a perceived world full of risks and threats. The book outlines three pathways to recovery from trauma.

➤ **Top down.**
   We can process traumatic memories by engaging in communication, re-connecting with others, and gaining self-awareness and insight into our internal experiences.

➤ **Medicines.**
   We can regulate our alarm reactions by using medication to suppress excessive alarm responses, or by utilizing other methods that alter the brain's information processing.

➤ **Bottom up.**
   By providing the body with experiences that directly and strongly oppose the feelings of helplessness, anger, or defeat caused by trauma, we can work through its effects.

   Talking, medicines, and bottom-up approaches can all play a role, but each has its limitations:

➤ **The limitations of *the talking cure*.**

   • Trauma is preverbal, meaning that few psychological problems re-sult from defects in understanding, and improving understanding does not necessarily help.

- Traumatized subjects can experience shutdown of Broca's area in the left frontal lobe, which is a speech center.

- The right hemisphere, which is responsible for memories of sound, touch, smell, and emotions, becomes active during flashbacks of trauma, bypassing the brain's executive functions and making them feel like intuitive truth.

➤ **The limitations of the *medicines*.**

- Antipsychotic medicines can help patients return to reality, but they do not solve the underlying problems that led to the development of their mental illness.

- Antidepressants can help with symptoms of depression, but they do not treat the root cause of the depression.

- Antianxiety medicines can help with anxiety symptoms, but they do not address the root causes of the anxiety.

➤ **The limitations of the *bottom-up procedure*.**

- The bottom-up recovery pathway can be a slow process as it involves rebuilding one small part at a time, and can take a considerable amount of time to see meaningful progress.

- The bottom-up approach may not significantly impact overall recovery as it only focuses on small, isolated parts, rather than taking a comprehensive approach to the entire system.

- The bottom-up recovery pathway may be limited by resource constraints such as financial resources, manpower, and technology. Rebuilding small parts at a time requires a significant amount of resources, and if these resources are not available, the recovery process can stall or be hindered.

KEY LESSONS

1. **Trauma affects the body as well as the mind.**
   Understanding that traumatic experiences can cause physical responses and sensations can help individuals identify and address the root causes of their symptoms.

2. **Trauma can lead to negative coping mechanisms.**
   Trauma can cause individuals to develop unhealthy coping strategies, such as substance abuse or self-harm, exacerbating its effects.

3. **Healing requires a holistic approach.**
   To effectively heal from trauma, individuals must address its impact on their mind, body, and spirit.

4. **Building a sense of safety and stability is key to healing.**
   Creating a stable environment, both internally and externally, can help reduce feelings of fear, anxiety, and hypervigilance associated with trauma.

5. **Connecting with others can be healing.**
   Building meaningful relationships and seeking support from others can help individuals process their experiences, reduce feelings of isolation, and promote resilience.

6. **Healing from trauma is a process, not a destination.**
   Trauma recovery is a lifelong journey, and individuals must be patient, compassionate with themselves, and willing to seek help when needed.

ACTIONABLE STEPS TO TAKE

➤ **Engage in physical activity regularly.**
Exercise helps release pent-up energy, improve physical and mental well-being, and increase self-esteem.

➤ **Practice deep breathing and mindfulness.**
By focusing on the present moment, mindfulness can reduce stress and anxiety levels, improve sleep, and provide a sense of calm.

➤ **Connect with others.**
Building supportive relationships with others can help you feel less isolated, reduce stress, and promote resilience.

➤ **Create a sense of safety and stability.**
Having a routine, structure, and predictability in your life can help calm your nervous system and provide a sense of security.

➤ **Practice self-compassion.**
By treating yourself with kindness and understanding, you can develop a healthier relationship with yourself and reduce feelings of shame and guilt associated with trauma.

➤ **Express your emotions.**
Allowing yourself to feel and express your emotions safely and healthily can help you process them and release their hold on you.

➤ **Challenge negative thought patterns.**
Recognizing and changing negative thought patterns can reduce anxiety and depression and increase feelings of self-worth.

➤ **Seek professional support.**
Talking to a mental health professional can provide a safe space to process trauma and gain a deeper understanding of its impact. It can also help you develop new coping strategies and work through difficult emotions.

Why We Sleep

by Matthew Walker

"Sleep is the single most effective thing we can do to reset our brain and body health each day — Mother Nature's best effort yet at contra-death."

T HIS book explores the science behind sleep, discussing how it affects the brain and the body. The book covers topics such as the evolution of sleep, the impacts of sleep deprivation, the connection between sleep and diseases such as Alzheimer's and cancer, and the importance of good sleep for overall health and well-being. The book highlights the benefits of sleep, such as improved memory, better mood and cognitive function, and reduced risk of numerous health problems. The author argues that sleep is crucial for human survival and that society should prioritize sleep and take steps to improve sleep habits.

Throughout the book, the author makes a compelling case for the importance of sleep in promoting physical and mental health. He emphasizes that sleep is not a luxury but a fundamental biological need essential for human survival and well-being.

One of the strengths of the book is its use of scientific evidence to support its arguments. It draws on a wide range of scientific studies to illustrate the benefits of sleep and the consequences of sleep deprivation. He also provides practical advice for improving sleep based on this scientific evidence.

The Science Behind Sleep

Routinely sleeping less than six or seven hours a night demolishes your immune system, more than doubling your risk of cancer. Insufficient sleep is a key lifestyle factor determining whether or not you will develop Alzheimer's disease. Inadequate sleep — even moderate reductions for just one week — disrupts blood sugar levels so profoundly that you would be classified as a pre-diabetic. Short sleeping increases the likelihood of your coronary arteries becoming blocked and brittle, setting you on a path toward cardiovascular disease, stroke, and congestive heart failure.

Sleep disruption further contributes to all major psychiatric conditions, including depression, anxiety, and suicidality.

Too little sleep swells concentrations of a hormone that makes you feel hungry while suppressing a companion hormone that otherwise signals food satisfaction.

Two main factors determine when you want to sleep:

➤ **The suprachiasmatic nucleus.**
An internal 24-hour clock is located deep within your brain.

➤ **Adenosine.**
A chemical substance that builds up in your brain and creates a *sleep pressure*.

Circadian Rhythm

Circadian rhythm refers to the natural physical, mental, and behavioral changes that occur in a 24-hour cycle, driven by an internal biological clock. The hypothalamus in the brain regulates it and influences processes such as sleep-wake patterns, hormone release, metabolism, and other physiological processes. The circadian rhythm is affected by both internal and external cues, such as light exposure, temperature changes, and behavior. It can be influenced by environmental factors such as travel and shift work. Disruptions to the circadian rhythm, such as jet lag or sleep deprivation, can lead to negative health consequences. Maintaining a regular sleep-wake cycle and exposure to natural light is important for synchronizing the circadian rhythm and promoting overall health.

Adenosine

Adenosine is a naturally occurring molecule that builds up in the brain throughout the day and regulates the sleep-wake cycle. As adenosine levels increase, they signal the brain that it is time to sleep. Caffeine works by blocking the effects of adenosine, which is why it is often used as a stimulant to increase alertness and delay sleep. During sleep, adenosine levels naturally decrease, allowing the brain to be more alert and awake the next day. This process helps to maintain the body's circadian rhythm and ensure adequate sleep. Adenosine is also involved in other physiological processes, including regulating blood flow and regulating the release of hormones such as adrenaline.

Melatonin

Melatonin is a hormone produced by the pineal gland in the brain that helps regulate the sleep-wake cycle. It is often referred to as the *sleep hormone*. Melatonin levels rise in the evening as darkness falls and signal to the body that it is time to prepare for sleep. Light exposure, especially from electronic devices, can suppress melatonin production and disrupt the sleep-wake cycle. Melatonin supplements are sometimes used as a sleep aid to help people with sleep disorders or jet lag fall asleep more easily. Melatonin is not a powerful sleeping aid in and of itself, at least not for healthy, non-jet-lagged individuals. There may be little, if any quality melatonin in a pill. That said, melatonin has a significant sleep placebo effect, which should not be underestimated.

Two Types of Sleep

According to the book, your brain switches between two types of sleep: Rapid Eye Movement (REM) and non-REM (NREM) sleep. The author explains that each type has different functions:

REM Sleep

REM sleep is a stage of sleep characterized by rapid eye movements, increased brain activity, and vivid dreaming. It typically occurs several times throughout the night and makes up 20-25% of total sleep time in adults. During REM sleep, the brain is highly active and processes information from the day, consolidate memories, and processes emotions. This stage of sleep is important for overall brain function and has been linked to improved learning and memory. REM sleep also has an important role in regulating mood and reducing symptoms of depression. During this stage of sleep physical paralysis occurs, preventing individuals from acting out their dreams and potentially injuring themselves. Disruptions to REM sleep, such as sleep deprivation or certain sleep disorders, can negatively impact brain function and overall health.

NREM Sleep

NREM sleep is a stage of sleep characterized by slow brain waves and minimal eye movement. It is divided into three sub-stages: N1, N2, and N3. NREM sleep makes up the majority of total sleep time and is important for physical recovery and restoring energy levels. During NREM sleep, the body's muscles relax, breathing becomes regular, and heart rate slows. It also provides an opportunity for the brain to process information from the day, consolidate memories, and regulate emotions. NREM sleep is also thought to play a role in regulating growth hormone release, which is important for the physical development and repair of tissues. Disruptions to NREM sleep, such as sleep deprivation, can negatively physical and cognitive functions.

Why Prioritize Sleep?

Sleep should be your number one focus ahead of anything else you do. It has a fundamental role in your health, weight, exercise, recovery, illness, etc. — it touches everything you do. The book is packaged with information, but there are some science-backed reasons from the book why sleep should be a priority:

➤ **Sleep improves cognitive function.**
Sleep helps consolidate memories, improve focus, and enhance decision-making skills. Lack of sleep impairs these functions leading to poor performance and accidents.

➤ **Sleep protects physical health.**
Sleep helps regulate hormones that control hunger and metabolism, reducing the risk of obesity, diabetes, and cardiovascular disease. It also helps boost the immune system and fight off infections.

➤ **Sleep regulates mood and emotions.**
Sleep helps regulate the release of hormones that affect mood and emotions, such as serotonin and cortisol. Lack of sleep can lead to an increased risk of depression and anxiety.

➤ **Sleep reduces the risk of chronic diseases.**
Chronic sleep deprivation increases the risk of developing several dis-

eases, including Alzheimer's, Parkinson's, and some cancers. Adequate sleep has been shown to reduce the risk of these conditions.

➤ **Sleep promotes longevity.**

Studies have shown a correlation between sleep and lifespan, with people who get adequate sleep having a lower risk of premature death. Sleep helps maintain overall physical and mental health, contributing to a longer life.

KEY LESSONS

1. **Sleep is essential for physical and cognitive health.**
   Sleep is vital in restoring energy levels, regulating hormones, and consolidating memories. It is also essential for physical recovery and has been linked to reduced risk of chronic diseases.

2. **Sleep quality is important.**
   The quality of sleep is just as important as the quantity. Good sleep quality is characterized by consistent, uninterrupted sleep that allows for adequate time in each stage of sleep, including NREM and REM.

3. **Light exposure affects sleep.**
   Light exposure, especially bright light, can suppress melatonin production and delay sleep onset. Limiting exposure to light before bed, especially from electronic devices, can improve sleep quality.

4. **The circadian rhythm regulates the sleep-wake cycle.**
   The circadian rhythm, an internal biological clock, regulates the sleep-wake cycle and is affected by factors such as light exposure and daily habits. Maintaining a consistent sleep schedule can help regulate the circadian rhythm and improve sleep quality.

5. **Sleep disorders can have serious impacts.**
   Sleep disorders, such as insomnia and sleep apnea, can significantly impact sleep quality and overall health. Seeking treatment, such as medication or lifestyle changes, can help improve sleep quality and reduce the risk of chronic diseases.

6. **Sleep is a critical aspect of overall health.**
   Sleep is critical to overall health and well-being, affecting physical, cognitive, and emotional functioning. Prioritizing sleep, by creating a sleep-conducive environment and adopting healthy sleep habits, can improve overall health and quality of life.

ACTIONABLE STEPS TO TAKE

➤ **Establish a consistent sleep schedule.**
Going to bed and waking up simultaneously daily helps regulate the circadian rhythm and improve sleep quality.

➤ **Create a sleep-conducive environment.**
A cool, dark, and quiet room promotes sleep and reduces disruptions. Earplugs, blackout curtains, and a comfortable mattress can improve sleep quality.

➤ **Reduce exposure to light before bed.**
Exposure to bright light, especially from electronic devices, suppresses melatonin production and delays sleep onset. Reducing exposure to light before bedtime can improve sleep quality.

➤ **Avoid caffeine and alcohol before bed.**
Caffeine stimulates the central nervous system and delays sleep onset, while alcohol can disrupt sleep quality. Limiting the consumption of these substances before bed can improve sleep quality.

➤ **Reduce napping.**
Napping during the day can disrupt the sleep-wake cycle and make it harder to fall asleep at night. If needed, limiting naps to 30 minutes or less can help improve sleep quality.

➤ **Reduce screen time before bed.**
The blue light emitted by electronic devices can suppress melatonin production and delay sleep onset. Limiting screen time before bed, or using blue light filters, can improve sleep quality.

➤ **Practice relaxation techniques.**
Relaxation techniques like deep breathing, meditation, or yoga, can help reduce stress and improve sleep quality.

➤ **Avoid large meals and drinks before bed.**
Eating a large meal or drinking fluids before bed can cause discomfort and disrupt sleep. Limiting food and drink intake before bedtime can improve sleep quality.

Not a Diet Book

by James Smith

*"It's not about perfect. It's about making the effort. And when
you bring that effort every single day, that's where transformation
happens."*

T HIS book is a refreshing and evidence-based guide to achieving long-term
health and wellness. Rather than promoting fad diets or quick fixes, it
offers practical advice on how to make sustainable changes to our eating habits,
exercise routine, and mindset.

One of the key themes of the book is the importance of balance. The author emphasizes that there is no one-size-fits-all approach to nutrition, and that
a healthy diet should include a variety of food groups. He also debunks common myths about diets and explains how to determine the right portion sizes for
different types of food. Additionally, he provides strategies for making healthy
choices when eating out or on the go, and for dealing with cravings and emotional eating.

In the section on exercise, the book stresses the importance of finding a
form of physical activity that we enjoy and can stick to long-term. He provides
a range of workouts and training plans to suit different fitness levels and goals,
but also emphasizes that exercise doesn't have to be intense or time-consuming
to be effective. He also provides tips on avoiding injury and staying motivated,
as well as the importance of rest and recovery.

Gaining Muscle or Losing Fat

According to the book, building muscle and losing fat are two different processes that require specific approaches. It is difficult to achieve both simultaneously since they have opposing requirements. When building muscle, a caloric
surplus is necessary to provide the body with the energy it needs to grow new
muscle tissue. On the other hand, when losing fat, a caloric deficit is necessary
to prompt the body to tap into stored fat for energy. Attempting to do both simultaneously will only lead to frustration and slow progress, as the body cannot

efficiently build muscle and burn fat simultaneously. Therefore, it is recommended to focus on one goal at a time.

Fat Loss

The book emphasizes that losing fat is not just about following a particular diet or exercise routine but a holistic approach involving various lifestyle factors.

The author suggests three ways to eliminate fat:

➤ **Create a calorie deficit diet.**
This means consuming fewer calories than the body requires to maintain its current weight. This can be achieved through a combination of reducing calorie intake and increasing physical activity. However, ensuring that the body still receives adequate nutrients and fuel to support its basic functions and physical activity is important.

➤ **Be aware of the quality of the food consumed.**
The author emphasizes the importance of choosing whole, nutrient-dense foods and avoiding processed and high-calorie foods. This helps reduce calorie intake and provides the body with the necessary nutrients for optimal health and metabolism.

➤ **Manage stress and getting enough sleep.**
Chronic stress can increase cortisol levels, contributing to fat gain, while poor sleep quality can interfere with metabolism and hormonal regulation.

Muscle Gain

Muscle gain is a complex process that requires discipline, patience, and consistency. According to the book, building muscle is a journey that involves pushing your body through stress, allowing it to recover and grow stronger. It is not just about lifting weights but also understanding how your body works and what it needs to grow stronger.

To effectively build muscle, certain rules must be followed:

➤ **Focus on progressive overload is crucial to building muscle effectively.**

This means gradually increasing the weight or intensity of your exercises over time to continue challenging your muscles. Without progressive overload, your muscles will become accustomed to the stress and stop growing.

➤ **Compound exercises are essential to promoting overall strength and muscle growth.**
These exercises work for multiple muscle groups simultaneously, such as squats, deadlifts, and bench presses. Compound exercises engage a larger number of muscle fibers and promote greater muscle activation, resulting in more efficient muscle growth.

➤ **Protein is a vital component of muscle growth, providing the necessary building blocks for repair and recovery.**
The book recommends consuming 1 gram of protein per pound of body weight daily. This ensures that your muscles have enough amino acids to repair and rebuild stronger after exercise.

➤ **Recovery is just as important as the exercise itself.**
Adequate rest and proper nutrition are critical to allowing your muscles to repair and grow stronger. Overtraining can lead to injury and hinder progress, so taking rest days and listening to your body's signals is essential.

Importance of Sleep

Sleep is an essential part of our daily routine that does great things for both the mind and body. It is a critical component of our overall health and well-being, and getting enough of it helps us recover faster, perform better, think better, have more sex drive, and indirectly helps us lose weight. The benefits of a good night's sleep are numerous, and the best part is that it doesn't cost you anything other than the time you spend awake. Studies conducted by *Michael Greger* concluded that:

> *"Sleep deprivation tends to lead people to overeat by about 180–560 calories a day."*

— Michael Greger

When we get enough quality sleep, we can make better decisions, which usually means we choose the right foods. In contrast, when we don't get enough sleep, we can't think as well, and our ability to make good decisions is impaired. This is compounded when we also have bad health habits, such as consuming foods that are high in fat and sugar. To ensure you get enough quality sleep, it is important to follow certain rules, such as establishing a consistent sleep routine, creating a sleep-conducive environment, avoiding caffeine and alcohol, and avoiding blue light exposure before bed.

Understanding the Sleep Hormones

Cortisol, a hormone often associated with stress, is essential to the body's survival mechanisms, contrary to common belief. This hormone, secreted by the adrenal glands, regulates blood sugar levels, blood pressure, and even inflammation. Without cortisol, our bodies wouldn't be able to respond to perceived threats, such as running away from a predator or waking up in the morning. However, when cortisol levels become too high or too low, it can lead to several health problems, including weight gain, anxiety, and depression. Therefore, maintaining stable cortisol levels is as crucial as controlling insulin levels. Another hormone that plays a crucial role in our well-being is melatonin, commonly known as the sleep hormone. Melatonin production is influenced by light exposure and regulates our sleep-wake cycle. Additional melatonin supplements can enhance sleep quality and help manage sleep disorders such as insomnia. Along with melatonin supplements, simple changes to our sleep hygiene practices can also promote better sleep quality. These changes may include setting an alarm, utilizing electronic wellness tools, listening to audiobooks or podcasts, and using magnesium and lavender oil on the skin to promote relaxation.

Calorie Deficits by Cutting Macronutrients

Creating a calorie deficit, also known as an energy deficit, is essential to weight loss. This concept is based on the scientific principle that when the body burns more calories than it consumes, it reduces body fat. Therefore, the calorie deficit principle is a fundamental aspect of weight loss diets.

Calories come in three different forms: fat, carbs, and protein.

➤ **Protein.**
Foods such as chicken, fish, red meat, and some dairy products.

➤ **Carbohydrate.**
When digested, all things primarily composed of sugar (glucose) are also referred to as carbs.

➤ **Fat.**
The process by which essential hormones are produced.

It's important to remember that none of these macros are always bad. Protein and carbohydrates both have 4 calories per gram, but fat has 9 calories per gram. The author explains how you can cut back on one of these macros to get a diet with fewer calories:

➤ **Creating a calorie deficit by reducing carbohydrates.**
When carbohydrates are broken down, glucose is made, the body's main and preferred energy source. Small amounts of glucose can be used immediately by the muscles or stored as glycogen in the liver. Since carbs are easier for the body to break down than fats or proteins, it prefers to do so. So, when we work out hard, our bodies break down more carbs; when we work out less hard, we tend to use more fat as a fuel source. Also, carbohydrates help keep muscle tissue from breaking down. This is called *protein sparing*.

➤ **Creating a calorie deficit by reducing protein.**
The author stresses the importance of protein as the most crucial macronutrient. However, the idea of protein making you feel full can be seen as a potential downside. Experiencing early satiety, a feeling of fullness that occurs before a meal is finished, can lead to malnourishment, hinder muscle mass growth, and negatively impact recovery. Nonetheless, this is not the typical outcome. The author emphasizes the significance of

protein as the primary macronutrient as it provides the body with essential amino acids for tissue repair and growth, boosts metabolism, and enhances overall physical performance. The Greek term *"proteios"*, which means *"first"* or *"most important,"* accurately reflects the importance of protein in our diets.

➤ **Creating a calorie deficit by reducing fat.**

Switching from red meat to lean meat can be a helpful option when trying to cut down on calorie intake. However, it's important to note that reducing fat intake too much can be detrimental to our health. While many associate fat with negative connotations, dietary fat is crucial for various bodily functions, such as hormone regulation and vitamin absorption. In particular, consuming enough dietary fat is essential for absorbing fat-soluble vitamins like A, D, E, and K, which are vital for maintaining healthy bones, eyesight, immune function, and much more.

KEY LESSONS

1. **It's important to know how to keep track of the calories you eat.**
   Eating the right number of calories can keep your weight healthy.

2. **There are no foods that are low in calories that you can buy.**
   People who eat modern foods are more likely to gain weight because these foods aren't made to limit the number of calories they contain.

3. **Fibre-rich foods have been shown to assist in weight loss, particularly in unfavorable circumstances.**
   Fiber is important for our bodies because it helps us stay healthy in many ways, like keeping us from getting fat.

4. **A low-fat diet can help you keep your weight at a healthy level.**
   Consuming a moderate amount of healthy fats can help with weight loss by promoting satiety and providing the body with sustained energy.

5. **In order to lose weight, it is often necessary to make significant changes, such as reducing sugar intake.**
   Reducing sugar from your diet is one of the best ways to shed pounds.

ACTIONABLE STEPS TO TAKE

➤ **Drink water.**
Staying hydrated helps flush out toxins, boost metabolism, and regulate hunger.

➤ **Eat more fiber.**
Fiber-rich foods provide a feeling of fullness, regulate digestion and reduce the risk of chronic diseases.

➤ **Reduce sugar.**
Reducing sugar can improve overall health and prevent conditions like obesity, type 2 diabetes, and heart disease.

➤ **Incorporate protein.**
Protein provides energy, helps build and repair muscle, and helps with weight management.

➤ **Reduce processed food.**
Processed foods are often high in salt, sugar and unhealthy fats, consuming them in moderation can improve overall health.

➤ **Get enough sleep.**
Adequate sleep is important for physical and mental health, helps regulate hormones, and supports weight management.

➤ **Get active.**
Regular physical activity improves overall health, helps with weight management, and reduces the risk of chronic diseases.

➤ **Reduce stress.**
Chronic stress can lead to overeating, weight gain and other health problems, reducing stress through relaxation, exercise or therapy can help improve overall health.

➤ **Build healthy habits.**
Adopting healthy habits like regular meal planning, mindful eating and regular physical activity can help with sustainable weight management and overall health improvement.

The Power of Now

by Eckhart Tolle

"You attract and manifest whatever corresponds to your inner state."

T HIS book's central theme is the importance of living in the present moment and achieving inner peace and happiness through mindfulness.

The book is divided into ten chapters, each of which focuses on a different aspect of living in the present moment. It argues that the mind is constantly focused on the past or future, which leads to anxiety, stress, and dissatisfaction with life. Living in the present moment can achieve inner peace and happiness.

The author introduces the *"pain body concept,"* which is the accumulation of past emotional pain that can manifest as negative thoughts and behaviors. He encourages readers to become aware of their pain body and to observe their thoughts and emotions without judgment.

It also introduces the concept of the *ego,* which he defines as the false sense of self-created by the mind. He argues that the ego is responsible for much of the suffering and conflict in the world and encourages readers to transcend the ego and connect with their true nature.

One of the main strengths of *The Power of Now* is its emphasis on practical application. The author's advice is clear and actionable, and his exercises are designed to help readers achieve a greater sense of mindfulness and inner peace.

Negative Thinking and Your Ego

You may have noticed that your mind is always busy with thoughts. Our inner voice speculates, complains, judges, compares, etc. We often think about and worry about the future in our daily lives. When we don't do that, we often think about the past. Our inner conversations and monologues are always going on, and they pretty much take up most of our lives. We don't even know this is happening, which is strange.

Our ego is in charge and only cares about the past and future. Because of this, it tries to keep the past alive. So, it tells your story and shows you what you were like in the past. Ultimately, it looks back at the past and looks ahead to the future. This means that it doesn't care about anything right now.

A person's ego comes from a lot of different things, like their possessions, their social status, their job, their physical appearance, their knowledge, their education, their relationships, their history, their beliefs, and so on. But none of these describes you. How do you feel about that? Most of these things will go away at some point, so you should be ready to let go of them anytime.

Being present is the only way to stop the ego and negative thoughts from controlling you. For the antidote to work well, we need to keep in mind the following:

➤ We waste our mental and emotional energy on things we cannot control. We can only change what is going on right now.

➤ When you think about the past, you feel things like guilt, regret, anger, sadness, bitterness, and the inability to forgive.

➤ When you think about the future too much makes you anxious, tense, stressed out, and worried.

➤ Our ego says that we are made up of our memories, experiences, religion, upbringing, education, jobs, gender, political views, and nationality. In your mind, your ego tries to take charge of your thoughts, feelings, and actions.

➤ Your ego is distracting you, which makes it hard for you to connect with your true self.

➤ If you let your ego run your life, you can't be at peace with yourself or be in the moment.

➤ Most of our pain and suffering comes from ourselves because we feed our bodies' negativity and let our egos fill our minds with worries about the past and the future.

Be Present in the Moment

The author emphasizes the importance of being present at the moment as a key to achieving inner peace and happiness. He argues that too often, individuals become consumed with thoughts of the past or future, which can lead to anxiety, stress, and a sense of disconnection from the present moment. Individuals can tap into a deeper sense of inner peace and fulfillment by learning to be fully present in each moment.

Here are four ways on how to live in the present:

1. **Learn to quiet the mind and focus on the present experience.**
   This may involve practices such as meditation, deep breathing, or mindfulness exercises, which can help individuals to become more aware of their thoughts and emotions in the present moment.

2. **Learn to embrace the present moment without judgment or resistance.**
   This may involve accepting difficult emotions or situations as they arise, rather than trying to push them away or avoid them. By acknowledging and accepting the present moment, individuals can develop a deeper sense of inner peace and contentment.

3. **Cultivate a sense of gratitude and appreciation for the present moment, regardless of circumstances.**
   This may involve actively seeking out moments of beauty, joy, or connection in everyday life, and taking time to savor and appreciate these experiences.

4. **Learn to let go of attachment to the past or future.**
   By releasing attachment to thoughts or expectations about the future, individuals can free themselves from anxiety and worry, and fully embrace the present moment as it unfolds.

Accept the Tragedies in Life

The author highlights the importance of accepting the tragedies and challenges that life inevitably brings. He argues that while it can be tempting to resist or deny difficult circumstances, such reactions only serve to perpetuate suffering and prevent individuals from experiencing true inner peace.

Here's how to get past opposition:

➤ **Learn to let go of the need for control.**
   This may involve recognizing that many aspects of life are beyond our

control, and learning to accept this reality with grace and humility. By letting go of the need for control, individuals can cultivate a greater sense of surrender and trust in the universe, allowing them to navigate difficult circumstances with greater ease and resilience.

➤ **Develop a sense of detachment from outcomes.**
his may involve recognizing that while difficult circumstances may be painful or uncomfortable, they do not define our fundamental sense of self or worth. By cultivating detachment from outcomes, individuals can learn to experience difficult circumstances without becoming consumed by them, allowing them to maintain a sense of inner peace and equanimity even in the face of tragedy.

➤ **Develop a sense of presence and mindfulness in everyday life.**
This may involve cultivating a greater sense of awareness of one's thoughts and emotions, and learning to observe them without judgment or attachment. Then individuals can develop greater resilience and adaptability in the face of difficult circumstances, allowing them to navigate tragedies and challenges with greater grace and ease.

KEY LESSONS

1. **Keep your mind on the present moment to make your life better.**
   It's more important to enjoy the moment you're in than to think about the past or the future.

2. **Don't let your ego keep you from being happy by making you do things that hurt you.**
   The ego is part of a person's mind that keeps them from being happy and even makes them hurt themselves by being selfish and making a big deal out of things.

3. **Pay more attention to your body than your mind to find peace of mind.**
   When the mind dwells on bad memories or worries about what might happen, it can cause pain.

4. **If you watch your thoughts without judging them, your mind will stop controlling you.**
   You can stop the flow of your life and watch your thoughts to see how they affect you.

5. **Always act like you are looking forward to something.**
   You can avoid living in the past and daydreaming about the future if you can stay aware all the time, as if something important is about to happen.

6. **If you live in the present, your relationship with your partner will get better.**
   At first, your partner's ego can drag you down, but over time, they will see how your inner peace helps them.

7. **Living in the present can't keep you from all pain.**
   The sooner you realize that you can't avoid all pain, the less you will have to go through.

8. **Giving in to the present moment doesn't mean you have to live a passive life.**
   The ability to live passively on the inside and act on situations on the outside is still there.

ACTIONABLE STEPS TO TAKE

➤ **Practice mindfulness.**

Mindfulness helps to increase self-awareness, reduce stress and anxiety, and improve overall well-being.

➤ **Focus on the present moment.**

Focusing on the present moment helps to reduce stress and increase happiness, allowing you to better handle life's challenges.

➤ **Practice self-observation.**

Self-observation helps to increase self-awareness and reduce stress, allowing you to better understand and manage your thoughts and emotions.

➤ **Let go of negative thoughts.**

Letting go of negative thoughts helps to reduce stress and increase happiness, allowing you to better handle life's challenges.

➤ **Cultivate gratitude.**

Cultivating gratitude helps to improve overall mood, increase happiness, and reduce stress and anxiety.

➤ **Develop a spiritual practice.**

Developing a spiritual practice helps to increase self-awareness, reduce stress and anxiety, and improve overall well-being.

➤ **Practice acceptance.**

Practicing acceptance helps to reduce stress and increase happiness, allowing you to better handle life's challenges.

➤ **Cultivate inner peace.**

Cultivating inner peace helps to reduce stress and increase happiness, allowing you to better handle life's challenges.

➤ **Let go of the past.**

Letting go of the past helps to reduce stress and increase happiness, allowing you to better handle life's challenges.

The 4-Hour Body

by Tim Ferriss

"The decent method you follow is better than the perfect method you quit."

THIS book provides readers with a wide range of information on how to improve their health and fitness, achieve their goals and optimize their life. The book is based on the author's personal experiments and research on human performance and covers a wide range of topics, including diet, exercise, sleep, and sex.

The purpose of the book is to provide readers with practical advice on how to achieve their health and fitness goals more efficiently, by implementing evidence-based strategies and techniques. The book aims to empower readers to take control of their own health and fitness, and to make significant improvements in their lives by adopting the techniques and principles outlined in the book.

Readers can benefit from *The 4-Hour Body* by learning about effective strategies for weight loss, muscle gain, improved sex life, and enhanced athletic performance. The book also provides insights into other areas of health and wellness such as sleep, stress reduction, and general health maintenance.

Fear and Motivation

According to the author, leveraging external pressures can be an effective strategy for motivating oneself to take action. This can be achieved by setting ambitious deadlines that require considerable effort to miss. Additionally, the author suggests exploring the use of contractual agreements to ensure the successful attainment of a given goal. To maintain momentum, rewarding oneself upon completion of a task is also advised. To ensure optimal results, the following four rules are recommended as essential safeguards against potential setbacks:

1. **Consciousness is key.**
   Focusing on the present moment is of greater significance than fixating on the end goal, according to experts. While food journals can be a useful

tool in weight management, studies suggest that utilizing visual aids such as photographs can yield more favorable outcomes.

2. **Turn it into a game.**
   While measurement can provide an initial burst of motivation, it is often short-lived. To sustain motivation over the long-term, it is crucial to monitor changes in the measured data. By regularly tracking progress and keeping an eye on the numbers, individuals can remain motivated to pursue their goals.

3. **Competition is very important.**
   The possibility of failing is a bigger motivator than the reward itself. Use peer pressure to improve your performance.

4. **Keep it simple and short-term.**
   One of the most significant barriers to achieving our goals is often the tendency to overlook the small, incremental changes that can lead to significant progress over time. When striving for long-term improvement, it can be tempting to focus on major changes that promise immediate results.

4-hour Diet Plan

The Slow-Carb Diet also emphasizes the importance of consuming adequate protein and engaging in regular exercise to support fat loss and muscle gain. The book provides detailed guidance on how to calculate your daily protein needs and offers a range of exercise protocols designed to maximize results in minimal time.

One of the key components of the book is the *Slow-Carb Diet*, also known as the *4-Hour Diet Plan*, which is designed to help individuals lose fat and gain muscle in a sustainable and efficient manner.

How to Execute the Diet

➤ **Eliminate *White Carbohydrates*.**
   All types of bread, white and brown rice, cereal, potatoes, pasta, tortillas, and fried foods that are breaded are included.

➤ **Avoid drinking calories.**

Avoid sugary drinks and fruit juices, which can contribute to weight gain and negatively impact blood sugar levels. Hydration is a crucial aspect of any healthy diet, and the program in question emphasizes the importance of drinking plenty of water, tea, coffee, and other low-calorie or calorie-free beverages.

➤ **Avoid eating fruits.**

While fruit may be a healthy source of vitamins and minerals, it is also high in fructose, which can interfere with fat loss and promote insulin resistance.

➤ **Repetition of the same few meals.**

By simplifying your diet and sticking to a few staple meals, you can minimize decision fatigue and maintain consistency in your eating habits. The author recommends meals that include these ingredients:

- Lean chicken, fish, beef, or pork.
- Variety of greens: spinach, mixed cruciferous vegetables, asparagus, peas, broccoli, and green beans.

➤ **Give yourself one day off per week.**

One of the key components of his Diet Plan involves designating Saturdays as a *"Dieters Gone Wild"* day. During this time, he allows himself to consume any type of food he desires, including large quantities of ice cream and other indulgent treats. While this may seem counterintuitive, the author argues that this approach helps to prevent binge eating and supports metabolic stability.

Dietary Mistakes to Avoid

In the pursuit of optimal health and fitness, it's important to be aware of common dietary mistakes that can derail your progress. According to *The 4-Hour Body*, there are several key mistakes to avoid when it comes to your diet.

➤ **Avoid processed foods and excessive sugar intake.**

These foods can be high in calories, unhealthy fats, and artificial ingredients, which can contribute to weight gain, inflammation, and other health problems.

➤ **Avoid skipping meals or drastically reducing your caloric intake.**
While it may seem like a quick way to lose weight, this approach can actually slow down your metabolism and lead to muscle loss.

➤ **Avoid over-reliance on low-fat or diet foods.**
These products may be marketed as healthier options, but they often contain hidden sugars, unhealthy additives, and other artificial ingredients that can have negative effects on your health.   ·

➤ **Avoid excessive alcohol consumption.**
This can contribute to weight gain, dehydration, and other health problems.

➤ **Avoid overeating.**
It's important to be aware of portion sizes and to avoid overeating, even when consuming healthy foods.

➤ **Consuming too little water.**
Ensuring adequate hydration can enhance the liver's ability to metabolize fat, resulting in improved efficiency of fat burning processes within the body.

How to Prevent Fat Gain

The book outlines a number of principles and strategies for achieving optimal health and fitness. One of the key areas he addresses is the prevention of fat gain. According to the author, there are a number of factors that contribute to weight gain, including hormonal imbalances, poor nutrition, and lack of exercise. To combat these factors, it recommends a number of key rules that can help prevent fat gain and promote weight loss:

1. **Limit your intake of carbohydrates.**
   Carbohydrates are one of the primary sources of energy for the body, but consuming too many carbs can lead to insulin resistance and weight gain. By limiting your carbohydrate intake and focusing on high-quality

protein and healthy fats, you can improve your body's ability to burn fat and promote weight loss.

2. **Exercise regularly.**
Exercise helps to increase your metabolism, burn calories, and build muscle, all of which can help prevent fat gain. He recommends a combination of resistance training and high-intensity interval training (HIIT) for maximum fat-burning benefits.

3. **Maintain adequate hydration.**
Drinking enough water helps to boost metabolism, support healthy digestion, and flush toxins from the body. By ensuring that you are properly hydrated, you can optimize your body's ability to burn fat and prevent weight gain.

4. **Get enough sleep, reduce stress, and avoid processed foods and sugary drinks.**
Sleep is essential for regulating hormones that control metabolism and appetite, while stress can lead to overeating and weight gain. Processed foods and sugary drinks are often high in calories and low in nutrients, making them a major contributor to weight gain and poor health.

SUMMARY OF WHAT YOU CAN EAT AND NOT

WHAT TO EAT	WHAT NOT TO EAT
Chicken Breast	Bread
Beef	Rice
Fish	Cereal
Pork	Potatoes
Egg Whites	Pasta
Whole Egg	Tortillas
Legumes	Breaded fried foods
Vegetables	Sugar-sweetened beverages
Tomatoes	Candy
Olive Oil	Chips
Avocados	Cake & cookies

The Art of Sex and Sleep

The book highlights that many people neglect the importance of sexual health and satisfaction, and that by understanding and practicing the art of sex, individuals can experience numerous physical and psychological benefits. The art of sex is a multifaceted and complex subject, involving both physical and psychological factors. By learning how to control and maximize your sexual energy, communicate effectively with your partner, and take care of your body and overall health, you can experience greater sexual satisfaction and well-being. The author recommends the following:

1. **Learn how to control and maximize your sexual energy.**
   This involves understanding the various stages of sexual arousal and learning how to maintain a high level of arousal for as long as possible. The book recommends a number of techniques for achieving this, including deep breathing, visualization, and muscle control exercises.

2. **Learn how to communicate effectively with your partner.**
   This involves being open and honest about your desires and preferences, as well as listening to and responding to your partner's needs. It emphasizes the importance of creating a safe and supportive environment for sexual exploration and experimentation, and recommends practicing active listening and non-judgmental communication.

3. **Take care of your body and overall health to maximize your sexual performance and satisfaction.**
   This includes eating a healthy diet, engaging in regular exercise, and getting enough sleep and rest. The author recommends specific supplements and practices, such as taking magnesium and zinc supplements, practicing intermittent fasting, and engaging in cold exposure therapy, as means of improving sexual health and performance.

The book argues that numerous women have reported never having experienced an orgasm, with many indicating that they have never achieved one in a sexual relationship. However, there are various steps and techniques that women can implement to enhance their sexual pleasure and potentially achieve orgasm. Some of these methods may include:

➤ **Penetration angle.**
Altering the angle of penetration during sexual activity can potentially stimulate the female G-spot, which is an erogenous zone located within the vagina.

➤ **Alter the pressure.**
During sexual activity, adjusting the pressure exerted can increase stimulation and pleasure for both partners.

Importance of Sleep

The book emphasizes the importance of sleep as a critical component of overall health and wellness. It argues that adequate and restful sleep is essential for maintaining optimal physical and mental function, and that it is often overlooked or undervalued in today's fast-paced society.

Here are a number of ways to improve sleep:

➤ **Establish a consistent sleep schedule.**
This involves going to bed and waking up at the same time each day, even on weekends or days off. By establishing a regular sleep schedule, the body is better able to regulate its natural sleep-wake cycle, which can lead to better quality sleep and increased energy and alertness during waking hours.

➤ **Create an optimal sleep environment.**
This may involve minimizing distractions such as noise, light, or electronic devices and keeping the sleeping environment cool and comfortable. It recommends engaging in relaxation practices such as meditation or deep breathing exercises before bed to promote relaxation and reduce stress and anxiety.

➤ **Focus on quality, not quantity.**
This may involve practices such as avoiding caffeine or alcohol before bed, reducing screen time in the hours leading up to sleep, and implementing techniques such as intermittent fasting or cold exposure therapy, which have been shown to improve sleep quality and duration.

KEY LESSONS

1. **The author learned a lot about health and fitness by letting himself be used and taken advantage of for fitness education.**
   During this process he learned that anything more than giving the minimum effort can be used to achieve the desired results.

2. **The Slow Carb Diet has helped a lot of people lose weight.**
   You can lose weight if you stay away from white carbs and eat the same kind of meal every day.

3. **If you want to improve your sexual life, you should move around.**
   Achieving an optimal angle and pressure during sexual activity can significantly enhance a woman's overall sexual experience.

4. **Don't take a hot shower before bed.**
   Getting into a cold bath right before bed can help you sleep better.

5. **Practice not only to get farther, but also to get better at your work.**
   Using the right technique when lifting weights is much better than doing too many reps.

ACTIONABLE STEPS TO TAKE

➤ **Track calorie intake.**
Tracking calorie intake helps to ensure that you are consuming the right amount of food for your goals and helps to identify areas for improvement.

➤ **Focus on nutrient-dense foods.**
Focusing on nutrient-dense foods helps provide the body with the essential vitamins and minerals for optimal health and performance.

➤ **Use the Slow-Carb Diet.**
The Slow-Carb Diet is a scientifically proven diet that helps to reduce body fat and increase muscle mass.

➤ **Incorporate strength training.**
Strength training helps to build muscle, increase metabolism, and improve overall fitness.

➤ **Experiment with HIIT training.**
HIIT is a highly effective form of exercise that helps to improve cardiovascular health and increase fat-burning potential.

➤ **Utilize cold therapy.**
Cold therapy helps to improve circulation, boost energy levels, and improve overall health.

➤ **Take advantage of sleep optimization.**
Sleep optimization helps to improve sleep quality, increase energy levels, and improve overall health and well-being.

➤ **Use strategic supplementation.**
Strategic supplementation can help enhance performance, reduce recovery time, and improve overall health.

➤ **Take advantage of advanced techniques.**
Advanced techniques such as the Pomodoro Technique and Parkinson's Law can help to improve productivity, reduce stress, and increase success.

TO THE AUTHORS...

"It always seems impossible until it's done."

— Nelson Mandela

THE credit for this book belongs to the authors of the fantastic books you have just read a summary of. Thanks to Debra Fine's book, *The Fine Art of Small Talk*, people now understand the importance of listening and smiling during a conversation. People now understand the importance of financial responsibility thanks to Vicki Robin's book, *Your Money or Your Life*. Thanks to Michael Matthews' book, *Bigger, Leaner, Stronger*, people now understand the concepts of fat loss and muscle growth. Thanks to James Clear's book, *Atomic Habits*, people now understand the massive impact small habits can have over time.

In the absence of these books, I could not have written the book and you could not have developed new life concepts and principles. These remarkable self-development books deserve all the praise. My role has been to distill the most crucial principles and concepts from each book and present them in a comprehensive and accessible manner. I am thankful to these authors for their exceptional work and the lessons they have imparted to me. Without their influence, this book would not have been possible.

Further Readings

HOPEFULLY, reading this book was the start of a lifetime of learning, and I enlightened your inner flame to take steps toward becoming the BEST version of yourself. To access further readings by me, kindly take a look at my other books listed below.

701 LIFE LESSONS

—

701 LIFE QUOTES

In undertaking your mission, I have provided you with a list of recommendations on the next page that I think will be beneficial for you. Good luck on your journey and hope the list proves useful.

LEADERSHIP

➤ *LEARNING TO LEAD* by **Ron Williams**

➤ *HUMBLE LEADERSHIP* by **Edgar H. Schein**

➤ *THE FIFTH RISK* by **Michael Lewis**

➤ *LEADERSHIP IS AN ART* by **Max DePree**

SUCCESS

➤ *THE SUCCESS PRINCIPLES* by **Jack Confield**

➤ *THE FOUR AGREEMENTS* by **Don Miguel Ruiz**

➤ *THE MOTIVATION MANIFESTO* by **Brendon Burchard**

➤ *THE OBSTACLE IS THE WAY* by **Ryan Holiday**

ENTREPRENEURSHIP

➤ *THE E-MYTH* by **Michael F. Gerber**

➤ *LOST AND FOUNDER* by **Rand Fishkin**

➤ *OUTLIERS* by **Malcolm Gladwell**

➤ *GRIT* by **Angela Duckworth**

BUSINESS

➤ *ZERO TO ONE* by **Peter Thiel**

➤ *PROFIT FIRST* by **Mike Michalowicz**

➤ *THE PERSONAL MBA* by **Josh Kaufman**

➤ *THE HARD THINGS ABOUT HARD THINGS* by **Ben Horowitz**

MARKETING

- *BUY.LOGY* by **Martin Lindstrom**
- *SOCIAL MEDIA ROI* by **Olivier Blanchard**
- *SELLING THE INVISIBLE* by **Harry Beckwith**
- *POSITIONING* by **Al Ries & Jack Trout**

DIGITAL MARKETING

- *CONTAGIOUS* by **Jonah Berger**
- *WHAT CUSTOMERS CRAVE* by **Nicholas J. Webb**
- *THEY ASK, YOU ANSWER* by **Marcus Sheridan**
- *HACKING GROWTH* by **Morgan Brown & Sean Ellis**

BLOCKCHAIN

- *CRYPTOASSETS* by **Chris Burniske & Jack Tatar**
- *BLOCKCHAIN REVOLUTION* by **Don & Alex Tapscott**
- *THE BLOCKCHAIN DEVELOPER* by **Elad Elrom**
- *THE BOOKS OF SATOSHI* by **Phil Champagne**

DROPPSHIPPING & E-COMMERCE

- *DROPSHIPPING* by **Ronald Anderson**
- *E-COMMERCE BUSINESS MODEL* by **Jim Work**
- *DROPSHIP INSTITUTE* by **Cory Eckert**
- *OWN YOUR NICHE* by **Stephanie Chandler**

ARTIFICIAL INTELLIGENCE

➤ *SUPERINTELLIGENCE* by **Nick Bostrom**

➤ *LIFE 3.0* by **Max Tegmark**

➤ *ARTIFICIAL INTELLIGENCE* by **Peter Norvig**

➤ *THE MASTER ALGORITHM* by **Pedro Domingos**

PROJECT MANAGEMENT

➤ *MAKE THINGS HAPPEN* by **Scott Berkun**

➤ *THE LAZY PROJECT MANAGER* by **Peter Taylor**

➤ *PRODUCT-LED GROWTH* by **Wes Bush**

➤ *DOING AGILE RIGHT* by **Darrell Rigby, Sarah Elk & Steve Berez**

PUBLIC SPEAKING

➤ *THE ART OF PUBLIC SPEAKING* by **Dale Carnegie**

➤ *TALK LIKE TED* by **Carmine Gallo**

➤ *PRESENTATION ZEN* by **Garr Reynolds**

➤ *SPEAK WITH NO FEAR* by **Mike Acker**

NEGOTIATION

➤ *REBEL TALENT* by **Francesca Gino**

➤ *BARGAINING WITH THE DEVIL* by **Robert Mnookin**

➤ *THE ART OF NEGOTIATION* by **Michael Wheeler**

➤ *3-D NEGOTIATION* by **David A. Lax & James K. Sebenius**

PSYCHOLOGY

➤ *THINKING, FAST AND SLOW* by **Daniel Kahneman**

➤ *THE MAN WHO MISTOOK HIS WIFE FOR A HAT* by **Oliver Sacks**

➤ *MAN'S SEARCH FOR MEANING* by **Viktor E. Frankl**

➤ *PREDICTABLY IRRATIONAL* by **Dr. Dan Ariely**

CONSULTING

➤ *THE MCKINSEY WAY* by **Ethan M. Rasiel**

➤ *VALUATION* by **McKinsey & Company**

➤ *THE TRUSTED ADVISOR* by **David H. Maister, Charles H. Green & Robert M. Galford**

➤ *CASE INTERVIEW SECRETS* by **Victor Cheng**

PROGRAMMING

➤ *CLEAN CODE* by **Robert C. Martin**

➤ *THE PRAGMATIC PROGRAMMER* by **Andrew Hunt & David Thomas**

➤ *CODE* by **Charles Petzold**

➤ *CODE COMPLETE* by **Steve McConnell**

LANGUAGE

➤ *THROUGH THE LANGUAGE GLASS* by **Benjamin Lee Whorf**

➤ *THE LANGUAGE INSTINCT* by **Steven Pinker**

➤ *THE FIRST WORD* by **Christine Kenneally**

➤ *THE GENIUS OF LANGUAGE* by **Amy Tan**

DECISION-MAKING

➤ *DECISIVE* **by Dan & Chip Heath**

➤ *THINKING IN BETS* **by Annie Duke**

➤ *SMART CHOICES* **by John S. Hammond, Ralph L. Keeney & Howard Riffa**

➤ *THE PARADOX OF CHOICE* **by Barry Schwartz**

ENJOYED THE BOOK?

T HANK you for taking the time to read my book. I hope that the ideas and insights presented in these pages have been valuable to you and that they have inspired you to make positive changes in your life.

As an author, there is nothing more rewarding than knowing that my work has positively impacted someone's life. Whether you were looking to improve your health, mindset, relationships, or career, I hope this book has provided you with the guidance and inspiration you needed to move forward.

I greatly appreciate your time reading my book and would love to hear your thoughts. Your feedback is invaluable to me, as it helps me improve my work and better cater to my readers. Please consider leaving a review, whether you enjoyed the book or found areas that need improvement. Your perspective is essential in helping us continue to create content that resonates with you and other readers. Thank you for your support and for sharing your insights! Feel free to contact me below:

🏠　https://www.honerod.com

✉　phonerodb@gmail.com

NOTES & COPYRIGHT

[1] https://fs.blog/2015/03/carol-dweck-mindset/, 2015.

[2] R. Prajapati, B. Sharma, and D. Sharma, "Significance of life skills education," *Contemporary Issues in Education Research (CIER)*, vol. 10, p. 1, 12 2016.

[3] C. Segrin, "Communication and the study of personal well-being," *Gazette*, vol. 67, pp. 547–549, 12 2005.

[4] S. Ravindranath, "Importance of life skills training for corporate sector," *Bonfring International Journal of Industrial Engineering and Management Science*, vol. 2, pp. 05–07, 09 2012.

[5] https://vikaspedia.in/health/women-health/adolescent-health-1/management-of-adolescent-health/life-skills, 2020.

[6] M. Navickas, T. Gudaitis, and E. Krajnakova, "Influence of financial literacy on management of personal finances in a young household," *Verslas: teorija ir praktika*, vol. 15, pp. 32–40, 03 2014.

[7] M. F. Zerihun and M. Makgoo, "The effects of financial literacy on financial management outcomes: Evidence from the south african employed youth," 07 2019.

[8] E. Rasure, "Money and the pursuit of happiness: In good times and bad," *Journal of Financial Therapy*, vol. 2, 01 2011.

[9] https://www.frbsf.org/cash/publications/fed-notes/2019/june/2019-findings-from-the-diary-of-consumer-payment-choice/.

[10] C. Davis, J. Mantler, B. Doyle, B. Sc, M. Ca, C. Cirp, P. Or, and Salewski, "The consequences of financial stress for individuals, families, and society," 05 2004.

[11] G. Putri, R. Rahadi, and A. Tiara, "A conceptual study on the impact of parental influence in improving financial literacy of university students," *Asia Pacific Journal of Social Science Research*, vol. 5, 04 2020.

[12] https://www.forbes.com/sites/lizfrazierpeck/2019/08/29/5-reasons-personal-finance-should-be-taught-in-school/?sh=438f16495178.

[13] https://www.youtube.com/watch?v=KMj9wsrPE5U.

[14] K. Andrews and K. Flanagan, *Social Isolation*. 01 2010.

[15] https://en.wikipedia.org/wiki/Paretoprinciple, 2020.

[16] K. Faro and M. Grimes, "Engaging consumers in the era of the eight-second attention span," 09 2017.

[17] C. Williams, "Use of written cognitive–behavioural therapy self-help materials to treat depression," *Advances in Psychiatric Treatment*, vol. 7, no. 3, p. 233–240, 2001.

MONEY

COMMUNICATION

PRODUCTIVITY

Deep Work by Cal Newport, copyright © 2016. Reprinted by permission of Grand Central Publishing, an imprint of Hachette Book Group, Inc.

Eat That Frog! by Brian Tracy, copyright © 2017. Reprinted by permission of Berrett-Koehler Books, an imprint of Berrett-Koehler Publishers, Inc.

Atomic Habits by James Clear, copyright © 2018. Reprinted by permission of Avery Publishing, an imprint of Penguin Random House LLC.

The 4-Hour Workweek by Tim Ferriss, copyright © 2009.
Reprinted by permission of Harmony Publishing, an imprint of Penguin Random House LLC.

The Power of Habit by Charles Duhigg, copyright © 2014.
Reprinted by permission of Random House Trade Paperbacks, an imprint of Penguin Random House LLC.

The Power of Less by Leo Bahauta, copyright © 2013. Reprinted by permission of Bard Press.

The ONE Thing by Gary W. Keller, copyright © 2009. Reprinted by permission of Hachette Books, an imprint of Hachette Book Group, Inc.

The Lean Startup by Eric Ries, copyright © 2011. Reprinted by permission of Crown Publishing, an imprint of Penguin Random House LLC.

HEALTH

Made in the USA
Middletown, DE
14 August 2023